BLOOD RED SNOW

BLOOD RED SNOW

The Memoirs of a German Soldier on the Eastern Front

Günter K. Koschorrek

FRONTLINE BOOKS

A Greenhill Book

Blood Red Snow: The Memoirs of a German Soldier on the Eastern Front

A Greenhill Book

This edition published in 2011 by Frontline Books,
an imprint of Pen & Sword Books Limited,
47 Church Street, Barnsley, S. Yorkshire, S70 2AS
www.frontline-books.com, email info@frontline-books.com

Original German edition: *Vergiß die Zeit der Dornen nicht* © 1998
by v.Hase & Koehler Verlag, Main, Germany
English-language translation copyright © Greenhill Books, 2002
This edition © Pen & Sword Books Limited, 2011

ISBN 978-1-84832-596-8

PUBLISHING HISTORY
Vergiß die Zeit der Dornen nicht was originally published in 1998 by
v.Hase & Koehler Verlag. The first English-language translation was
published in paperback by Greenhill Books in 2002. This edition was
translated by Olav R. Crome-Aamot.

For more information on our books, please visit www.frontline-books.com,
email info@frontline-books.com or write to us at the above address.

Printed in the United States of America

Contents

Illustrations

Maps

Introduction

IT'S NOT EASY to pull your experiences of the Second World War from your memory and then write a chronologically accurate report about them: either you satisfy yourself with the incidental events which you have with difficulty sifted out, or you simply fill the gaps in your memory with lively fantasy. Many books have been published using the latter mixture, either glorifying the war by telling of what are indisputably acts of heroism, or interpreting it by means of malicious obituary with the result that the reader is persuaded to regard soldiers as bloodthirsty murderers. I want neither of the above; I intend neither to glorify nor to judge. I will describe the reality—how I, as an ordinary soldier, personally experienced and perceived the war on the front lines in Russia from the autumn of 1942 until the bitter end, interrupted only occasionally because of injury.

This book is an authentic report, with descriptions of my own unforgettable experiences, impressions and perceptions—the perceptions of an ordinary front-line soldier, referred to, in the slang of the day, as a *Landser*. Unlike many books, which rely on contemporary documentation, it does not discuss responsibility (or the lack of it) from the point of view of the command staffs in charge of the conduct of the war, nor even from the point of view of the leaders who had been specifically trained to be examples to their men (and who, as a general rule, fought alongside them in the front lines).

The book is intended to be a tribute to the countless anonymous soldiers who spent most of their war in filthy foxholes in the Russian soil, relinquishing them only when they needed to engage the enemy directly—whether it be in summer in the boiling hot sun, during the rains in knee-deep mud, or in a winter blizzard with the ground frozen hard or covered in deep snow. The only hope for these men was the promise of a brief respite when they were permitted to rest with the rear-area supply trains. But, until that happened, their home was the front-line trench or the foxhole—there, on the main battle line, where day after day they worried about their survival and killed their enemies in order to avoid being killed; where each man fought as a unit but in the end had to rely upon himself; where the earth around them often turned into a burning hell; where they sensed the ice-cold touch of death when a glowing hot splinter or a fizzing bullet searched out their living bodies; where the shredded corpses of their enemy were heaped in front of them; and where the piercing screams of the wounded would mix with the barely audible calls of the dying, touching them as they cowered deep within the ground and pursuing them in their nightmares. There cannot be many still living who, after half a century, can say that they survived the murderous war on the Russian front, or survived an inhuman imprisonment afterwards. But there most assuredly are still fewer who, thanks to some miracle, escaped the hellish inferno and who, because of notes they made during those days, can now write about it.

After my training I graduated as a heavy machine gunner. As a result, my superiors employed me primarily in this speciality and as a heavy weapons gun team leader for most of my front-line service. I will not deny that, using this rapid-fire weapon—mounted on a gun-carriage and equipped with an optical sight—I killed many of the enemy during the war on the Eastern Front.

During this period I made a number of notes with a view to writing up a factual report after hostilities had ended. Initially I also kept a diary, although this was against regulations for the common soldier. I made my first comments in this diary as we, a freshly trained unit of young recruits, made our way to Stalingrad as replacement troops. Before we reached our destination we marched for days, with heavy loads on our backs, through the shimmering heat of the endless Kalmuck steppe.

During a massive Russian tank attack on 13 December 1942, at the edge of the Stalingrad pocket, our supply train and personal effects fell into enemy hands. Unfortunately my diary was amongst the booty. I didn't worry too much, as I had only written down my impressions, which the Russians would not be able to make much sense of. My name was not in it, nor was the name of the unit I belonged to, although from the material they took they would in fact have been able to discover my unit.

Later, while I was recovering from my first injuries, I again wrote down what I had experienced during this fateful period—the days and weeks in which we distraught Germans tried to escape the Stalingrad encirclement, finally fleeing headlong across the frozen Don under the shattering live fire from the approaching one hundred Russian tanks. This incident ended a never-to-be-forgotten experience as, almost deafened from the roar of the exploding shells and the incessant clatter of tracks, and blinded by the flashing close behind us, we made our way over mountains of emaciated corpses and wounded comrades whose blood stained the snow red, to the safety of the other bank of the Don, which, the day before, had seemed so peaceful covered in a mantle of fresh snow.

After I lost my diary I had made my notes on any scraps of paper which happened to be available at the time. I then folded these pages and slid them through a tiny slit in the lining of my uniform coat. During my short stay in the military hospital I twice had an opportunity to pass these observations on to my mother for her safe keeping. I was convinced that no one other than I would be able to decipher my scribble, which was partly in shorthand.

This hiding place in the lining of my uniform jacket apparently served its purpose, because when I returned home during my next leave I again deposited my latest notes in the same place. The only difference was that now the notes were in the lining of my new winter coat, which I had last worn at the end of 1940, before I was called up to spend a year at the NSKK Motor Vehicle School in Itzehoe. (This was preliminary military training to qualify for several different Army driver's licences.) Sometime or other I began to organise the notes chronologically and to formulate an idea out of them. It became my fervent wish to write a book, but this ambition was destined to remain unfulfilled for various reasons. The years passed, though the flame was often rekindled.

Then came the time when I mislaid my notes: I assumed that I had somehow lost them during a move, and it was only much later that I discovered that I had left them behind in our apartment in the 1950s when I had gone through a traumatic divorce from my wife. After the divorce my wife quickly did what she had longed to do—she married an American soldier, who took her and my daughter, and a further child, back to America.

The decades passed, but the painful memories of the war years remained deep in my soul. Moreover, changes in society's attitudes, from what was once acceptable behaviour to an unmistakable 'new wave' permitting lack of respect, aggressive attitudes, hatred and violence, did nothing to help me forget those fateful times. Then, one day, I quite unexpectedly held my long-lost notes in my hands again. Reading merely a few lines from them brought images from the 1940s back to stark reality.

It all had begun with a call from the United States. At first I found no words as an unknown woman's voice with a decidedly American accent asked me for my name and thereupon addressed me as 'Daddy'. It took a moment before I realised that the caller was my daughter from my first marriage—a daughter whom I had not seen since my divorce in the mid-1950s. It was a strange feeling to discover that I suddenly had a daughter who was married and who, overnight as it were, had also made me a grandfather of two.

She then visited my new wife and me in Germany, and she presented me with a wonderful gift—a folder containing all my wartime notes! These notes had been the only souvenir she had had of her father, and she had kept them all these years in the hope that one day she would be able to meet him again. It took almost forty years. Her repeated attempts to find me had been frustrated by the many changes in addresses which I had gone through. Contact has remained intact since then, however, and we have enjoyed several holidays at her home in Las Vegas.

Today, almost sixty years after World War II, we are fed images of hatred, acts of brutality and footage of war by the various media directly into our homes. These events may cause a sudden chill to run up and down the spine and perhaps bring tears to the eyes, but no one really understands the true hurt suffered by the victim. People see brutalisation and atrocities; they are aghast, and they may discuss what they have seen, but images are quickly forgotten. Only the parties who were actually involved at the time experience the concentrated impact of the tragedy deep within their consciousness—and often it is only time that heals the wounds in their souls and lessens the pain.

My wounds from World War II have healed as time has passed, but I can still feel the scars on my body and the injuries that remain implanted in my soul. And every time I am shown or read about some disturbing event or other in today's world, the awful images from those terrible experiences during the war well up from within to dance vividly before my eyes. It was exactly these memories which drove me, after several unsuccessful attempts, to write the present book, using my notes as the basis. Almost an entire lifespan lay behind me, and finally I had the time to write, from the soul, about that from which I could never really free myself.

It was not my intention to give the reader all the names, nor my unit's exact designation, as I wanted this book to concentrate on documenting my personal experiences and my mental impressions and observations, as well as my feelings and perceptions of the war: should any of the members of my unit happen to read my writings, they will in any case be able to recognise it.

I have written this book because I sensed an uncompromising duty to do so. It was time to set down that which for all who have survived will remain unforgotten. The survivors of the last war were tasked to become the admonishing emissaries of those who had perished on the battlefields, sentenced to eternal silence. This book is my contribution, and I feel that I have now fulfilled my obligation.

Günter K. Koschorrek

CHAPTER ONE

En Route

TODAY IS 18 October 1942. I am sitting on a bale of straw in a railway goods wagon, part of a troop transport. So far as the rattling and shaking allows, I am making the very first entries in my brand-new notebook. About three hours ago we boarded this train—we being about 300 freshly trained, 18-year-old recruits—along with some *Gefreiter*, *Obergefreiter* and *Unteroffiziere*.*

Finally we have a little time to ourselves. The last three days have been extremely hectic. On our way to the front we were first rushed through preliminary training at the Stablak centre in East Prussia. Yesterday the commander of the training battalion at Insterburg gave us a rousing speech about our contribution to the operation in Russia. For us this was a great moment—to have finally graduated and now be considered fully fledged front-line soldiers.

The commander's speech made us all feel extremely proud. He had spoken about the German Army's far-flung commitments, and its many successes, and about the mission that we were about to undertake on behalf of our *Führer* and our beloved Fatherland. We were to accomplish this with all the strength and military prowess we could possibly muster. Our attitude was first rate—not least because our daily suffering had also ended. The six months of training often

---

* In British Army terms, these would be roughly equivalent to Lance-Corporals, Senior Lance-Corporals and Corporals, respectively.

involved a pretty harsh routine, and as a result many of us won't forget it in a hurry.

But that's now all in the past. We look forward to a new era, a great future. Immediately after the commander's send-off, we exited the Insterburg camp through the main gates and headed straight for the railway station. Our marching songs never sounded as cheerful and confident as they did this sunny autumn morning!

The Stablak Troop Training Centre is well-known to old soldiers as a place where harsh military training is meted out. It now serves as a transit area for replacement troops destined for the front lines. No one knows which front line we are being sent to, as this sort of information is classified. We were loaded into these wagons with three days' combat rations. Ever since then the main question has been—what is our destination? The only person who might know is the *Obergefreiter* with the Iron Cross 2nd Class and the Wound Badge—he's in our carriage—but he's saying nothing and is calmly smoking his pipe. He and a couple of other fellows who also have one or two chevrons on their sleeves are supposed to have come from a convalescent company. They were assigned as senior occupants of each goods wagon by the *Transportführer*.* We take it they are returning to their old units, to which we then might be assigned as replacements.

Someone's heard that our unit is an old cavalry division, re-formed as a tank division with two infantry regiments. The evidence is the yellow piping on our epaulettes. Yellow is the traditional colour of this former cavalry outfit, which has been in the Stalingrad area for a while. I don't attach any significance to this rumour—we'll wait and see.

Of the sixteen men in our wagon, only six besides me are from our training company; I only know the others by sight. There is Hans Weichert, who is always hungry. Next there is a tall fellow called Warias, the flank man of the training company. Then there is Küpper, a muscular fellow with fair hair. The fourth man is a quiet, sensible chap

---

* Literally, 'Transport Leader'.

called Grommel. Then there is Heinz Kurat, who plays the harmonica. The last man, Otto Wilke, uses every free moment to play cards—even as I write, he is engrossed in a game with some of the others.

I think back to the days I spent in the training camp, where in spite of the physically demanding work I did enjoy some good times. I think about our strolls through Insterburg and the time spent at the Dance-Café Tivoli, where you could sometimes get to meet a girl. I admit I was a bit shy on these occasions and even blushed in front of girls, but I used to explain this away by using various slick excuses. I had no close friends at the time; I suppose I was a bit selective.

19 October. It's Sunday, but you'd never know it. It was a bit fresh during the night, but now, since sunrise, it has got warmer in here. Outside, the countryside is drifting past us. It looks a poor sort of area: everywhere you look you see wooden houses and dilapidation. We pass through some little villages, and you can see farm buildings with thatched roofs and broken-down brick buildings in many places.

There are some people at the next station, standing on the rails and on the platforms. In amongst them are some *Wehrmacht* uniforms. They look like guards. Some of us wave from the wagon, but no one waves back. Our train is moving very slowly and the figures in front are staring at us. There are a lot of women among them. They have headscarves on, while the men all have peaked caps. They must be Poles. They look very downcast. They have shovels and picks for working on the railway line.

At some of the main stops we're given hot coffee and occasionally fresh sausage; we are slowly getting tired of canned meat. We also find time to wash and freshen up a bit. We don't know exactly where we are, but last night we're supposed to have crossed into Russia.

In the early hours of the morning we suddenly hear rifle shots coming from the front of the train. The train stops and an alert is sounded. Partisans are supposed to be around here somewhere; they get quite interested in goods trains. But everything remains calm.

23 October. Day after day, the wide expanses of Russia pass by. There are harvested fields as far as the eye can see, and in between some huge barns and farmsteads—the so-called *kolkhozes*. In the distance I can see a group of figures marching in a long row. As they come closer I can see that they are mostly women, loaded down with bundles. Some men are walking along carrying nothing. Hans Weichert gets annoyed with the men for allowing the women to carry the heavy loads while they just walk along beside them. Our wagon chief, the *Obergefreiter*, explains: 'In this part of Russia that's normal. The *pajenkas*, the girls, and the *mattkas*, the mothers or women, are from childhood taught to do what the *pan*, or man, tells them to do. The men are real layabouts: *they* decide what's to be done. Whenever you see them they are always walking alongside the women. Indoors they are usually to be found lying on the clay ovens asleep. Nowadays you mostly see only old men—all the youngsters have gone off to the war.'

In the last few days our *Obergefreiter* has become more communicative, and in fact he turns out to be quite a decent chap. It all started when some of the men called him '*Herr Obergefreiter*'. He would tear them off a strip, telling them that we were no longer in training. Besides, addressing someone with '*Herr*' in front only began when he wore braid on his shoulders, starting with sergeants.

'Are we supposed to address you with "*Sie*"?,' asks little Grommel.

'Don't be daft! Don't use "*Sie*" to me—just call me plain "Kumpel".* That's the way we do things around here!'

'Or comrade,' a slim, fair-haired fellow interjected. I don't know him, but he later told me that he was a *KOB-Kriegsoffizierbewerber*†—for

---

* 'Mate'.

† A candidate for an officer's battlefield commission.

which he would first have to prove his aptitude by serving on the front lines.

The *Obergefreiter* raised his hands in protest. 'Heavens—not that! That word is better left for the armchair soldiers in the rear echelons or those back home rather than us front-line blokes. I am sorry, chum, but the comrades all get killed.'

He then went on to tell us about his unit. It was a former cavalry division which in spring 1942 had been designated a tank division. He had been with it since it was reorganised and transferred to Russia, and he took part in the advance on Woronesch in June. The fighting had ended with many dead and wounded. In July and August he had fought with his unit past Tschir and the Don and on into Stalingrad.

So it's Stalingrad after all—just as we had thought! However, we're not that near yet—we're only seven days into the journey, and the only sensation is one of being shaken up and down.

24/25 October. Our train is always being overtaken by other ones loaded with weapons and supplies for the front lines. Someone says that we passed Krementschug railway station last night. This means we are in the middle of the Ukraine, the granary of Russia. The *Gefreiter*—I now know his name: Fritz Marzog—says that we are being taken over the Dnyepropetrovsk and Rostow and from there in a north-easterly direction to Stalingrad. He's right: a day later, during the early hours of the morning, we reach Rostow on the Don estuary by the Sea of Azov.

The train stops in a siding near of the railway station. There is water nearby, so we can freshen up. The weather is nice and warm, but it's still hazy and we still can't see the sun. We're running around without shirts on, as we're told that we will be here for some time. I am just about to visit some friends in the next wagon when all hell breaks loose.

We hear the sound of engines, and, dropping suddenly out of the sky, three Russian fighter aircraft come for us with machine guns rattling.

Even before the command 'Aircraft—take cover!' rings out most of us are already underneath the wagons. I can see sparks flying off the rails and hear the *zing!* of the ricochets. Then everything is over . . . but immediately someone yells, 'They're coming back!'

Sure enough, I can see them turning and coming straight back at us. Suddenly all hell is let loose for a second time. The sirens wail and a storm of firing breaks out, so loud that my eardrums almost shatter. There must be several anti-aircraft batteries in the railway complex now laying down crossfire. The three aircraft immediately peel off and disappear, unscathed. We all look at each other a bit stunned: everything happened so fast, and it is all so different from training days when the instructor yelled 'Aircraft—cover!' This was the real thing, which explains why we'd never taken cover so fast as we did now. Someone says that somebody has been hit. It isn't serious—a graze on the leg which the medic can sort out.

'All wagon seniors report to the *Transportführer* for orders!' The message is passed down the train. *Obergefreiter* Marzog returns shortly afterwards with news. He says that two open flatbeds will be coupled to our train, each with a twin anti-aircraft gun, to protect the train against enemy air attack. So, they reckon there will be further air attacks! In addition, from now on we have to place two men per wagon on guard duty every night, due to the increased chance of an attack by partisans. We may also have to make detours, because we have to reckon on rails being blown.

The straw underneath us is flattened and we don't have any fresh, and the blanket which has been thrown over it doesn't help very much—it feels as if we're lying directly on the carriage floor. The tall fellow Warias and several others complain that their hips are hurting. The *Obergefreiter* smirks and tells us that it's good training: it's worse in the dirty foxholes on the front line.

We get him to tell us about the successful campaigns his unit fought in the summer, and this makes us even more impatient to get to our destination as soon as possible so as to not miss out on anything. Dieter Malzahn, the tall, fair-haired *KOB-Kriegsoffizierbewerber*, expresses in words what we're all thinking. Marzog replies somewhat laconically, 'Take your time, lad. When you are up at the front your arse will go from one to a hundred soon enough.' This is old news—we've heard this sort of remark before, usually from men from one of the convalescent units. What they meant was that we, the young squirts, will shit in our pants the first time we get fired upon. Nonsense! When so many others have made it, why shouldn't we? Besides, age has nothing to do with it!

Nearly every time the train stops we hear favourable *Wehrmacht* radio reports booming out over the loudspeakers from the *Transportführer*'s wagon. So it is today, 25 October—a report telling us all about German victories. It makes us feel good, and we start singing battle songs.

The countryside has changed since yesterday. We were passing villages every now and then, but today, on both sides of the line, there is nothing but brown-coloured steppe, with the occasional small hillock. Once in a while you can see large *kolkhozes*.

The driver brings the train to a halt in the middle of this landscape. We climb down from our carriage. The driver has noticed that a section of the railway line had been blown up. We now have to back up along the track for almost twelve hours so as to get on to another line. Progress is now a series of jerks: the engine wheezes like an old walrus as soon as there is the slightest incline.

We carry on like this for quite a while, until suddenly everyone sits up. There, over a hill in front of us, is a huge dark shadow, like a bird of prey, coming right at us! First we hear a low droning noise, then a crescendo roar like a swarm of bees . . . 'Take cover—air attack!' We lie flat on the ground, and overhead comes the rattle of aircraft cannon. I can see dirt being thrown up where the shells hit the ground, then our ack-ack begins to spit back. I look up and see small bombs falling from the plane. They explode in front of the train on the engine. Then again the mad buzzing noise—and he is gone.

Our anti-aircraft fire didn't manage to get the plane, but there's not much damage—a couple of splinters hitting various parts of the engine and making some holes in the sides of the wagons. Marzog tells us about it: 'That was the "Iron Gustav", a Soviet combat fighter, which Ivan also uses at the front lines. It's a nimble, low-altitude, close-support plane which appears from nowhere and sprays everything with its automatic cannon. It often also drops small bombs and sometimes larger ones. Standard ammo is quite useless against it as it has an armour-plated belly.'

After this incident we carry on, pushing the train uphill and riding it downhill. How long can this go on? But eventually we come to the end. Nothing more can be done—we can't move the train any further, even by pushing it. What now? We are stranded somewhere in the Kalmuck steppe, with 320 men and a good 40lb of personal gear for each one.

How far is it to Stalingrad? The *Transportführer* tells us: 'About another 140 or 150 kilometres.' Apparently, because of all the detours and delays, we're well behind schedule. We are informed that we will therefore complete the journey on foot. We have to reach our destination in four days. We're told that we will spend the night in the wagons and set off in the morning at 0600.

26 October. Reveille is at 0500, and it is still dark. We get hot coffee and half a loaf of Army bread per man and a piece of hard-cured sausage. We noticed yesterday that the rations had been decreased. A few men with injured feet will remain behind with the train and anti-aircraft crews. We load up our kit and, on the order 'Route march!', take off with compass and map. Now for real hardship, which will inevitably dent our enthusiasm.

We start off singing, but slowly and surely this dies away. The sun gets up and it becomes warmer. At lunchtime a longer rest is ordered. During the afternoon the sun really beats down. We still have some reserves, and, although we're very tired, we carry on well past nightfall. We just collapse to the ground in a hollow in the steppe, catch our breath and then unroll our ground sheets and blankets from our kitbags. That night we sleep like the dead.

27 October. This morning my legs are as stiff as an old pack horse's, and the rest of the men are feeling no better. I eat a slice of bread and take a sip of my cold coffee. Goodness knows when I'll get something to drink again.

'Up and at it!' The fellows up front start out at quite a rate of knots. The train company does not have that much to carry, but the rest of us are loaded down like pack animals—we carry the full kit with blanket and ground sheet, steel helmet and heavy winter coat thrown over it. We have a full ammunition pouch on the belt, on our backs the kitbag with the field canteen, and on the other side the folded entrenching tool. A gas mask is slung around our necks, resting on the chest, and the heavy rifle swings back and forth from its strap round the neck. Lastly, a ditty bag is carried in one hand, filled with clean socks, underwear and similar items. The whole lot weighs about 40lb.

Time passes. Men regularly fall to the ground exhausted. After a while, having caught their breath, they stand up again and struggle on. Many stragglers look pale and sickly: they are completely exhausted.

Suddenly a message comes from the head of the column. Relief! 'Village up ahead!' That means water and something to eat. We summon our last resources and drag ourselves on. Soon we can see the houses. There are only a few, but there are also several barns belonging to a *kolkhoz*, just like we saw on the wide Russian steppes. There is a well in front of the first hut, with a windlass and a dented bucket.

A *Feldwebel** stands a few feet from the well and waits until the first men get there. Those in front are dashing up to it, wanting to let the bucket down.

'Hold it!' yells the *Feldwebel*.

The man at the windlass lets go of the bucket, which now crashes down into the well. The *Feldwebel* suggests that the water may perhaps be poisoned. He goes up to one of the houses—one that has nice wooden carvings on the windows—and goes in the door. Not a soul can be seen.

The *Feldwebel* reappears with a scruffy looking fellow from the house. He is an old man with a bushy beard and is dressed in the typical quilted jacket. The *Feldwebel* is dragging him over to the well holding on to his sleeve with two fingers. The bucket is now full of water, up from the well, and reflecting the gleaming sunlight.

With a gesture of his hand towards the water, the *Feldwebel* now demands: 'Drink, Ruski!'

The old fellow looks at him with a crafty expression, smiles and refuses several times while repeatedly saying something like: '*Pan karosch, pan karosch.*' The *Feldwebel* now becomes impatient. He grabs the old fellow by the neck and shoves his face in the bucket; the old boy chokes and swallows. He looks a bit surprised, but not too concerned. In other words, the water's safe.

'Okay, you can drink the water,' says the *Feldwebel*. Bucketful after bucketful is now brought up and the old fellow starts to grin. He has finally realised what this was all about. We wallow in the water, drinking all we can, and then use some to freshen up.

The *kolkhoz* is a disappointment. We can't find any food anywhere. In one shed are a pile of mangold-wurzels and a few ears of corn. Küpper bites a chunk of mangold-wurzel but spits it right out again. Meanwhile a number of women have come out of the houses and are gawking at us. Weichert says the old Russian chap has mentioned

* Sergeant.

24

something about a garrison headquarters and confiscation. That probably means that some German unit or other has already taken off with anything that's edible.

28 October. We march onwards with empty stomachs. Hour after hour passes. We sweat, we swear, many of us shout out just to lighten our spirits, but we still have to drag ourselves forward—kilometre after kilometre. Then suddenly the peace of the countryside is broken by a dull, throbbing sound. 'Take cover—air attack!' someone yells. We try to run for cover just as we have been trained to do, but after a couple of paces we go down on the spot.

I scan the sky and on the horizon can pick out some aircraft coming towards us, their tails glinting in the sun. We can tell they're heavily loaded with bombs, ready for the kill. They are coming closer—then we can make out the cross insignia under their wings and realise that they're German bombers up on a mission, so we stand up and wave to them. They disappear in a north-easterly direction with their deadly cargo. That must be Stalingrad over there. We trudge on.

'How far is it now?' asks little Grommel, who has made himself comfortable between me and Marzog.

Marzog shrugs his shoulders. 'No idea, but I heard we're supposed to get there tomorrow.' As if in answer we hear a heavy muffled noise in the distance, followed by what sounds like rolling thunder. As it starts to get dark we can see a red glare in the sky in the far distance.

'That's Stalingrad!' someone says.

'What are those lights?' Warias makes a gesture with his hand.

We look towards where he is pointing and see a row of lights in the sky, just like lanterns. Then we hear more muffled explosions, and straight after that we can see long, bright strings of pearls which start from the ground, continue up into the sky and then disappear. Someone remarks, 'That's the Runway Raider!'

25

The old veteran explains that this is a light biplane, which generally operates at night over the runway, letting off flares suspended on little parachutes to illuminate targets. Then the plane drops a number of small bombs or fragmentation bombs. The pilot can turn off his engine and sail noiselessly towards his target like a glider. When the enemy discovers him it's usually too late. The front-line troops have called him the '*Nähmaschine*',* because that's what the engine sounds like.

The old soldier goes on: 'By the way, those strings of pearls in the sky are tracer rounds from the 20mm twin-barrel and quad anti-aircraft guns, which are trying to shoot him down.'

It's a great show. More flares appear and more strings of pearls follow in the night sky. It's odd, but we can't hear anything: it's like a silent movie.

29 October. A new morning is breaking, and our morale is at zero level. For an hour now a fine drizzle has been coming down, and some of our men are quite outspoken about their dislike for it.

The rain gets heavier and now it's windy as well. For the first time we are experiencing really lousy weather—something we hadn't expected. The gusts become stronger and stronger and the open countryside offers no protection. The raindrops lash your face like fine needles, drumming against the steel helmets that we've put on to protect us. The wind tears at the groundsheets which we've wrapped around us, and they don't make much difference. They slap against our wet trousers and the cold wind practically knocks us off our feet. We trudge on.

Several hours go by, then we finally spot a village. It has stopped raining. We find some empty barns and sink gratefully to the ground. It's quite busy in the village, with privates and other ranks all over the place. They snap to attention and salute each other. Have we reached the

---

* Literally, 'Sewing Machine'.

front line or not? There is plenty of evidence here that this area has been taken over by a headquarters and regimental staff—in other words the *Organisatorischen Schreibstubengefechtsstände*,* as Marzog puts it. Our *Transportführer* is supposed to be organising some rations for us.

It works, and we all receive a large helping of barley soup with meat chunks. They live quite well here. After the soup we feel a lot better. What next? We wait and we wait . . . Then there is an announcement: there are still eight or so kilometres to go. New strength is awakened in us. Although our bones ache and the blisters on our feet hurt, we manage to march the rest of the way in about an hour and a half—quite an achievement considering the weight of our kit.

Rumour has it that we will be picked up by vehicles from this point. However, they're not yet here, so again we have to wait.

They arrive at dusk. We drive into the darkness, then over a long bridge with lots of other vehicles—'the River Don,' someone behind me remarks. Then we continue on the MSR,† more commonly referred to as 'The Runway'. We drive without lights because of the Runway Raider. We can see his flares close up now and can quite clearly hear the bangs as his bombs go off.

After a few hours we stop somewhere amongst some cottages. We are quartered in them for the night. In the distance we hear the rolling thunder, and the sky is glowing red—that's Stalingrad all right! How is our enthusiasm compared to how we felt last week? It's definitely suffered because of the forced march we've just had to make, and we reckon that enthusiasm and euphoria are in short supply here. The reality is rather different—it's not something that gives you a good feeling at all.

Well, we've reached the first stage towards our destination, and we'll now have to see how things work out. For the moment, though, I'm off to sleep to forget everything . . .

---

* Literally, 'Organisational Administrative Orderly Room Command Post'.
† Main Supply Route.

CHAPTER TWO

Fighting in Stalingrad

O CTOBER 30, 1942. Reveille is at 0600 and it's still dark outside. We get some hot coffee and food. No one knows for certain what's happening, although there are lots of rumours. One says that we still haven't reached our destination; another says that this is only one regiment from the division. We'll go from here to our unit in Stalingrad. The unit's strength is reported to have been dramatically cut, and we are the replacements. We're told that the entire regiment doesn't even amount to two companies at the moment. Rumours are often the only source of information for the common soldier. Even if they don't exactly fit the facts, there is normally a certain amount of truth in them.

I miss *Obergefreiter* Marzog and the others from the convalescent company at Insterburg. It seems they have already been picked up. Now, for us, the usual routine starts up: 'Fall in—two ranks!' We line up so that we're always in the second row so that we can stick together, all except for Malzahn. The entire group is 90 men strong. 'To the 1st Battalion, Regiment 21,' orders a young *Oberleutnant*.*

Round about noon we are picked up by some trucks and four Mercedes personnel carriers. The vehicles are all wearing the division's tactical emblem, a leaping rider in a circle. I'm given a seat next to the driver of an eight-man personnel carrier. We set off along an MSR, a

---

* Lieutenant.

wide road packed with traffic. The road is undulating, the surface smooth and shiny like bacon rind, stretching away across the steppe almost in a straight line. Now and then roads branch off, the junctions plastered with unit designation symbols and the names of villages.

Rumours are flying: it's no longer certain that we're going to Stalingrad. I ask the driver, who is a *Obergefreiter*. He says that we are not going to Stalingrad, but rather to a so-called 'winter position'. This is where the baggage trains are situated—because they can no longer be brought into Stalingrad—from which the troops fighting in the northern suburbs of the city are supplied with food and ammunition.

31 October. The 'winter position' is close to a *kolkhoz* in the open steppe. Along one side there is a *Rachel*, a deep, often long, rectangular trench where the steppe suddenly dips down. These *Rachels* are natural, geological phenomena and are often 10–20 feet deep in the otherwise flat landscape. A *Rachel* can be small, or large enough to give protection to an entire battalion complete with vehicles and men. A *Hauptwachtmeister*—in soldier's slang also referred to as '*Spiess*' or 'Mother of the Company'—meets us. He informs us that we now belong to a division rich in tradition, which even in the Polish and French campaigns was still a cavalry unit. He explains that the unit is therefore particularly proud of its old cavalry designations: a *Feldwebel* is called a *Wachtmeister* and a company is called a *Schwadron*, whilst a battalion is called an *Abteilung* and a *Hauptmann* is a *Rittmeister*.*

'Yes, *Herr Hauptwachtmeister!*' we yell at his question whether we have understood him or not. After one more division we are thirty men in the 1st *Schwadron*, while the others are sectioned off to the other *Schwadronen*—located quite close to us actually. We are then informed that our *Schwadron* was fighting with a total strength of only 26 men.

---

* *Hauptwachtmeister* is a cavalry rank roughly equivalent to Sergeant-Major; *Schwadron* means 'Squadron'; and a *Hauptmann* is a Captain.

29

Our regiment was also understrength: it was fighting in the ruins of Stalingrad mostly in small combat units, which because of the scarcity of officers were frequently led by *Unteroffiziere*.* The engagements were said to be murderous. Brick walls were no longer standing and the piles of dead and wounded got higher every day.

This news certainly didn't breed enthusiasm. What had happened to tall he successes and the reports of the proud German Army's advances—the ones we'd heard only few days ago? Were they exaggerations, or was this merely a temporary set-back to the usual run of successes?

1–6 November. Considering the situation, we are all surprised to discover that we are not off to the front immediately. Instead, we have to put up with the normal Army 'Mickey Mouse' routine—salute the officers, stand to attention, take up formation, listen to guff from our leaders and so on. Even when their training is completed, recruits are only novices and have to prove that they are real soldiers. All well and good—but they should give us the opportunity to prove it.

9 November. The intermittent explosions and general racket from the Stalingrad front are barely audible here. At night the sky is always red, and the para-lights of the *Rollbahn UvD*† can often be seen out searching for likely targets. This evening stuff from the stores is being handed out. Each man gets a bottle of juniper brandy, some cigarettes or tobacco, a little chocolate and some writing materials. When I was sixteen I barely survived a bout of alcohol poisoning while on holiday helping a friend bottle cognac for his parents' restaurant. I now throw up if I so much as smell alcohol, so, being a heavy smoker, I'm swapping

---

* A German *Schwadron* would normally be expected to consist of between 100 and 200 men, although numbers could vary according to the type of unit.
† MSR 'Sergeant of the Guard', meaning the Russian aircraft patrolling the MSR.

my brandy with some of the non-smokers for extra tobacco or cigarettes.

The alcohol brings a bit of atmosphere into our bunker, and, after a while, song is in the air again. Grommel and I stay sober because we have to take over the next watch. It's cold and windy, and I'm glad I've got my heavy lined winter coat; during our march I cursed it on more than one occasion because of its great weight. I wake Grommel for his shift, and all the rest are sleeping. There is a stench in the bunker that knocks you over, so I let in some fresh air.

11 November. The weather is colder, but at least it stays dry. Overnight everything has been covered in white frost, like fine filigree. There is movement in the air every day. Our bombers are flying towards Stalingrad. You can pick out the Russian anti-aircraft defence zone from the puffs of smoke in the sky.

I am on watch with a friend from our bunker. The supply truck has just returned from Stalingrad, as it does every night. They unload two dead and three wounded. An *Oberwachtmeister* is said to be seriously wounded. They're loading the wounded into an ambulance which will take them to the main medical station.

Up to this point we hadn't seen any dead men. The bodies are always buried in a special spot—I saw all the wooden crosses days ago as we drove by them while on manoeuvres.

Three *Landser* have come back with the supply truck and are to be reassigned for health reasons. They are told to go to different bunkers, and one of them comes to ours.

I return to the bunker after my guard duty, and discover that my place on the mattress has been taken. The *Landser* from Stalingrad has taken it. I can hardly make out his face—it is covered with beard stubble. His peaked cap almost covers his eyes and the earflaps are pulled way down over his ears. He is in a deep sleep, though he doesn't snore. Every now and then he gives a twitch, as if he is having a bad dream. I lie down in Kurat's place; he is the guard who relieved me.

12 November. Today, at noon, our sergeant-major has taken me off manoeuvres and given me a special job. I've got to dig a new latrine because the old one is already full up. The two Russian prisoners taken out of Stalingrad a couple of days ago are supposed to help me with this task. This is the first time I have seen Russian soldiers up close, and I look at them with curiosity. In their dirty brown coats and greasy headgear with long earflaps, they do not look particularly trustworthy. They do not exactly ooze danger, but rather just give the impression of being more 'foreign'. One seems to be of Mongolian descent. Their faces are unshaven and grey, with restless eyes. I can sense insecurity and apprehension in their faces. I would probably feel the same if I were in their shoes.

Both Russians turn out to be quite lazy types. I reckon they are between twenty-five and thirty years old. I have to chivvy them quite often in order to get work out of them. We have just finished digging and I am just admiring our work when a Russian standing next to me throws his shovel down and lunges past me directly into the trench. The other leaps after him, and I crouch down, thinking, before jumping into the trench as well, landing directly on top of the first Russian. All three of us are now flat on our stomachs in the trench and can hear the rattle of aircraft cannon as the shells hit the ground directly above us. Then a shadow, accompanied by a droning noise—which I know all too well—flies sideways over and past us. The Iron Gustav must have crept up on us while coming in low over the *kolkhoz*.

The new latrine is some way away from the rest of the unit. I peer over the edge of the trench towards the bunker and the vehicle dugouts. The Iron Gustav is turning back at low altitude and he again opens fire with his two wing-mounted cannon. He also drops several medium-sized bombs. Then, suddenly, there are two more combat aircraft in the sky. They also spew metal from their wing-mounted cannon and drop bombs. The other part of our unit must be over there—or are they firing on the men on manoeuvres?

Machine guns from all over the place now fire back at the aircraft, and I can also hear the louder bangs from a 20mm anti-aircraft cannon. Sparks are flying from the bellies of the aircraft just as if someone is doing some welding. Normal bullets bounce off the armour . . . but suddenly there's a smoke trail. A hit! One Iron Gustav peels off, smacks into the steppe and bursts into flame. The rest flee.

I jump up and head for the bunkers and the vehicles. Except for the men in the orderly room, only a few sick and a couple of drivers have stayed in the bunker. I can see one or two bomb craters close by the vehicles, some of which have a holes through their side panelling. Petrol is escaping from one of the trucks.

The rest of the unit arrives back from manoeuvres late in the afternoon. They've heard nothing about an air attack; they were much too far away. Warias says that they were near Karpovka, along the Kalatsch–Stalingrad railway line. The damage to the bunker is quickly repaired.

13 November. The weather has hardly changed. It's cold and dry. It's supposed to be −15°C or +2°F in Stalingrad. The Russians are launching attacks in our unit's sector every day, preceded each time by a big artillery barrage. The attacks have so far been repulsed, but with heavy losses.

There are now only eighteen men left on the front line from our *Schwadron*. The entire regiment has been reorganised into a single combat unit and is moved around to where it is needed most. Hot meals and fresh ammunition arrive more or less on a daily basis. Besides the kitchen wallahs, and *Unteroffizier* Winter, the medical orderly, goes

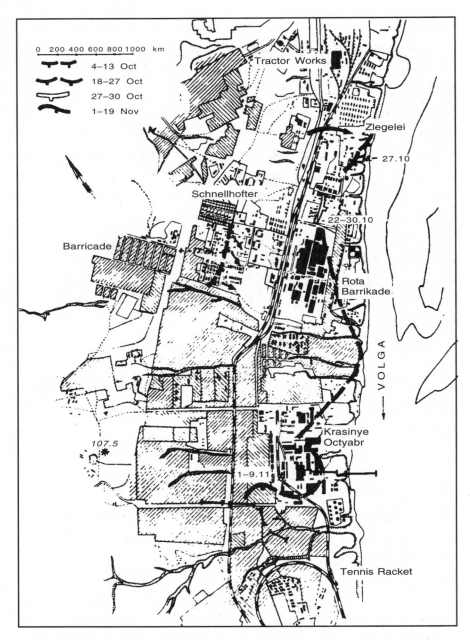

The 21st Panzergrenadier Regiment's war zone in Stalingrad,
October–November 1942

along, plus two drivers with their vehicles. Two volunteers are needed, to lug the mess buckets around. Küpper and I volunteered yesterday—the roster goes around from bunker to bunker and it's now the turn of our one.

It's almost dark when we move off. We've got one Steyr 70 MTW personnel carrier with a soft top and a 1½-ton Opel Blitz 4×4 with a tarpaulin cover. We drive off into the dusk with our lights dimmed. The kitchen wallah knows the way, but he says that there can be no talk about a *Hauptkampflinie** in Stalingrad as amidst all the ruins the front shifts hour by hour. Not long ago our line lay north of the tractor factory, but as of yesterday it is apparently further to the south, in a sector known as the Tennis Racket. The Russians are supposed to have a chemical factory there which they are defending, and so they have set up a bridgehead.

'We need to ask for directions,' *Unteroffizier* Winter says to us. Well then, let's go! We can only hope that we find them soon.

We are now driving purely by the light of the moon on an MSR. Traffic comes towards us and also overtakes. To the right is the railway line running from Kalatsch to Stalingrad. Just beyond Woroponovo station we turn off to the left, and after a few kilometres we're already well inside the ruins of the city. We drive through shallow craters and over heaps of rubble, avoiding debris and overturned telegraph poles. Thick, acrid smoke from smouldering fires chokes our lungs; to the left and right are burnt-out wrecks of various bits of military equipment. Our driver zigzags slowly towards what looks like a small forest or park.

We are now standing on top of a small hill and can see something of the city. More black smoke and smouldering fires—a terrible sight, and we can feel Stalingrad's hot breath. This must be how Rome looked after Nero put it to the torch. The only difference is that here the inferno is made worse by the screaming shells and lethal explosions, increasing

* Literally, 'Main Battle Line', or MBL.

the madness and giving the onlooker the impression that he's witnessing the end of the world. The further we penetrate into the city, the closer the shells fall around us.

'The usual evening blessing from Ivan,' remarks the medic.

It was supposed to sound lighthearted, but it falls flat. He is sitting cowering on ammunition boxes, as I am. My heart is hammering in my throat; fright has gripped me. Now there is a new noise in the air—like the rush of a thousand wings. It is increasing in intensity and seems to be coming directly at us.

'Get out! It's the *Stalinorgel!*' yells the medic.

We jump out of the wagon and dive for safety underneath a large burnt-out tractor. The rushing noise passes us, and then the explosions rain down around us just like fireworks. A splinter the size of a man's hand spins by my head and hits the ground beside Küpper.

'That was a bit of luck,' says the medic.

Behind us we hear yells and cries for the medic.

'Someone from the anti-aircraft position must have been hit—that's the one we drove by,' says *Unteroffizier* Winter, who has just jumped into a hole. 'Come on, let's go—we've got to get on.' We climb back on to the vehicles.

The medic says that the *Stalinorgel* is a primitive rocket launcher, mounted on the back of an open truck. The rockets are fired electrically. They can't hit a precise target, but by using this weapon Ivan can saturate a large area of ground—and God help those who find themselves inside it without any shelter.

We are now driving very carefully. Many places have had to be thoroughly cleared so that vehicles can get through the wreckage. We meet other vehicles, who seem to have the same idea as we do. Many of them are loading up with wounded and dead—they can only do this at night time, when, in theory, the Russians can't see what's going on. But the enemy *does* know what's going on, and he is pulverising the area with his artillery and other big guns. There are always some

'*Nähmaschinen*' in the air—we can often see these biplanes quite clearly, silhouetted against the fiery glow in the sky.

Tracer rounds climb high into the sky, and in front of us we can hear the rattle of machine-gun fire. I can tell it's Russian fire by the sound. Hand grenades are going off and we can hear yelling, so we come to a halt amidst the ruins. Winter disappears, returning some minutes later

'Our people are supposed to be in the same area they were in yesterday,' he says. We'll move in as close to them as we can, and then we'll have to carry the stuff the rest of the way.

The vehicles move off again, gingerly, a yard at a time. I can see two burnt-out Russian T-34 tanks. We pass them and come up to a large building with big open spaces, like a factory. In the background, standing out against the glow of the fire and rising out of the ruins, is a tall chimney, looking for all the world like a threatening finger pointing up to the sky. We pull up in the shadow of the factory.

We start to unload, but Russian artillery shells are falling precisely where we want to go. Some of them land pretty close to us as well. A fire flares behind us—a vehicle has been hit. There is another big blaze nearby—probably a petrol dump or something like that. We wait, all ready to go.

There are craters in front of us, lumps of stone and piles of debris, and between the screams of artillery shells and the thunderous roar as they explode I get goose pimples. We move in zigzags, clambering over stones and beams; stumble; lie flat on the ground; get up again; and continue on.

'Stay close together,' croaks Winter.

In the glare of a fire I can see men running, then some hand grenades go off. Several figures run past us, bent double. Winter gets up and speaks to them. I can recognise an officer's uniform.

'We've got to move further over to the right,' he says afterwards. 'A couple of hours ago they threw Ivan out of this area. Now there's hell to pay because he wants to take it back.'

We creep carefully forward, then we come to an open space littered with clods of earth and concrete blocks with iron rods sticking out. This was perhaps once a bunker, destroyed by our bombs. A long wall rises at the other end; three pillars are still standing.

'They are supposed to be there, somewhere,' says Winter, pointing to the wall.

We can't go any further. Ivan is firing like mad at the churned-up ground which we have to cross. Has he spotted us yet? We crouch down behind the concrete blocks, but the shells are landing so close to us that I can sense the hot metal on my face and can feel the muscles on my back cramping up. In front of us tracer bullets shoot up into the sky; rifles and machine-guns crackle. Is Ivan on the attack?

The shooting gradually dies away.

'Go, now! To the wall!'

It's Winter, barking out his orders. We run through the confusion of rubble, wire and lumps of iron. We can't see anybody. We slither along the wall and come to a basement entrance.

Suddenly there's a shout from somewhere, as if from the grave: 'Hey mate, get out of here! What do you want to do? Bring Ivan down on our heads?' A steel helmet sticks up from the ruins.

We're looking for our unit,' I hear Winter whisper.

'Which one?'

Winter tells him.

'No idea. We don't belong to that crowd. But if you're looking for the ones who chased Ivan out of here this morning, you'll find them about fifty metres further to the right in that large factory building. But get out of here—and thank your lucky stars it's quiet at the moment.'

The head with the steel helmet disappears again. He call this quiet? We hardly dare lift our heads out of the dirt! During a short lull we stumble on, pieces of broken glass crackling under our feet, shadows springing out of the ruins. Immediately tracer bullets zip towards us and bursts of machine-gun fire hit the wreckage all around like a hailstorm. We hurry onwards, the mess buckets clattering against the blocks of concrete. A shadow appears beside us.

'Are you the supply blokes from the 1st Squadron?' comes the question out of the darkness.

'Is that you, Domscheid?' Winter demands in return.

'Yep! I've been waiting for you for two hours to show you the way!'

Are we relieved! Domscheid is an *Obergefreiter*. He tells us that they carried out a counter-attack this morning and are now positioned a bit further forward in the factory building.

Winter swears. 'Every time we come you are somewhere else. One day we'll probably deliver these supplies straight to Ivan.'

'Oh, that's been done before,' says Domscheid. Last night, four men from the 74th Infantry Division walked right into Ivan's hands, with food and ammunition. During the counter-attack this morning only empty containers were found—there was no sign of the men.

We creep behind Domscheid, tracer whizzing in from both sides. I stumble and bang a metal strut with my canteen, making an awful row. Immediately a Russian machine gunner opens up and a strip of tracer bullets lights up the night. Ivan is pretty close! We lie down flat; the shots sing over my head and explode against the concrete block. The chalky spray drizzles down my neck, mixing with my sweat. I roll forward and pull the two mess buckets behind the block. Küpper has also let go of his mess bucket and is hauling it to safety. He is lying a couple of paces further forward, next to a protective wall. I want to catch him up and I take a pace forward—only to fall into emptiness. Hands grab me and pull me up.

'Hang on!' says a deep voice. And then: 'Where did you come from so suddenly? We were just about to fire on you—you were bloody lucky!'

Domscheid tells them.

'Christ, do you have to use this particular street? We've got Ivan sitting right on our backs here.'

'I came by here just two hours ago and Ivan was further forward,' Domscheid says.

'Yes, but in the last hour not so. Max, do you have your sprayer ready?' asks the low voice.

'Of course—as always,' comes the answer.

'Good, then we'll give you covering fire. You can get through behind us, across the street. Now—off with you!'

On their first burst of fire we dash off. Küpper is faster than me and nearly pulls my arm out of its socket because I'm still holding on to the other handle of the food container. Ivan shoots wildly back. Then the artillery opens up. In between I can also hear the *thud* of the mortars. The rounds loop towards us and explode all around. The bombardment seems to go for us like a wild animal, and we squeeze together in a bombed-out basement. I duck further down with each explosion, expecting the basement to collapse any moment and bury the lot of us. The earth above shakes—just like in an earthquake, I should think. My nerves are a-flutter. I'd never imagined I could be so terrified.

You can't do anything—not a thing. The only solution might actually be to get out and run. But where? The only advantage is that death will come more quickly. For heaven's sake, they are forever going on about the 'proud, successful German advances' in the Army news bulletins, but here in Stalingrad I haven't seen anything of that. The only thing I understand is that we are holed up in these ruins like cowering rats, fighting for our lives. But what else can we do, given the Russian superiority?

The driver and the medic are sitting next to me, with Winter and Küpper on the other side. Küpper is as white as a sheet, and we are all staring at the ceiling, which already has a huge number of cracks. Domscheid has the strongest nerves: he is standing by the entrance, staring out into the darkness. As far as Küpper and I are concerned, these few hours in Stalingrad have certainly dampened down our enthusiasm for war—and we haven't yet had any 'personal contact', as it is so nicely put. My thoughts now are concentrated solely on how and when we're going to be able to get out of here safely. We've been in this god-awful heap of ruins for hours, and we still haven't reached our unit.

Domscheid tells us from his position at the entrance that Ivan is shooting at the slightest thing. Because our machine guns opened up, Ivan probably thought we were mounting another attack and wanted to make quite sure that it was nipped in the bud.

'If only he knew that we are quite happy keeping our heads down for the moment—until we get our replacements that is,' says Domscheid. 'We're supposed to be replaced by fresh troops, according to our *Wachtmeister*.'

'He who believes is indeed blessed,' murmurs the medic.

Finally the barrage is lifted—after what seems to me like an eternity. We jump up—Domscheid knows the way. He makes for a ruined factory building, knowing that someone has been lying there under cover, watching everything. Softly, he calls out the code-word while we are still some distance away, and gives his name. We go to a basement entrance, which is half-covered by wreckage. Domscheid leads us through a corridor to a room, where, in front of the doorway, an iron plate has been placed. I can see two Hindenburg lanterns, which provide just enough light to clear the darkness in the room.

Domscheid makes a droll introduction: 'May I present our new battle headquarters.'

A heap of sacks and a few rags are strewn on the ground, and lying on top of them, curled up, are two *Landser*; another one is sitting on a couple of stacked-up ammunition boxes. Startled by the noise we have made, the two *Landser* jump up and help us into the room with our containers. Both men appear to be very tired—and who knows when they might next get some sleep? I can barely distinguish their faces under all the dirt and stubble. But I guess we all look about the same.

Then a *Wachtmeister* comes in. He says hello and offers his hand to Weichert. I recognise him—he's the one who pushed the old Russian fellow's head into the bucket at the well. He tells Winter that the one remaining officer in the group became a casualty this morning, and that now he was in charge of this sector. The men are positioned in front of and to the side of this area, hidden in the ruins. The fighting ebbs back and forth, and no one really knows where the *Hauptkampflinie* really runs. Casualties today are one dead and two wounded, and they're already on the way to the main medical centre.

'This is the craziest place imaginable. The Russians are often only twenty or thirty metres away, sometimes at hand-grenade range in front of us. No more than 200 metres in front of us there is a deep trench, and this trench leads right down to the banks of the Volga. From there Ivan gets reinforcements every night. For days now we've all been waiting impatiently to be relieved, or at least to receive reinforcements, but we're beginning to doubt whether they'll ever come.'

This last sentence is only whispered to Winter, but with my sharp ears I still understand what he has said. So they've got their doubts. That makes me think. The warm food and the coffee must by now be frozen solid, even though the containers have double skins and are supposed to be insulated. Winter has brought a fair supply of solid methylated spirits along, and a solid-fuel burner to heat up the food. The food is ice cold, but not frozen solid. It's a good, thick noodle soup with lots of canned beef—much better than what we get in the bunkers. These men have more than earned these decent rations.

Winter is pressing for us to start getting back. An hour has passed since we left our bunker. The *Wachtmeister* needs more ammunition, which we've got on the trucks. He details five men to go with us. On the way there the Russians lob more heavy shells into the area. We run after the lead soldier at the double and stop only briefly each time a large shell lands nearby . . .

We jump up on the trucks and sit on the empty ammunition boxes. The dead soldier we are taking back with us lies in the front, in his body bag. There is supposed to be another road we can take going back. The driver says that the route across the village of Petschanka and past another *kolkhoz* to Vavarovka is shorter going from here. Because of the frost, all the roads are quite passable. But first we have to work our way through the ruins. Every now and then the vehicles drive down into a trench and come up the other side, and we're catapulted towards the back and have to hang on to the tailgate, the ammo boxes sliding after us and slamming into our jackboots. Just keep going, I think—just get out of here. When it all starts up again we need to be well out of range.

We go through another deep trench and have to help push the truck back out again. We pass several other vehicles, and some VW jeeps with officers as passengers pass us. The MSR is rough, but hard and solid.

'How far is it now?' I ask the medic, who is looking back at us from up front through a slit in the tarpaulin.

'Just a few kilometres,' I hear him saying.

At that moment we all hear a thundering noise, as though the world were going split apart at any moment. I slide hastily towards the back and release part of the tarpaulin. I see a frightful spectacle—one that makes me cringe. Küpper joins me and stares open-mouthed. It would be a beautiful sight were it not for the sinister roaring and the continuous explosions which make you realise that thousands of lives are being sacrificed.

The sky is glowing over Stalingrad. Greyish-white smoke billows from the ground; flames shoot high into the sky in between. The long probing fingers of the searchlights tear at the half-darkness of the breaking day. There must be a lot of aircraft up. Bombs are ceaselessly raining down on a city that has been condemned to death. The explosions merge into one another, creating a devastating inferno. Tracer patterns from the anti-aircraft guns climb high into the sky for kilometres around. Two aircraft explode over the hellish fires and are swallowed up by them.

This is absolutely crazy—no one can survive this! And yet . . . Even in this inferno, some are managing to stay alive; not only that—they are defending themselves and fighting back. The proof is that, after every bombardment, the enemy counter-attacks once more and sometimes even gains a bit of ground, although usually he is stopped in his tracks and pushed back to where he started from. This is the way it has been since the beginning of September, ever since German troops forced their way into the city. But because of the strong defences along the Volga, the Germans have now been obliged to hide in the ruins.

When we return to the bunkers it is full daylight. We can hear only a far-off droning noise, just as before. But for me it is no longer the same. I now see the disaster that will come out of this hapless city. It is a stark warning to everyone languishing in the rear areas, wasting their time by making their quarters comfortable for the winter.

CHAPTER THREE

A Narrow Escape

T ODAY IS 17 November 1942. Yesterday we had the first snowfall, and a white blanket now covers the steppe as far as the eye can see. It seems as if everything around is muffled; even the rumble of battle is barely audible when the wind carries the sound over to us.

Last night a few soldiers came back from Stalingrad. I'm glad to see that the sickly *Stabsgefreiter** Petsch is among them. It's obvious that he wasn't much use at the front, owing to his nervous condition.

The unit has suffered a lot more casualties. These include *Unteroffizier* Seiffert, who has been badly wounded and has a splinter in his leg. Domscheid apparently was extremely lucky according to another soldier. A bomb took his helmet off and the only injury he suffered was a cut from his chinstrap: a fellow standing no more than two metres away was blown into the air. The only things left of him were individual body parts, which they gathered up in a groundsheet.

In the evening we have a chat with Meinhard about the general situation as far as it has affected us. It is more a mish-mash of rumours, assumptions and hopes that things will turn out in our favour. He's been drinking again—I can smell it on his breath—and he is therefore much more communicative. Warias is rubbing his back against a beam, and the noise he makes is so loud that we turn to look at him. We've all used

* Literally, 'Staff Lance-Corporal'.

lice powder, and we've even boiled our underwear, but it only helps for a while.

Seidel inadvertently crashes into the back of another soldier, who sprawls headlong on to the floor. Seidel helps him to his feet and mutters some excuse or other. We haven't seen the soldier with the chevron before. But before anyone can say anything else, Meinhard bellows: 'Hey, Swina, where on earth have you come from? I thought you were at the front with the others?' He in turn clutches his throat and croaks something unintelligible. He is short and quite chubby. He's got a scarf round his neck and a cap on his head which he has pulled down so far that it almost covers his somewhat dangly ears. He goes over to Meinhard at the table and our eyes follow him in curiosity. When he takes his cap off I get the feeling that everyone is kind of smirking. Even I can hardly hold it back.

The name 'Swina' brings to mind the image of the grunting creature whose meat we haven't had for a while, especially with his chubby pink cheeks and little red eyes, which look at us from beneath bristling white eyebrows! He has a rounded, good-natured, almost comical face, with a mop of straw-coloured hair on top.

Swina offers Meinhard his hand. He motions to his scarf and grunts: 'Got a bad throat—can barely speak. *Wachtmeister* Romikat sent me to the rear to recover.'

'That was very sensible of him. How long have you been here?' asks Meinhard.

'What?' grunts Swina, stretching his head forward like a bird.

Meinhard pulls Swina towards him and speaks directly into his ear: 'How long have you been here?'

'For an hour. Was supposed to come here to the 4th *Schwadron*, but the truck crashed. Had to wait all day before we could get a tow.'

'Did anyone else come with you?' Meinhard speaks right into Swina's ear.

'Yes—Gorny and Kirstein.'

'What, they're both here?' exclaims Meinhard in delight.

The chubby *Gefreiter* nods, but he looks dejected and, barely audibly, explains: 'Gorny only lost a bit of his arm, but Kirstein was killed outright—a shell splinter. They brought him to the cemetery straightaway.'

Meinhard must have known the dead soldier very well. He says in a thick voice: 'Bloody Stalingrad! Soon there won't be any of the old fellows left. Now Fritz has gone—and he always believed that nothing could ever happen to him. We were together for a month. Once his rifle was shot out of his hand and shortly after that a splinter tore open the side of his helmet, but he was quite convinced that no Russian bullet would ever have his name on it—he would die in his bed, an old man. Nothing would persuade him otherwise, despite the fact that many of our friends were falling around us. And now it has happened, old chum—even though you never thought it could.'

Meinhard mutters to himself. He starts sucking on his pipe and blowing out clouds of smoke.

Swina sits on the bench, staring into the flickering light of the improvised petrol lamp which was put in our bunker yesterday. Some clever individual takes wine bottles half full of petrol and sticks a cartridge case with two holes in the side up through the cork. The gas which escapes up through the cartridge case is ignited and burns evenly, lighting up the bunker better than the usual Hindenburg candles, which are in short supply anyway.

It's all a bit depressing here in the bunker right now. The faces around me no longer look carefree and unconcerned. We've heard about the heavy casualties, and also about the problems that exist resupplying the troops, particularly over the last few days. The Russians in the meantime are reported to have increased their strength considerably along the Volga.

'What does it look like at the front?' we hear Meinhard asking Swina.

Swina doesn't understand the question and cups his hand to his ear. The man must be almost deaf, and, realising this, everybody glances at everyone else.

Meinhard speaks more loudly, directly into Swina's ear: 'What's it look like up at the front?'

'Worse and worse,' Swina croaks. 'Two days ago two mortars in our sector were lost. We've only got one now in our battle group.'

'*Spiess* has told me that already!' says Meinhard. Then he bends forward and says in a loud voice: 'Hey, it gets worse with you all the time. Last time we were together at least you could hear better!'

Swina points to his throat: 'It's because of my throat!'

What does his throat have to do with deafness, we wonder?

Meinhard is thinking exactly the same thing. More to us than to Swina he says: 'What do you mean, your throat? They should be packing you off home when you are this deaf. I don't understand why they are always sending you back up to the front lines. By the way, which bunker are in?'

'The first one, with the young sub-machine gun blokes,' croaks Swina. 'But I don't like it there.'

We look at each other and Meinhard smiles.

'These fellows spray everything,' he says, 'but they don't like it when you tell them that.'

The chubby Swina shifts uneasily. Scratching himself and shrugging his shoulders, he croaks: 'That's what everyone tells the new boys.' We all laugh.

'D'you want to come into our bunker?' Meinhard again has his mouth close to Swina's ear and at the same time is looking at us. We nod. Why not? It's big enough. If we pull our stuff a bit closer together we can get another two in. Swina says 'Yes' to the question and looks up at us.

'Okay—go get your stuff. You can stay here,' says Meinhard out loud.

The chubby little *Gefreiter* grins and trots like a walking flour bag out of the bunker. If it were not so tragic, this whole incident would have been comical.

Meinhard says that he cannot understand how Swina could have got into the Army in the first place. In the summer, he tells us, Swina came to the *Schwadron* with a group of returning convalescents. He couldn't hear very well even then. At first people thought that he was being anti-social because he never answered anyone's questions, but then it was realised that he couldn't even hear the shells screaming overhead and had to be pulled to safety at the last moment. His deafness became even worse after an shell exploded right next to him. So he can't do very much. Most of the time he's been bringing up ammunition stocks and fetching rations, and for these tasks he has been absolutely dependable. He seems to get a little bit anxious when he is at the front, but this is only because of his hearing difficulties—Swina is certainly not a coward.

Meinhard puffs away at his pipe—he only actually lets it go out when he's asleep. He fumbles around under the table, pulls out a half empty bottle and takes a long swig. In the dark I hadn't even noticed it was there.

'Why do you call him Swina?' Grommel wants to know.

'Very simple—that's his name,' laughs Meinhard.

'What? I thought it was a nickname!' Warias retorts, surprised.

'Well, it's not his full name. We've shortened it actually. His full name is Johann Swinowski.'

So, that's the way it is. Outside someone is kicking up a racket at the entrance, and then Swina comes waddling back in. He is carrying his kitbag and he's got some blankets under his arm. Seidel shows him to the spot beside Meinhard which he has cleared for him.

The night passes quietly. Once in a while I wake up as I subconsciously hear a new noise in the bunker—which turns out to be a satisfied grunt.

18 November. The night is cold and frosty. I have dressed for warmth for my guard duty, with a scarf round my neck. The frost bites at my ears; with each step the frozen snow crunches under my boots. I think about home and about going skiing in the glistening winter sun with its crunchy snow. I was a good skier and could often make around thirty meters at our ski jump. Here in the steppe everything is flat, as it is on our lake. In order to reach our ski jump we would have to cross the frozen lake on skis for about three kilometres. By that time we would have worked up a pretty good sweat. Those were a wonderful times.

As I do on so many clear nights, I am staring up into the night sky. I'm searching for the Little Bear, and tracing up to the Pole Star to find north. I have at least a general idea of the direction where home is. I can often hear, even late at night, *Unteroffizier* Döring on his harmonica, playing his favourite tune, 'Home, Your Stars'. Tonight Döring is the duty NCO and is making his rounds of the bunker area. He also leads our combat training. He is a real old timer, released from his service at the front to give us training. We have no problem with him and have learned a lot from him—not exercises, but first-hand experience in trench training.

19 November. Towards morning the wind picks up. The weather is hazy and light snow clouds are moving over the steppe. Meinhard tells us that he has to return to Stalingrad today—the *Spiess* told him so yesterday. He'll drive over with Winter; it is also his turn to go.

'Ah well,' says Meinhard, reflectively. 'That's life.'

'True,' says Kurat, 'but it could take a hundred years.'

'Could be,' agrees Meinhard, 'but I don't want to grow that old. I shall be quite happy if I can survive this bloody war.'

'You will,' says Grommel with conviction.

We all want to give him a bit of courage, but we probably fail, as Meinhard doesn't talk much after this. He is smoking even more than usual. Then he sits down and writes a letter home. The next drill is after lunch, so until then we get busy cleaning our weapons and getting all our equipment in order.

As we report to our formation, something is different in our bunker area. Drivers are running backwards and forwards and are busy with their vehicles. A courier scurries around on his motorcycle and disappears in the direction of the *kolkhoz*. We also have to wait longer than usual for the *Spiess* to show up. Something is happening. But what? We look at each other. Our neighbours from the next bunker don't know anything either. Then the *Spiess* arrives with maps in his hands.

He tells us, not beating about the bush, that we are now at the highest state of alert because the Russians have attacked the left flank of the front with strong tank units and broken through the Romanian lines around Kletskaya. The entire Romanian front has reportedly caved in, with the remnants fleeing in the direction of Kalatsch.

'Shit!' I hear one of our instructors exclaim.

The *Spiess* waters down our first shock by telling us that steps have already been taken to start pushing the Russians back—our tanks and air force have already engaged them. More we are not told.

Meinhard tells us later that he and Winter will not be sent back into Stalingrad, because no one knows where our combat group is at the moment; they were pulled out of the ruins and reassigned somewhere else. We have to wait. He also tells us that the *Schirrmeister** reckons that the vehicles will be able to get going, but he doesn't have enough fuel for all of them because for the last few weeks there has been a big shortage of petrol and other supplies.

'Is it really that bad?' asks Meinhard.

The *Schirrmeister* shrugs his shoulders. 'No one knows anything for sure, but it could be that we'll have to move our vehicles out of here if we can't stop the Russians.'

'In that case, sod it!' says Seidel in his flippant style.

* Motor Sergeant.

We sleep uneasily. When I begin my guard duty at about 0500 I listen intently for any noise coming from the north in the dark. The wind brings muffled rolling noises to my ear, but no more than usual. If fighting is taking place near Kletskaya, we wouldn't be able to hear anything anyway because it's too far away. Or could it be that the breakthrough has been stopped by our own troops?

20 November. As daytime emerges, things get busy. We've never seen so many He 111 bombers and Ju 87 Stukas. In other words, something serious must be going on up north. The skies are filled with the roar of engines, and we can also hear a faraway rumbling noise. It increases hour by hour, becoming more distinct and swelling to a rolling thunder. It's coming from the north, where the Russians are supposed to have broken through. But soon we are also hearing it from the south as well—something is happening down there. We are on full alert and are waiting. Some men are in their bunkers; others are, like me, standing on the top of the bunker waiting for whatever it is coming towards us.

'Alarm!' someone is yelling. 'Everybody out of the bunkers!'

We dash down into the bunkers, pick up our weapons and all our equipment, and struggle into it while we run back up again. Many have to go back down in the bunkers to pick up their winter coats. What's going on? You can read the questions in our faces. Then one of the drivers says that the Russians have also broken through the Romanian lines in the south and are coming at us from both sides, trying to take us in a pincer movement. Their tanks have already reached Sety, and we are supposed to hold them back.

I suspect that things will now become serious for us and for everybody else around Stalingrad. We felt secure for the winter in our shelters and bunkers, but the rumbling has grown steadily right through into the night. Anybody who doubted what was happening now knows better: even the most inexperienced soldier here realises that we are about to be taken in a pincer movement. It's still quiet at the moment—but for how long? Is it the lull before the storm?

21 November. And so it proves. It begins in the early morning with the whining of heavy shells over our heads and their crackling explosions. Anybody still in his bunker runs out into his prepared position. But we see nothing.

'Their artillery are just firing to get the range,' says the driver sitting beside me.

Most of the rounds are landing to our right, and further to the rear. *Stalinorgel* rockets zoom overhead, landing near the *kolkhoz*.

Slowly it gets lighter and we can see a little better. In amongst the howling and the explosions, we can now hear other noises—the droning of diesel engines and the squeaky clatter of tank tracks. Russian T-34s are circling round. They can see the situation better. Their shots ring out, making a harsh, metallic sound in the frosty air. The shells cut through the air with a *swish!* and explode on their targets. Often the shells hit the ground as hot glowing balls, only to ricochet with a *swish!* high into the air and then boring back into the ground. 'Tank shells!' yells someone.

Then the T-34s emerge from the haze. I count five of the steel giants. They are still some 100 metres away and moving only slowly. Their guns swivel, searching for targets. When they have found them, they fire. The artillery barrage is also increasing; again, their targets seem to be to our side and behind us. The tanks are also firing there. Haven't they seen us yet, or do they have a better target over there?

Someone is creeping up behind us in the trench. It's Jansen, the truck driver. He is followed by two Russian volunteers bringing up ammunition. Jansen works his way over to Meinhard at the machine-gun. I can hear what he's saying—fuel has been provided and orders have been given to move all the trains out, with all the vehicles, over the bridge at Kalatsch towards the west. The *Spiess* and Döring want to wait until nightfall, because we've got no anti-tank support—otherwise the Russian tanks could knock us over like ninepins.

Then, over our heads, we hear the deep droning noise of Russian combat aircraft. They drop their bombs and smoke billows up behind us. From the side, three small aircraft are diving down towards us. We can easily identify the Soviet star on the fuselages and wings.

We stare towards the front; my nerves are fluttering. Everything is different compared to all the combat training. Various thoughts flash through my head. The tanks in front of us are moving very slowly. I sneak over to Meinhard and peer through his field glasses.

The soldiers look like dirty brown lumps of clay glued on to the white camouflaged tanks as, for the first time, I see our enemies in front of me. A faint shudder goes through my body. If they get me, everything is over, because we have often heard in gruesome detail what they do to German soldiers. There is a mixture of excitement, fright and rebelliousness about what could be happening to us. My mouth is dry and I grip my carbine more tightly.

Meinhard, who has carefully lifted his white-chalked helmet over the edge of his trench, seems to think that they are moving towards the right, past us. They are at the receiving end of heavy fire from there. The stream in front of us stops and the infantry dismount. They would be much too far away for our machine guns and carbines. Maybe they have not even seen us? Our counter-fire slackens and the tanks and infantry move almost parallel to us, further towards the right.

We wait and watch. The enemy tanks go out of sight, and the shooting dies down. The haze in front of us increases and slowly spreads over the white plain.

We wait for a while longer, then comes the command 'Everyone to the vehicles and mount!' We wait until the vehicles are out of their covered positions and then we climb aboard. 'Go!' We look round; we are a bit downcast. The bunkers were sort of shelter for us. We had got used to the straw bedding and the cracked clay walls. Now we are off into the cold across the hard frozen snow with its great unknowns. The general direction is Kalatsch.

The driver of the lead vehicle knows the way, and has often driven it. In spite of our winter coats we are freezing cold in the vehicle, even though, on Meinhard's suggestion, I have put on a second shirt and an extra pair of underpants. I am not alone in my misery. Our empty stomachs don't help: the body needs fuel. We received only cold rations this morning, but still haven't had time to eat. We try to eat now, but we abandon the idea of drinking anything as the coffee in our canteens is frozen solid.

On the way we meet up with other traffic—trucks, personnel carriers, motorcycles, jeeps, half-tracks with gun carriages and guns. They are all moving like we are, in great haste to escape something which we sense rather than see. Beside us there are the remains of destroyed or defective vehicles. The *Rollbahn-UvD* recently dropped his parachute flares and his bombs and a quad anti-aircraft gun had finally chased him away.

We are told about this by a driver who wants to jump up on to our vehicle. Warias unceremoniously hauls him up. There are many others along the road who try to jump up on our vehicles. As we come to a rail line, we take another soldier on board. He says that his supply vehicle was hit not far from here, just about half an hour ago, by a shell from a T-34. His sergeant was killed immediately and he was wounded in the head but had escaped on foot.

'It's about ten kilometres to the Don bridge at Kalatsch,' he says.

The vehicles which have converged on the bridge have built up into a huge traffic jam trying to get across. Everyone is pushing, and the traffic is barely creeping along. It'd probably be quicker to walk, but then, in the darkness and in confusion, we'd probably be hard put to find our places again. So we stay where we are and freeze. The other vehicles with Döring and the *Spiess* are out of sight.

22 November. In the morning the fog lifts from the Don and a milky white veil slowly envelops the bridge. We have just made it across when we hear the harsh metallic report of a tank gun. A Russian tank is firing into the vehicles which are making for the bridge ready to cross. We can only see the action as weak shadows. There are explosions.

'The 88-millimetre AA gun has been hit!' says Küpper, who has been sitting at the back all the way and can see a bit more clearly.

The vehicles in front of us give fuel and drive into the mass ahead of us, which is getting ever thicker. We follow! After a few kilometres we stop. Everything is quiet. We get down, walk around a bit to get the circulation back in our limbs and wait. For what? For the other vehicles? In this fog it would only be sheer luck if we found them again. We are now only three vehicles: the *Schirrmeister* with his Steyr and four men and two Opel Blitz trucks with fourteen men and three soldiers from other units.

Our nerves are on edge. We are running beside the vehicles, so that our feet don't get frozen. Stop—turn the engines off! The *Schirrmeister* orders a halt, gesturing to the other drivers. We can hear the sound of engines quite clearly now. They are pretty rough, and I reckon they are diesels.

'T-34s!' whispers the *Schirrmeister*, who knows about these things.

'We must go back—we can't get through here!' he whispers. The Russians are already across the Don and are blocking our way. We can also hear tank engines to the right of us. We assume that they are advancing in line. The noises disappear now and then, but they always come back.

We start up our engines. They run smoothly and we drive very slowly back. Two soldiers are leading the way and are waving our vehicles on. It is a nerve-racking business, and I get the impression that we're going round in circles. At any moment a Russian tank could be standing in front of us, his engine cut, ready to blow us to pieces. But he can't see in the mist any better than we can, and has to rely on what he can hear. That at least is something in our favour—though it's not much.

Again there are noises in front of us. A flare goes up. We keep stock still! Have they seen us? The light from the flare hardly penetrates the fog, giving it a ghostly appearance. The drivers immediately cut their engines. The yellowish light falls and is extinguished in the snow. Silence! My heart is pounding in my throat. Then a diesel starts up with a low droning noise. Tank tracks squeak, and slowly the tank moves and disappears to our left.

Wow—that was a bit of luck!. But he is in the same situation as we are. It's possible he's heard us, but for him too it must have been scary. Where to now? Have we been driving around in circles? That's always a possibility in these conditions.

We carry on driving at walking pace through the milky soup, just like before. Then one of the soldiers who has been walking ahead of us comes back, out of breath, to report that he has noticed a weak light from a fire or something to our side. We must assume that the Russians are there, and he suggests a recce. I am in the patrol. We creep very carefully in the direction of the suspect area. We don't see the red glare of the fire until we are quite close. The flames are flickering. In the fog it looks as if it is burning in a hollow. The thick fog gives the illusion of walls. To right and left the dark outlines of houses and barns appear. We glide over the snow, closer to the fire, and can make out several figures talking together. Then one of the soldiers beside me gives a start and blurts out happily: 'Thank God! They're ours!'

I too have recognised them by their language. It is the *Spiess* with Döring and two personnel carriers. Among the twelve men are Meinhard, Swina and the sick *Stabsgefreiter* Petsch. Just like us, they have been fumbling around in the fog, and then ended up here in the *kolkhoz*. Where the rest of our vehicles have ended up they don't know either.

The *Spiess* and some of the others discuss the matter. They agree that an advance party should try to find a gap. The vehicles will then move

57

forward quietly as far as they can, and then make a run for it through the gap at full speed.

We pray that the fog won't lift, otherwise it would be our undoing. After the fire has been put out we slowly follow the advance party. We walk quietly beside the vehicles, in order to keep warm. I have to rub my eyes continually—the constant staring into the fog and the cutting cold is affecting my sight. Whenever we watch we imagine figures in front of us and clutch our weapons that much more tightly.

Then Russian voices can clearly be heard, coming from the left. Then there is a loud yell and a question. In response a tank engine starts up with a droning noise. Then the engine of the Steyr screams into life and Jansen pushes the accelerator pedal of the Opel Blitz to the floor. Our truck leaps forward and then drives on. Then we hear the engines of our other vehicles to the right of us.

We can see nothing in front of us; the milky mass is just like a wall. Driving across the bumpy steppe, we are thrown up to the canvas roof over the truck and hold on to the framework of the flatbed for all we are worth. We hope the truck won't break an axle. Behind us we hear the sharp report of the tank gun firing. The rounds swish overhead. The T-34s are shooting blindly into the fog. It would have to be sheer luck if they were to hit us.

'We made it!' yells Warias, and all our pent-up excitement is released.

Although we have broken through the tank barrier, the question still remains—are we out of the encirclement? The gunfire from behind has stopped and Jansen eases his foot off the pedal as the engine has run hot. Where are we? And where are the others? We haven't seen anyone lately.

The fog hasn't lifted at all—it's just as thick as ever—and we're swimming in the middle of it. We dismount again and walk about to warm our feet up. The snow crunches underfoot and we are leaving tracks all over the place. Grommel finds tyre tracks from two vehicles.

We follow them, and soon we come across the second Opel Blitz and the Steyr personnel carrier. The truck is hanging with a rear wheel over a hole on the rim of a *Rachel*.* We hadn't thought of this problem—we ourselves could easily have ended up in one.

We get the truck out of the hole and rest up in the next *Rachel*. Slowly the fog lifts. Behind us there is nothing but snow-covered steppe. We hear fighting in the distance. What now? No one knows.

'We were supposed to drive south to Nishne Tschirskaya,' an *Obergefreiter* reminds the *Schirrmeister*. That's the village where the rear-echelon supply vehicles were supposed to assemble after the Russian breakthrough. Okay, fine! Off to Nishne Tschirskaya!

A really disheartening feeling comes over me. I would prefer to just get off the vehicle and disappear, as many have already done. It's not that I am a coward, but the retreat from the Russians, the soldiers around me with their frightened, pale faces, many of them without weapons, all add up to a very uneasy feeling. Then there is the sight of the little *Leutnant*,† who seems to be an administrative official or a teacher, and who, as the only officer, is probably now obliged to take on a job he is not up to. In his buttonhole he wears the red-striped ribbon of the so-called *Gefrierfleischorden*,‡ which was awarded to more or less everybody who survived the Russian winter campaigns of 1941/42. I assume he has no front-line experience, and everyone else sees it the same way.

He divides us into groups and sends us out to secure the MSR using tank positions left over from earlier combat. What a situation! We have neither heavy weapons nor sufficient small arms or ammunition. The holes are partially filled with snow. I work with Küpper like a wild thing to clean up a tank shelter, just to keep warm. I have to give the *Leutnant* full marks because he has been able to scrounge a hot meal for us. We

---

* A 'trench' formed by faulting of the steppe crust.
† Lieutenant.
‡ Order of the Frozen Meat, a derogatory reference to the Russian campaign medal.

have no idea what it is—is much too foggy and dark to tell—but it's made from meat and tastes delicious. In the next hole, Seidel starts to laugh. He thinks it's the old horse which we saw on the railway line earlier. This could be true, but in any case this hot meal—the first in three days—tastes terrific!

23 November. It's quiet this morning, although German bombers and fighters are up and about. A small, wiry infantry *Unteroffizier von der Infanterie*, who has been assigned as our *Gruppenführer*,* peers through his field glasses at the troops coming towards us. We expect a Russian attack, but as they get nearer we realise that they are in fact stragglers from our own forces. They join up with us, increasing our strength. Several more vehicles arrive, including a 75mm anti-tank gun, a quad anti-aircraft gun from our regiment, which we can use for ground defence, and an 88mm from an anti-aircraft gun battalion. Many of these men know each other and are pleased to meet up with friends again.

We also have a stroke of good luck, because the personnel carrier with Döring and the others reach us. They got lost in the fog and again ran into another tank. They kept their heads down for the entire night, and first thing this morning they drove off as if the devil was after them. To our delight, our *Spiess* and two further vehicles, including our field kitchen, also reach us. Our unit is now well represented. From what we are told, some of our supply vehicles were able to make it across to the south side of the Don yesterday and should even now be on their way to Nishne Tschirskaya.

---

* Group Leader.

CHAPTER FOUR

A Last-Minute Reprieve

D URING the early afternoon of 23 November our combat group was, surprisingly, reinforced by a larger pioneer (engineer) unit under the leadership of a *Hauptmann*.* They suddenly appeared in front of us from nowhere, driving forward a platoon of Russians they had taken prisoner while on the way over here to us. The unit came from a pioneer school which had been stationed near Kalatsch on the Don heights. They were able, with a strength of nearly three companies, to save themselves from the T-34s.

The experienced *Pionierhauptmann* takes over command of our combat group and brings some organisation to the confused and demoralised men. It turns out that most of the demoralised soldiers and NCOs have no combat experience, while those in the Stalingrad area mainly served in supply, maintenance and administrative units. Even though we, the replacement troops since October, also don't have much front-line experience, we are the best-trained and -armed unit and are well prepared for any serious incident. For that reason we have the only combat-proven men—assistant machine gunners—assigned to us. During the breakthrough they were either sick or on their way back from leave, and were in the rear areas.

I'm not particularly happy when a leader assigns me *Obergefreiter* Petsch—the one whose nerves have failed him—as my number two.

* Captain.

Küpper is assigned as number two to Meinhard, who has the second MG 34 light machine gun in our squad. Our morale is boosted by the knowledge that most of the men in our unit will be taking up positions close to each other.

In the meantime we've been able to find out where we are. We're on the so-called Don Heights Road. Behind us is a village called Rytschov. This lies directly on the Don and on the railway line to Tschir and Stalingrad. A few kilometres to the south-east there's an important railway bridge which crosses the Don. We can see this bridge clearly only if we use of field glasses. On the other side of the Don there is reported to be another combat unit. Only a few kilometres west of us is Tschir railway station. Tschir has a fuel depot and other war supplies. Two drivers coming to us from this direction report that the Russians have already secured the area.

We also learn from Meinhard that our combat unit has formed a bridgehead in order to stop the Russians securing the important railway line which leads to Stalingrad, and the two bridges which lead south over the Don. For defence we have one 88mm AA gun, two 75mm AT guns on mounts and one quad AA gun for use against ground targets. The pioneers have in addition several mortars and hollow charges for anti-tank work. Three tanks and another 88mm gun are supposed to be joining us. Hopes are raised more because a rumour is going around that *Generaloberst** Hoth and his Fourth Tank Army is on his way to break the siege and the encirclement. With that our situation here will also loosen up.

This news and the slogans which follow—'Soldiers, hang on! The *Führer* will get you out!—improve morale only for a short while. We quickly realise that we are entirely dependent upon ourselves. Our early hopes disappear like the melting snow as soon as a shell explodes. The almost daily Soviet attacks and the constant fight to stay alive drain us visibly. To these privations must be added the hunger we suffer for

---

* No precise equivalent in the British Army; one rank above General.

days on end when no food can be delivered, forcing us to search through the dirty bread bags of dead Russians lying in front of us in order to find anything edible. Occasionally they'd have more German rations on them than we'd ever been given.

It's all very difficult—a time that I and the few who survive it will never forget. It's particularly demoralising for us because, after the loss of our few AT weapons, no more replacements are available. What is more, contact with other combat units south of the Don is non-existent.

24 November. At about midday one of the machine guns on our right flank suddenly starts hammering away. Then we hear rifle fire. The firing becomes more intense, and next we see Russian infantry appearing through the haze. I am meeting the enemy face to face for the first time, and, apart from an undeniable curiosity, also feel an enormous amount of nervousness and excitement. The brown, huddled figures remind me somehow of a great herd of sheep moving over a snow-covered field. As soon as the herd comes under fire from us, they hesitate for a moment, move apart from each other, and then immediately move forward again.

We are firing from all positions; only our machine gun is silent. What is the matter? I have concentrated so fiercely on the Russians that I've paid no attention to Petsch. Why doesn't he shoot? His ammunition belt is in place, his machine gun is okay. Then I hear Döring call over: 'What's wrong, Petsch? Why don't you shoot?'

Yes, for God's sake—why doesn't he shoot? Some of the enemy fall, hit by rifle fire and fire from Meinhard's machine gun, but the mass continues undeterred towards us. I am in a turmoil and feel fear in every part of my body. Why is Petsch dabbling with his hands all over the machine gun instead of pulling the trigger? The questions are screaming out within me. His entire body is shaking as if in a fever, and the barrel of his machine gun is wandering backwards and forward. He's had it! His nerves are gone and he can't open fire! What should I do? I can't just push him away from the weapon and take his place. I still have too much respect for him. But every second is precious!

Finally it happens—a burst of fire comes from the barrel! Every third bullet is a tracer round. The stream of light passes way over the heads of the attackers, disappearing into the haze. The next burst is also poorly aimed and goes high into the clouds. By now the attackers have located our machine gun. The bullets swarm around our heads and bury themselves in the embankment behind us. Petsch suddenly yells out. He holds a bleeding ear and falls into the trench. Seidel, who has seen what has happened, looks after of him.

This is my chance! I immediately get behind the machine gun and fire some short, carefully aimed bursts, just as I learned how. I aim into the mass of the advancing Soviet infantry. Grommel is now beside me, helping me by feeding in the ammunition belt. My aim is good, and several of the brown-clad figures fall to the ground. The waving mass stops for a moment, but then moves ahead, bent double, step by step, right for us.

My mind goes blank. I only see the advancing stream of enemy soldiers coming directly at us. I again fire straight into it Only fear is there—fear of this dirty brown heap of destruction constantly moving closer, which wants to kill me and everyone around me. I do not even feel the burning pain on the inner surface of my right hand, which I have caught on the hot metal while changing barrels seconds after getting a jam.

This is crazy! We are firing with four machine guns and at least eighty carbines from secure, covered positions into the advancing horde. Our machine gun bursts rip openings in their ranks. Dead and wounded are hitting the ground all the time. But more of them are coming through the haze, and we can't see them clearly. The first ones are now so close to our positions that we can readily make out the plump, bent figures with rifles and Russian Kalashnikovs. Then, suddenly, two of the machine guns on our right flank are silenced.

Immediately the mass moves towards that flank from which they're now getting only rifle fire. Together with Meinhard, I continue to fire into it as it moves towards the right. Their move now becomes their undoing: the heavy, hard-hitting fire of the 20mm quad anti-aircraft guns also comes as a surprise to us. Their bursts sound like low, regulated beats on a drum. We can see how the tracer rounds spew out of all four barrels and hit the middle of the attacking mass, tearing huge gaps in its ranks. Our two machine guns on the right flank start firing again; I assume that their silence was deliberate.

The quad machine gun is now raking the attackers in front of us, and when it stops firing stillness descends over the battlefield. We can hear calls and crying in Russian. I take a deep breath. The first battle with the enemy has affected me deeply, but now all my thoughts are working again. I raise my head out of the trench and peer into the field ahead. In front of us lie innumerable brown clumps on the snow. The quad's fabulous fire power still amazes me—I never imagined it would have an effect like that.

The terrain in front of us is quiet, and I, in my innocence, believe that all the attackers are either dead or wounded. As I move a bit further out of my trench to get a better look, a Russian machine gun opens fire. The bullets zip around my ears. Then a second machine gun starts firing and spraying us. Shortly after this I hear a sound that I recognise from Stalingrad, and the mortar rounds start landing all around.

'Mortars!' someone yells, and shortly afterwards: 'Döring and Markowitz are wounded. We need a medic!' Someone calls back that the medic is on his way.

I later discover that *Gefreiter* Markowitz, who was once a driver in our *Schwadron*, has taken a bullet through his shoulder and has had to be evacuated. *Unteroffizier* Döring, however, is only slightly injured on the cheek. At his own request, he stayed where he was. Petsch has lost

65

his right ear. We're all delighted when they bring him back to the village.

The mortar fire is so intense that we dare not stretch our heads over the trenches. But then we hear the familiar *plop!* of our own mortars. The pioneers have moved into position and are now beginning their own counter-fire. Their rounds rise up and over us and are exploding somewhere in the haze, where, it is assumed, the enemy is located. Gingerly I raise myself out of my trench, in order to watch what is going on—and I cannot believe my eyes. Many of the brown lumps, which I thought were dead or wounded, are now standing up and are moving off: under cover of their own machine-gun and mortar fire, they are retreating.

Warias has also realised this, and he calls out from the neighbouring hole, 'Hey, the Russians are leaving!'

Now our mortar rounds are landing right in the middle of the retreating Russians. For the quad machine-gun crews, either the range is too great or they are saving their ammunition for later. It's not long before the Russians have disappeared in the fog.

I have just filled my pipe with tobacco when the order to counter-attack comes. We are to clear the area in front of our positions and stay on the heels of the Soviets for a while longer. Before I jump out of my hole and throw the machine gun, ready to fire, over my right shoulder, I light my pipe and take a couple of deep drags. Tobacco never tasted so good, and it feels as if I have gained new strengths. We fan out on a broad front and get only sporadic counter-fire. We fire back and move slowly forward. Close behind, the quad machine gun follows on its carriage.

As we get to the fallen Russians, we discover that the wounded have been taken away. For the first time I see the dead enemy in front of me. The bodies are lying spread out over the snow and sometimes close together, just as they fell: wearing thick coats, they are either stretched out or bent over. Red puddles of blood are frozen on the snow.

66

My stomach is churning, and I cannot bring myself to look at their colourless faces. Now, for the first time, when I see the lifeless bodies before me, my consciousness really grasps the meaning of death. As a young person you tend to push these thoughts far away from you, but here there is no way to escape them. These people are our enemies, but, even so, they are flesh and blood, just like us. And just as they are lying here now, so could I or some of us be lying here dead and motionless in this ice cold snow.

I glance over at Grommel, who is carrying two ammunition boxes for me. The poor chap is as white as a sheet, and his eyes are staring towards the front, so as to avoid looking at the corpses. The others are doing the same. Küpper, Wilke and I go up to a dead soldier who only has a bloody half of his head left because the other half was probably torn away by an exploding shell. Wilke turns away, just as I do, while Küpper has to summon all his strength to stop himself throwing up. For us newcomers, the first view of a dead body gives a feeling of confusion, fright and helplessness—unless perhaps someone is of such a robust character and is so insensitive to human feelings that he is not affected: someone like the little black *Unteroffizier von der Infanterie* who looks like a gypsy. His name is Schwarz, and I saw him two days ago in position on the MSR. I met up with him again here, as Grommel and I were advancing against the weak but still dangerous enemy fire, behind some flat ground rising over on our left flank. While we were here we also stumbled across a circular-shaped earthwork. Round a centre circle dug out fairly deep in the ground was another rim dug down to the height of a man.

Meinhard had mentioned these features while we were still in our defensive positions. He said that while the division was advancing they used them for their artillery and anti-aircraft guns, and we could now expect the Soviets to use them for themselves. This was obviously correct, for scattered around there were a number of dead Soviet soldiers. This is when I hear this black *Unteroffizier* tell a soldier to shoot

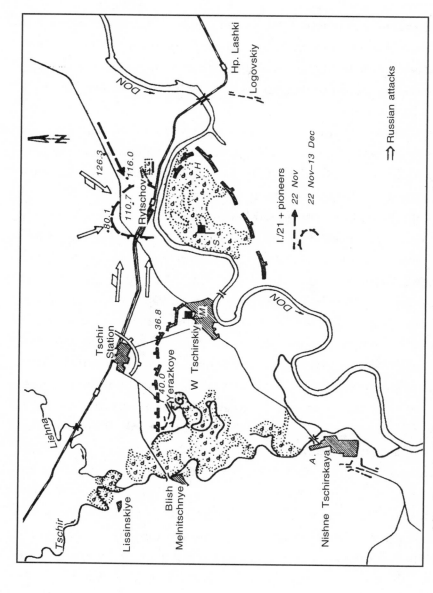

After the retreat from the cauldron of Stalingrad to the defensive positions near
Rytschov, up to 13 December 1942.

⇒ Russian attacks

a crumpled figure in the head; he himself had the muzzle of his sub-machine gun against the back of another soldier's head. Both shots sound muffled and unpleasant, much as if one had shot into a sack. I was shocked, and I shuddered. Is the man so full of hate that he even has to dishonour the dead? After this he walks past me towards another fallen soldier. He kicks the body, which is lying on its side, really hard in the stomach and mutters angrily, 'This one too is still alive!' He places his barrel directly on the forehead of the soldier and fires. The body, which I had assumed to be dead, convulses.

'Why don't we take them prisoner?' I ask him angrily.

The black sergeant just looks at me in disgust and growls: 'Then just try to get them up when they are playing dead! The swine think we won't realise they're alive and will cut us down from behind. I've seen it before!'

How can I answer him? I'm still not conversant with all the underhanded things that are done in warfare. But I would never shoot at any unarmed soldier, even if it was to my personal disadvantage. What I consider unworthy and terrible, the *Unteroffizier* only looks upon as a safety measure for our own protection.

He simply says: 'Him or us!'

Nevertheless, I can't bring myself to fire if I am not attacked. And I don't intend ever to change my mind!

Grommel is also upset, and so he presses on, and I have to hurry to catch up with him. All the time I can hear these muffled shots to the head, and they really shake me to the marrow. Although this *Unteroffizier* may have a very logical argument, I still reckon a large part of his thinking comes from his rather sadistic nature, which such people can satisfy in time of war under the pretext of legitimacy.

Meinhard says that the Soviets commit atrocities on our soldiers and often do not take prisoners. So our side behaves in the same manner. He says this is the way of war, with its constantly increasing avalanches of hate. It begins with an attack and then combat. The two enemies fight

69

for their lives, and it develops into grim determination and over-reaction from both sides. That leads to revenge and retaliation, in accordance with the motto 'As you do unto me, so I do unto you!' Oh, and heaven help the loser. I've never heard Meinhard speak like this before, but I suppose he's right. I haven't been in the war long enough to be able to form an opinion.

Our counter-attack is over as we arrive at the jumping-off point of the Soviet attack. The enemy has in the meantime withdrawn far behind these positions, so we take them over, keeping on the alert.

After dark we are given hot coffee and our rations. The vehicles take five wounded back to the village. On one of the vehicles are one dead and one slightly wounded soldier. We don't know either man. Some of the soldiers tell us that they have found German rations and cigarettes in the Soviet soldiers' kitbags. On the wrist of a *Kommissar* they also found a German Thiele wristwatch, with a name inscribed under the second lid. The driver from the supply vehicle will give them to the *Pionierhauptmann*.

We spend the night in the new positions. It's bloody cold, and an icy easterly wind penetrates into our very bones. Anyone not on watch at an observation post sits huddled in his cold foxhole and dozes until morning.

25 November. Even before it gets light, we have orders to board our vehicles. We make for the village and re-occupy the old positions and trenches scattered around on the steppe. That saves us a lot of hard work, because the ground is frozen so hard in the top layers that you can only break up the soil with picks.

In good weather we can see for many kilometres across the steppe, but unfortunately in some places the enemy can also see into our trenches. We have almost daily incidents involving snipers hitting our men. These snipers are extremely well hidden and we have a very hard time seeing them. Rations and ammunition supplies are therefore always brought in at night, although even then it's dangerous. We assume that the snipers are aiming their rifles at the critical points during the daylight hours and then occasionally pulling the triggers also at night.

It is quiet at first this morning, but later on the Soviets launch an attack on Tschir station with tanks and infantry. To begin with we were only spectators to the action, but then we were also attacked with mortars and machine guns. The enemy came for us very suddenly, as if they had risen out of the ground. We learned later from prisoners that they had crawled up to within only a few hundred metres of us and had dug themselves in under the protection of a small hillock. The breezy easterly masked any noise made by their digging.

While we hold down the infantry in front of us with aimed fire, a T-34 tank leaves its formation of five and comes at us from the other side of the *Rachel*, firing continuously. He stops at the edge of the *Rachel* with his broadside towards us. I've never seen an enemy tank this close before, and it looks very menacing. It has white camouflage paint and its steel turret swings round as the gun is lowered towards a target. The thundering shot shakes it up a bit, and there is a small jet of flame from the muzzle followed by a brief smoke trail. The hit behind us registers at just about the same second. Then the powerful diesel engine revs up and the monster moves off, its tracks clanking along the edge of the *Rachel*.

I am showered with debris. Just don't get spotted! He knows that we're lying here, but maybe he hasn't noticed our well-camouflaged bunker. He must have realised that we haven't got any anti-tank weapons here in this sector. In spite of this, he moves carefully before he drives through the flat swell at the end of our *Rachel* before entering it. One shot from an AT or 88mm AA gun would knock him—he is standing with his broadside towards us—but I know full well that our AT weapons are guarding the railway line and the village.

71

Suddenly he backs up and tries to turn, but he doesn't manage it very well and then puts a track on the edge of the *Rachel*, causing bits of it to break off. Now I can see some pioneers in the *Rachel*. They're working with something—it looks like a bar or a pole. Then I'm interrupted by Weichert, who is beside me and is making me aware of the infantry, who have advanced under the protection of the tank. What should I do—shoot? Yes, I have to, otherwise they will overrun us— even if it means that the T-34 will discover our position.

I squeeze myself behind the machine gun and pull the trigger. Weichert feeds in the belt. At about the same time Meinhard and the others also fire at the attacking infantry. The first row of men falls to the ground and the others throw themselves down. There is no cover for them on the snow-covered steppe. What is the tank doing? He has spotted us and is turning his turret towards us. Then he lowers his gun and aims directly at us. He is barely 50 metres away. It would be crazy to stand there and fire, so I pull down the machine gun from its position and cover myself with the others in the trench. The resulting explosion is mixed with shrapnel as the shell strikes home just metres behind us.

'This time we were fortunate, but next time we'll have had it!' says Weichert. A chill runs down my spine.

Swina brings relief from the terrible excitement. 'The tank is destroyed!' he calls out.

We move up and can see that the tank is hanging over the edge of the *Rachel* with a broken track. From the rear of the vehicle comes thick, black smoke, which quickly dissipates.

Someone calls out, 'The pioneers got him with a hollow charge!'

We breathe more easily and are grateful to the men in the pioneer unit. Later the *Unteroffizier der Pioniere* tells me it was a piece of cake because the T-34 didn't notice them under the edge of the *Rachel* and had positioned itself directly over them, so they could attach their home-made charge of hand grenades under the track quite easily. Even so, they were almost killed by the broken bits of track.

Today we have been fairly fortunate. The tank fire caused only three lightly wounded. The pioneers were forced to smoke the crew out. They had kept still for hours inside their vehicle, hoping for rescue by their own people. They crawl out and I take a look at them. I have a strange feeling—a mixture of curiosity, threat and respect. I'm quite surprised to see their helmets, which can best be described as a number of blown-up bicycle inner tubes sewn together, one next to the other. What purpose they serve I don't know; perhaps they're a form of sound insulation and a protection against the cold.

26 November. Today begins with ground fog. It dissipates in the winter sun, giving us good fields of views. German bombers, accompanied by fighter escorts, drone around unmolested in the clear blue, cloudless sky. Grommel identifies them as He 111s and Do 17s. I have often seen the slim Me 109s, the escort fighters, in air combat. Once in a while we also recognise the heavy Ju 52, the so-called '*Tante Ju*', which is used for freight and as a troop transport. All of them are flying heavily loaded to Stalingrad, and when they are lucky they come back empty.

Warias and Swina were down in the village early to get clean underwear and lice powder from our kitbags. The little beasts have multiplied incredibly quickly on me and I have already rubbed my entire upper torso.

Warias says that two days ago the *Führer* declared Stalingrad to be a fortress. Some of the soldiers—those who were in Stalingrad—are furious when they hear it. They are angry at the way the war is being conducted, and because they are no longer given any opportunity to escape the encirclement. They speak quite openly of being sacrificed in a pocket which is surrounded by an enemy force superior to any before. Others believe the encirclement will shortly be breached by the approaching tank units commanded by *Generaloberst* Hoth. I, and most of the reserve unit personnel, believe the latter.

However, this optimism is built on wishful thinking and it falls to pieces like a pack of cards. As even the lowliest soldier knows, the combat strength of our enemy grows steadily day by day while we, with our inadequate weaponry, become weaker. Added to this come the days when we are only able to satisfy our rumbling stomachs with a handful of *Hartzwieback*.* It is not lost on anyone that we remain here in a totally isolated outpost and are to be sacrificed for some strategic purpose or other. It will be at the beginning of December—only a question of days away—when Soviet superiority will grind us to pieces.

On the afternoon of this day, 26 November, we have however received a boost to our morale in the form of an 88mm anti-aircraft gun which is to be used in the ground defence role. We also get a 20mm quad AA gun on a wheeled carriage. Before the 88mm is taken into position on the hillock, the ground is dug out so that only a little of the white-painted protective shielding of the gun can be seen from the front. As of yesterday there are supposed to be three tanks in the village to give support, but because of a shortage of ammunition they are to be used only in an absolute emergency.

27 November. During the early hours an enemy reconnaissance patrol is able to gain entry into the village. We hear the gun shots. The emergency response unit manages to take some prisoners. Afterwards the Soviets pound the village for hours with heavy artillery. During the morning we're also bombarded with mortars and *Stalinorgeln*. However, they do not attack. Yesterday the pioneers mined part of the village, but unfortunately one of our drivers, in a personnel carrier, ran on to one of the mines and was blown into the air.

Because of the heavy shelling we are sitting like moles in the ground for much of the time, occasionally checking to see whether the enemy has started his attack yet. It is my turn to keep watch, and I carefully

* A kind of hard biscuit or rusk.

74

raise my head up over the lip of the trench, but just then a grenade explodes right on the edge. The hot splinters zip past my head, and my ears ring like mad. Dirt and debris rain down on heads and down the necks of those in the trench. But the roof holds.

The snow around us has for the last few hours been no longer white, but rather mixed in with brown dirt because of all the explosions. It is bloody hard, and wearing, to sit in a hole in the ground and wait. What for? No one knows exactly; only that it is about our lives—that much we know for sure. Maybe we will take a direct hit, which will end what little is left of our lives. When that happens we'll probably not notice anything. It would be bad enough if the enemy were attacking *en masse*: at least you can defend your self. But here, in this awful hole, you can do nothing except wait.

I try to think about other things, but can't. The howling and the crashing explosions over and around us banish all other thoughts and there is only the fervent wish that this nerve-racking din will finally stop. The only person seemingly unaffected is Swina. I can't see excitement and fear in his face like I can with the others. But then how could he feel these emotions? The poor devil can't hear the crashes and the whining of the shells: he looks at us unconcernedly and asks us what we're doing. To talk to him you must go right up to him and shout: then he understands.

The artillery barrage lasts almost two hours—proof that they do not have to be too sparing with their ammunition. They haven't achieved much. Apart from a damaged machine gun and a filled-in trench there's no harm done.

28 November. The night of 27/28 November passes quietly, but Meinhard brings bad news early in the morning. He says that our *Spiess* and another *Wachtmeister* from the unit fell yesterday morning. Although we weren't that close to our *Wachtmeister*—he always kept his distance

from us newcomers—we were stillpretty shocked. What's more, he was our linchpin and our superior, and in spite of his serious nature he always concerned himself with our well-being—as much as he was able to here in the bridgehead anyway. Now he is among us no more. There are only two service grades left in our company, the *Schirrmeister* and *Unteroffizier* Döring. Meinhard says that in peacetime the *Spiess* served with the cavalry and that the job of the soldier was made for him.

It doesn't seem to get all that light today. It stays hazy and cloudy, and the visibility is so bad that we have to be really careful in case the enemy suddenly looms up in front of us. Döring therefore sends several men to man the observation posts up ahead. Meinhard reckons that the Soviets will make use of the weather to get up close to us. As it turns out, he's right.

Shortly after this the observers come back to report that they've heard noises coming from the north and have heard commands in Russian getting louder and louder. They hadn't, however, been able to see anything, but there is no doubt that the enemy is on his way from the north. They hadn't heard any tank engines. Okay, so it's the infantry first. We're ready—and we'll give them a warm welcome.

Döring sends word that we will open fire only on his command. He intends to let them come close, to within a certain range, and then take them by surprise with crossfire. We are standing with our weapons and getting excited. No one knows what will come at us. These are the worst minutes before combat, when everything in your body is at the highest level of excitement. The minutes become eternities . . .

Then—they're here! The first figures approach, bent double, out of the haze, coming right for us. Everyone's waiting for the signal to fire. Pity I don't have any field glasses, because something seems odd—something that I can't quite understand.

Someone yells, 'Those are our boys! Don't fire!'

Then Döring: 'Keep your heads down! Everyone stay down!'

We do as we're told and keep looking. The soldiers in front of us are coming closer, and I can see those in front waving. Where have they come from, I am thinking, because their uniforms and steel helmets appear so new? Then Meinhard's machine gun hammers away and someone is yelling, 'They're Russians—in our uniforms!'

The figures in the German uniforms are storming forward in an attempt to overrun us; behind them come the others, in mud brown overcoats and dirty camouflage uniforms. We lay down cross-fire from all our machine guns and carbines. Those who have not been hit throw themselves to the ground. The attack stops. In front of us we hear shouts. Then two Soviet machine guns let loose. A rain of bullets comes towards us and mortar rounds explode all over the place—another centimetre and one of them would have taken out my machine gun. I pull it back and crouch down.

'They are attacking again!' calls Weichert as he feeds another belt of ammunition in.

It's a weird sensation firing on an enemy wearing your own uniform. It's as if you're shooting traitors. They are trying to overrun us in a second and third wave, but they don't make it—especially when the pioneers fire at them from the flank.

There are an awful lot of dead bodies lying around on the snow in front of us which are gradually freezing solid and getting covered by whirling snowflakes. We can hear the wounded groaning and calling out for help, but we can't do anything for them. Some of the dead even have German felt boots on, which we ourselves are in desperate need of. Where possible these are removed from the stiff frozen feet of the dead and put to use again. I can't find a pair to fit me and so I keep my own boots on. Many of the soldiers even help themselves to the primitive earflaps the Russians are wearing. They seem to be made out of a single piece of pressed felt, but they serve their purpose in the cold. My boots were too large during the summer, but if I hadn't put on an extra pair of very thick socks and placed some newspaper wadding in the boots, my toes would undoubtedly have got frostbite at the start of the winter, like so many other people's did. For this reason, a couple of days ago we received some rather unpretentious looking overshoes made out of woven straw, which Swina dubbed *Strohpotschen*.* Although we can't take very big strides when we're wearing them, they do insulate our feet quite well against the cold ground when we are standing around in our foxholes.

Weichert and some of the others are also checking the kitbags of the dead Soviet soldiers, as we have not received any rations since yesterday evening other than a piece of Army bread and half-warm tea. Weichert suffers from hunger more than any of us. He finds some black Russian Army bread and some pieces of smoked meat, which also originate from German supplies. Swina brings a large bag of *Machorka* for me, as he has noticed that I've been turning my pockets inside out all morning to salvage a pinch of tobacco for my pipe.

Tonight we again place the observation posts way out ahead. When Grommel wakes us at about 0300 it is quite cosy in the bunker but, to make up for that, very much colder outside. Everything is covered with rime because of the fog. The machine gun, wrapped in a canvas ground sheet, appears as a white, indeterminate lump. Behind us, on the hillock, a flare goes up. The view from there is better.

The fog is thicker in the hollow in front of us. Often we can't even see our hands in front of our faces. I trudge with Swina into the haze. The snow crunches under our boots, and we follow the tracks. Then comes a muffled request for the password. 'Railway!' I answer quietly.

'Come over here.' I hear a voice which seems to be familiar, but I can't see anybody.

'We are to your right, in the foxhole.' says the voice.

Then, suddenly, a figure stands in front of us, and another is climbing out of the foxhole. Damn this thick fog! If they had not challenged us, we might have stepped on them.

---

* Straw pots.

They report that it's been quiet out front. As soon as the fog has swallowed them up, Swina leaps into the foxhole; I still need to orient myself a bit. I'm only a few metres away from Swina, but I can't hear or see anything of him. I only know roughly where he should be. Bloody fog!

I stumble over a dead body and realise that I am too far out front. I do not feel very well, and crouch down as I think I can hear crunching footsteps. More dead bodies are scattered around. An uncanny feeling is coming over me, and I am regretting that I left Swina. I can't call him, because he can't hear me. But again I hear those crunching footsteps and muffled voices. Soviets! The thought flashes before me. Now don't panic, I think. My nerves are stretched to the limit. I reckon the Russians often stand around and then call to each other: they manage to keep in contact with each other in the thick fog in this way.

Slowly I back away from the noises—and almost step on Swina's head! For him it must be an awful feeling, to be unable to see or hear in the fog. I indicate to him that something is happening in front of us, and it seems almost grotesque when he cups his hand and places it behind his ear to listen. We then creep back and tell the others.

We wait until we can hear the voices quite clearly. Then Döring fires off a flare. It lights up only a small area, cold and ghostlike. Some figures stand stiff and immobile as if with roots in the ground. Then suddenly they disperse. The first ones throw themselves on to the ground. We fire into the darkness. The Russians are yelling something to each other. Then we hear some clatter, which retreats rapidly. A second and then a third flare go up. Five figures are still lying on the snow; the others have disappeared.

We assume they are from a Soviet reconnaissance unit or men who have lost their way. It's only a small group. We fire a few rounds. In the light of another tracer I see two figures leap up and run back. One is hit and falls down. Three are still lying in the snow. Someone from our side is calling out something in Russian—it must be one of our Russian volunteers who was with the supply trains and now is helping us. A Russian is answering him, then stands up and raises his hands. The other two follow him.

Among the three prisoners are two women, which we refer to as *Flintenweiber*.* They are said to be more fanatical even than the Soviet soldiers. They do not have much to hide and say they got lost in the fog with a group of fifteen soldiers. We are well aware of their front lines, and also of he fact that their positions are being strengthened day by day.

2 December. After thick morning fog it is now clearing up. There is considerable enemy activity in the direction of Tschir station. I walk along the trench towards Meinhard's position. He has been talking to Döring, who has been scanning with his field glasses.

'Döring thinks the Soviets are preparing for an attack,' says Meinhard. 'He has seen lots of vehicles and tanks. Apparently they are moving replacements in by transport.'

Meinhard is annoyed that the Russians have the audacity to form up in front of us, calm as you like.

'Those swine know full well that we have no artillery, otherwise they would never have the cheek,' he grumbles.

We watch the enemy for another hour, then we realise that the bulk of their formation is moving south-east towards Werchne Tschirskiye. Another combat unit is supposed to be securing the bridge over the Don. When the Russians take the bridge they will be in our rear and will have us in the bag. The flashes tell us that their attack is supported by well-equipped tank units. Three of these dreadful steel monsters are coming along the railway line towards us right now.

Suddenly there are loud engine noises overhead.

'Our Stukas are here!' some of the soldiers cry out excitedly.

* Female partisans (literally, 'gunwomen').

The stress and anxiety within us is vanishes in a trice, and we start cheering like children who've just opened a present. So there is some contact with High Command after all! Can it have come from the south bank of the Don? Only later do I find that there is in fact no connection: the pilots had realised what was going on from the air and had acted accordingly. Later, Stuka support is again carried out without any reference to us. Nevertheless, each time they come they are greeted excitedly, and they help lift our spirits, if only temporarily.

First there is flight of three Stukas, which dive down; then three more follow. Their attack in front of us is a real spectacle but, even for us non-participants, it brings a cold, creepy feeling to the spine. The fearsome shark mouths painted on the engine cowlings give the enemy a premonition of the catastrophe that is about to be visited on them. The aircraft first roll to the side, then with the deafening wail from their sirens getting louder and louder, swoop down on their target. As soon as they have released their bombs the planes climb steeply, only to dive again on another target. The effect on the morale of those on the receiving end must be terrible. It is just like the inferno of hell, even though the action is taking place far away from us.

Within the next few minutes black clouds of smoke billow into the clear sky. We notice that some of the tanks are moving in zigzag fashion to escape the attacking dive bombers. They don't really have a chance, because the Stukas are over them again and again, sending their bombs down.

When they have dropped their bombs the aircraft turn and disappear over the horizon. Smoke clouds, large and small, show how many targets were hit and destroyed—mostly vehicles, tanks and heavy weapons. The Stukas have accomplished a great deal, and the Russian infantry has been halted by the combat group south of the Don. We can quite clearly see that the Don bridge has not been captured by the enemy. But how long will things last?

3 December. The ration orderlies bring us thin, cold coffee, which we first have to heat on the stove. Each four men receive half a can of beef and a canteen full of *Zwieback*; that has to last until tomorrow evening. Grommel counts out each mouthful of *Zwieback* so that everyone receives exactly the correct amount. It is more than we received yesterday, when we got one loaf of bread, already mildewed, among three men.

Typically during this period of the war, hunger so completely dominates our thinking that even the constant worry about our survival takes a back seat: the main topic of conversation is food. Even at night I dream about food, and even dream about a delicious roast being cooked in the oven. Waking up is therefore that much more difficult, particularly when I discover that the noise is only a loud rumble in my empty stomach!

Our lives are re-energised when we get enough dry Army bread to eat. I chew it slowly in my mouth and savour the exquisite taste. I would even forego the best cakes—I would never have thought bread could be so delicious. But on many days even bread is unavailable. It is taken for granted in normal times, but it's really precious now.

CHAPTER FIVE

Blood Red Snow Falls
Not from the Sky

D ECEMBER 4, 1942. The day begins like yesterday—not many clouds in the sky and clear visibility. Later the clouds gather and get grey. During the afternoon it begins to snow and the cold wind blows and forms drifts. Before long the brown and white checked ground around us is again white and clean. I'm shovelling the snow out of the connecting trenches and the work is warming me up. Weichert is making sure that the field of fire for our machine gun remains unobstructed.

I go to visit Warias, Seidel and the others in the neighbouring bunker, and walk through the connecting trench. They have fired up their oven, so much so that it's glowing. When I see Warias I have to laugh. He is lying stretched out in the bunker with his lower legs disappearing into the clay wall, as if cut off. Their bunker is just like ours—an enlarged, covered trench—but it is too narrow for Warias's long legs so he has excavated a hole in the wall to accommodate the rest of his stilts. Two other soldiers are lying on the straw-covered ground beside him, both snoring. I can hear their stomachs murmur, and Warias says that if you sleep you save power and energy. Seidel is standing by the oven, stirring something in his mess tin. He says that when you cook up a hot soup of bits of *Zwieback* and snow melt it lasts longer in the stomach than it would if you force it down dry. He might be on to something here— I will have to try it some time! You can hear the harmonica again, in

Meinhard's bunker. Kurat's playing some really sad tunes, bringing back memories from home.

They were forever telling us at training camp how to service and use our weapons in order to kill our enemies, and we were trained, and proud, to fight for *Führer,Volk undVaterland*, and, if necessary, die. But no one told us what you might have to go through before you got killed. Nor that death might not be instantaneous—there are many forms. In the few days we've been here we've heard the awful screams of the wounded—how terrible it must be to die lying on the frozen ground. The thought fills us with horror—we might lie there, with nobody to help us. We weren't told that this might happen, nor were we told how we could cope with the anxiety that eats away at you like fire and is far more powerful than the impulse to do your duty. Each soldier will have to solve that problem for himself, they said. But, more than anything, he will have to hide his anxiety, so that the others don't notice it; if he doesn't hide it, his anxiety might be interpreted as cowardice—as in the case of little Grommel, who even while under attack can't bring himself to fire on the enemy.

Weichert has also noticed that Grommel can't aim and pull the trigger. Even when he is forced to shoot, he closes his eyes as he pulls the trigger, so he can't see where he's shooting. Yet he was one of the best shots in the training camp. What is the matter with him? Do his nerves fail when he sees the enemy, just like Petsch? Weichert has noticed that every time the enemy attacks he acts as if he's lame, and his eyes flicker and water as though he is in a fever. Maybe I'll talk to him about it, particularly as it affects the safety of all of us. Unfortunately I never get the chance, because over the next few days we are constantly under attack. The few peaceful moments we have—those of us not on guard duty—are used for sleep; we are always overtired.

This evening I go and see Meinhard in his bunker again. *Unteroffizier* Döring is also there, and tells us he'll be returning to the village to pick up his harmonica as soon as he has the chance. On the way to the bunker

I hear soft tunes wafting from Kurat's harmonica. I cannot know that I will see him alive only one more time—he and another chum will be casualties in a day or so.

5 December. It snows again during the night. When Weichert and Swina wake me in the morning there is a wild firefight going on in the village. According to Weichert, it has just begun. He and Swina came back from the observation post and hadn't noticed anything particularly unusual, but now all hell is let loose in the village. The frosty air is filled with the sharp *crack!* of tank and anti-tank guns, with the rattle of rifle and machine-gun fire in between.

A soldier comes running up, yelling that they need the quad anti-aircraft gun. The engine of the towing vehicle is quickly started up and the quad moves along the hillock towards the village. Flares are constantly shooting up from over there. The thin flaky snow makes the darkness seem even hazier. 'Just the weather for a Russian attack,' comments an old *Obergefreiter* as he crawls through the trench.

Then the quad gets into action; there is no mistaking its low staccato firing. Fires are blazing at two places in the village. Soon the firefight dies away and the only firing now comes from the railway line in the direction of Tschir. It is machine-gun fire.

During the sudden lull, loud engine noises can be heard coming from the *Rachel* and heavy diesel fumes penetrate our noses. Küpper and Warias come over towards us. We assume it must be a T-34 stuck in the *Rachel*, because the droning noise of the engine starts up and then dies down again, always coming from the same spot. We crawl up to the edge of the *Rachel*, which falls away steeply. We can see nothing—it's much too hazy—but we're in no doubt that the tank has got bogged down.

'This is our chance to blast it—but how, and with what?' asks Warias.

As if in answer to his question, there is an explosion and the tank is literally blown apart. We are blinded by the fire and throw ourselves flat on to the ground. The tank's ammunition explodes in the heat, ricocheting back and forth between the walls of the *Rachel*. In the pale light of the breaking dawn we can see thick smoke oozing out of the engine compartment. The pioneers call over to us that they have destroyed it with a couple of mines.

In the counter-attack that follows we capture a lot of weapons, but we find very little food in the kitbags. Weichert manages to scrounge a few bits of black Soviet Army bread which tastes of dough and because of its texture feels like sandpaper when it is chewed. However, we still gulp it down, in order to satisfy some of our hunger. From time to time I can again hear, away to the right, those revolting muffled shots to the head, being carried out by the black sergeant, who will no doubt justify his brutality the same way as before.

6 December. Three of us are dozing away in the warm bunker. Weichert has been on night duty outside. We can hear his footsteps in the hard frost coming closer. As he stands in front of the bunker and lifts the blanket away from the opening, we are wide awake. In spite of being permanently overtired we still sleep mostly like rabbits, with one eye open and ears alert for any unusual noises. Weichert tells us that Döring has been issued with several cases of ammunition and that we are to pick up our share.

It is still quite dark when Grommel and I go over to see Döring. Kurat is still not back. Apparently his observation post still has twenty minutes left on this shift. Everything seems to be quiet, and we hope it will stay that way. As I go to enter the bunker, I seem to hear Kurat's harmonica. But that is not possible—Kurat is at an observation post in a foxhole out in front. Am I mistaken? Are my nerves so frayed that I'm hearing things? I walk back to Warias. Both he and Seidel have heard it—not a tune, just two loud notes, as if someone has just breathed into it. They also were wondering what it was. When we tell Döring about it he at once takes action.

'Something is wrong. Alert! Give the alarm! Ready to fire!'

I run over to my machine gun and pull the cover off. The entire unit is now on the alert and waiting. For what? Everything is quiet in front of us. Could Kurat accidentally have blown into his harmonica? If he'd noticed anything he would have warned us with a rifle shot, as per the usual procedure. Could this be a false alarm? The shift should now be finished, so perhaps they are waiting for the new shift to take over? Döring holds everything up. Then a tracer spirals up in the air.

What's that? Less than 50 meters in front of us we see figures in white, snow-camouflage battledress. When we fire our machine guns and rifles at them they throw themselves into the snow. As it gets lighter we can see more Russians They lie behind the first group, also in camouflaged battledress, ready to jump up. The pioneers are shooting at them too, from the flank. They stay lying in the snow, waiting. Half an hour passes. Why don't they attack? What next? What are they waiting for?

We know soon enough—tanks! First we can make out only two, then another three emerge from the haze of the breaking dawn. They advance towards us and fire at our positions. What is our 88mm doing? It is camouflaged and certainly awaiting its chance. The thought calms us only a little. What good is one gun against five T-34s? The Soviet infantry follows up under cover of the tanks in a dispersed file. We try to keep them down.

Then, like a bolt of lightning from the clear sky, comes firing from the 88mm. We see a glowing armour-piercing shell slam against a T-34, causing a jet of flame and then thick, black, acrid smoke. The barrel of the 88mm has already been lined up at the next target. The shell goes right into the track of the tank; the vehicle can now only spin in circles. The tank crew has just got enough time to jump out before a second shot, a bull's-eye, destroys the tank. Another tank tries to escape into the blind spot of the 88. Two T-34s fire on the 88. Their shells come close: one ricochets like a fireball from a snowdrift and slams into the bunker to our right. We hear yells and calls for the medic. Then the third tank is hit; he can't work his turret any more. With his barrel angled and immobile, he tries to escape to the rear. Minutes later the other one follows him. The tank which had crept into the blind spot of the 88 now steps out of the frying pan into the fire. As he tries to move into a firing position to wipe out the 88, he is standing exactly under the guns of two of our tanks, which have been waiting for him behind the hillock. Before they destroy him, however, he manages to damage one of them quite seriously.

Although we have again managed to counter the enemy attack, we have had to pay dearly. The T-34 hit on our bunker has killed the promising tank rifleman Dieter Malzahn and a *Gefreiter*. Three others are seriously wounded, one having had half of his arm torn off. Only later in the day, when the heavy Russian shelling eases off, can we again move into the area in front of our position.

Beside the foxholes at the observation post we find Kurat and his chum in their own frozen pools of blood. The Soviets have slaughtered them and taken their boots and rifles. Kurat can't have been killed instantly because he managed to warn us with his harmonica. As we carry the two corpses back with us to give them a decent burial, Kurat is still holding his harmonica in his limp hand. He has saved our lives, for without his warning the enemy would surely have taken us by surprise and massacred us.

Today has been another bad day for us, and we, the survivors, have again been granted a reprieve by Him above. Grommel reminds us that today is St Nicholas's Day and Sunday. What is that? For us there are no more holidays, only survival, and every day we remain alive is a good day. I will sleep rather fitfully tonight.

7 December. The weather this morning is hazy again. During the morning it clears up, so that the visibility gets quite good. The enemy snipers are firing like mad again. We have three incidents during the morning. At the station the Soviets are attacking separately and are firing their mortars into the village. When our Stukas arrive, everything becomes quiet. They bomb the Russian positions in front of us. The Soviets have camouflaged themselves so well in the white snow that we are surprised how close they've been able to get without our noticing them. The dive bombers throw themselves at the Russians in several waves. We have become used to their wailing sirens when they dive. The many black clouds of smoke make it obvious that they have also hit vehicles and heavy weapons, but they still couldn't stop the enemy attacking us that afternoon with artillery and mortar fire. Only the *Stalinorgeln* were not involved. Were they perhaps destroyed by the dive bombers?

For our evening meal we unexpectedly receive bean soup with potatoes and some bread. Jansen managed to bring back some food supplies for us over the Don.

8 December. Today is pretty much the same as yesterday. The visibility is good and the dive bombers start bombarding the Russian positions early. This time they are operating further back: the Russians must have pulled together strong forces on the heights behind Tschir station. The dive bombers attack for a second time, in several waves and lob their bombs on to their targets, and inky black smoke rises up into the blue sky.

9 December. A grey morning, and the enemy is firing with all his heavy weapons into the village and into our positions. Until noon we can peer only with the utmost of caution over the edges of our bunkers. The

terrible waiting game has begun again. The Soviets are undoubtedly getting their own back for the dive-bomber attacks, which today will not take place owing to the poor visibility. During the afternoon they attack the village both from the east and along the railway line from the south. We, however, are not involved. If they do manage to take the village, they'll be able to attack us from two sides and leave us vulnerable to a pincer movement. We wait and pray that they will not succeed.

The fight for the village lasts several hours. Then the reserve unit manages to counter-attack and drive the Russians back out of the village again. The losses are great—six dead and many wounded.

11 December. The entire sky is grey today, and so visibility is limited. Since early morning shells have been exploding all around us. The Russians don't want to give us any respite, it seems. Because of the explosions we don't hear any engine noises and don't realise the danger which is about to descend on us. Suddenly, like phantoms, five T-34 tanks are standing in front of us. They surprise not only us but also the crew of the 88mm gun deployed for ground support behind us on a knoll. Before the crew can traverse the long barrel to aim at the tanks, all five of the latter fire simultaneously. This surprise fire, at this short range, means the end for the 88. Surprisingly, the crew manages to destroy one of the five tanks before receiving two direct hits. We see pieces of armour and bodies fly through the air. The men are killed instantly. The four T-34s now advance triumphantly directly towards us, the Russian infantry clinging on like grapes, but the quad AA is still firing. Its tracer rounds are hitting the tanks and are forcing the infantry to get down and seek cover behind their vehicles.

Two T-34s are nearing the edge of the trench in front of us but turn away. They drive along it with their sides towards us until they come to Meinhard's position. This is an opportunity every tank destroyer dreams about. However, they know that we no longer have any means to destroy them. We fire from all barrels on the infantry following the

90

tanks, but the latter keep on rolling until they come to Meinhard's position. Some of the Russians who have dared to advance towards us are cut down by our fire. Hand grenades explode close to Warias and Meinhard. Then, suddenly, Meinhard's machine gun stops firing, although all the others continue. The tracer rounds from the quad AA swish over our heads, aimed at the waves of Soviet infantry soldiers bearing down. Without the quad we would have been overrun long ago. The sappers are also firing their two machine guns from our flank into the decimated ranks of the Soviet infantry.

The first tank halts on top of Meinhard's position. The engine roars more loudly. He is now turning on the spot and churning up the ground with his tracks as he does so. The quad AA is now firing at point-blank range at the T-34 with explosive rounds, but they have no more effect on the thick turret armour than firecrackers. Then it happens! The tank that has broken through our lines to our right is firing at close range directly at the quad. The second round hits and smashes the weapon. Pieces of metal and various body parts fly through the air and land back on the snow over a wide area. A torn-off leg, still wearing a felt boot, hits the ground only a few metres from us; the blood pumping out of the leg slowly colours the snow red. We look at each other helplessly, our faces flushed. Despite the cold, sweat is running down from my forehead into my eyes. My mouth is dry and my tongue is glued to the roof of my palate.

Now the tanks are free to roam about, roll up our positions and take them over. Then there will be nothing to prevent them from advancing into the village and wreaking havoc there. But at least they have mines in the village, and one of the tanks might not be serviceable. More than that we don't know.

One of the tanks stays near us and continues to churn up the ground, another ploughs up the ground near Seidel and further over on the right flank, while a third tries to get to the village over the hill. The fourth tank has already managed to negotiate the hill and is firing continuously into the village. In spite of our determined defence several Soviet soldiers still manage to break into our positions. They are disarmed by Döring and his men in hand-to-hand fighting. Now only my machine gun and those of the two sappers are still firing. Weichert, who feeds my ammo belt, complains about the poor quality of the ammunition and the many cartridges which are torn by the ejectors in the breeches. We only have one replacement barrel left in reserve.

Swina stands beside me, firing a carbine as fast as he can. He stays there, reloading with nervous hands. I don't see Grommel, as he is standing several metres beyond Weichert. He quickly throws him two machine-gun barrels with cartridges plugged in the breeches.

'Unplug the casings, *Kleiner*.* You are good at that!' he calls to him.

Just then he ducks down and exclaims in astonishment, 'Bugger— now the T-34 has discovered our machine-gun nest!'

The T-34 turns its turret towards our position and comes at us, its engine roaring. I pull my machine gun into the trench and throw myself down. Grommel and Weichert dash into the bunker. Swina is already lying behind me in the trench.

A harsh metallic shot, and a tank shell explodes exactly where my machine gun once stood. Frozen dirt and hot splinters rain down over my head. There is a loud ringing in my ears and it feels as if my eardrum has just been perforated. The acrid powder is sucked into my nose and fills my lungs. But I live, and so does Swina—I can hear his convulsive coughing behind me. And there it is again—the rattle and the roaring as steel tank tracks grind squealing on their rollers. A deathly noise! I press myself like a worm on to the ground. In the trench everything goes dark: the steel monster is parked directly on top of me, blocking out the daylight.

Now the sharp steel tracks are tearing up the edge of the trench. Frozen blocks of dirt fall on to my back and half cover me. Will the monster bury me alive? I remember soldiers telling me that tanks have

* Little fellow.

92

turned on top of foxholes until the men below could no longer move and suffocated in the dirt. A hell of a way to die!

I'm panic-stricken! Maybe it's safer with the others in the bunker. I crawl on my knees to join them, and Swina follows me. The bunker is almost dark and I can hardly recognise the faces of the others, but I sense the fear and the restlessness in the air. The tank now stands on top of us. What will he do? Will he turn and try to collapse the bunker? The earth is frozen solid, but will the roof of the bunker be able to take the weight?

Terrible minutes tick by, during which we can do nothing but wait. Wait for death? We might try to dispatch it with a mine or a magnetic shaped charge, but we have neither of these to hand so we can only hope and pray that the death will pass us by.

I hear Swina starting to pray out loud, and I feel that I also need to steady my nerves by prayer. I haven't prayed since I was a child, believing in my youth that I was strong enough not to need the help of a higher being. But now, facing death and fearing for my life, those long-forgotten words come to mind. I don't say them out loud like Swina and the others: I pray quietly within, without moving my lips. I pray that we will be saved from serious injury and from a ghastly death.

Although nothing in our situation has changed, I do sense after my prayer an inner peace and faith, which I can't explain very well in words. Swina has also finished. He looks over at Weichert, who sits in a pile of sheaves on the ground and stares up at the ceiling. Grommel's breathing is loud and excited; he also gazes upwards. Whenever the tank fires a shot, the roof vibrates and dirt and snow fall down between the beams and planks on to our steel helmets. As the engine roars and the steel colossus again moves off, clods of frozen earth fall into the bunker and give us more of a glimpse of the tank track.

Not buried alive! That's my main concern! Weichert and the others are panic-stricken.

'Out of here!' he cries in alarm, and is the first one to the door.

93

There are lumps of ice in front of the door. Weichert pushes them away with his feet and manages to squeeze out. The trench is half full of dirt and snow, and my machine gun is buried underneath it all. Further over in the trench several Russian soldiers are moving around, and Warias and Seidel are lobbing hand grenades over there. We can hear the sappers, still firing from their trench. Grenades explode over us and land in front of our position. The sappers are trying to provide cross-fire with their mortars. It stops the Russian infantry but not the tank.

The tank finally departs and moves towards the village. We realise that we have been dead lucky, because the tracks show that the tank actually missed our bunker and only churned up the earth at the left edge. It is now firing at the sappers' machine-gun position. We watch in horror as their position takes a hit and realise that the machine gun is now useless—then he turns and comes back!

The T-34 is now shooting at will in the connecting trenches. He rolls over them and turns round, churning up the frozen ground and filling them. Two soldiers, frightened and desperate, jump up and try to flee the trench, but seconds later they are cut down by the tank's machine gun. Another soldier bravely throws a hand grenade against the tank's turret. It smashes against it like a snowball on a wall. The man does not get away quickly enough and is ground down by the tank's tracks. The turret hatch opens and several hand grenades are lobbed into the trench.

While I desperately try to dig my machine gun out from the dirt, Swina throws a hand grenade at two Russians who are storming towards us. They fall and writhe around in the snow. Weichert has no time to reload his carbine, so he snatches Grommel's out of his hands and fires at the Russian who is about to jump into our trench. I hit the second Russian with a pistol shot. Blood drips from the wound in his throat; crying, he runs back. Others run with him. Again we have a little air. There are only a few Russians in the trenches now, but the T-34 churns on. He grinds down everything under him—and there is no one able to destroy him.

Will this be the end? Will a single T-34 be able to destroy us all? The air is filled with terror, and also with anger and helplessness in the face of this steel monster. Another soldier whose nerves cannot stand the pressure of being in the trench gets up and out, and the tank turns around and runs him down, tearing him in half. A terrible sight to behold! Grommel's stomach turns and he crawls back into the bunker.

The tank churns over the position again and again, then he slowly approaches our bunker. Are we next? Does he know that we're still in there, and still alive? What should we do? Running away is no good, but the bunker could be our grave! In my subconscious I hear several detonations in the village, and I remember the other tank. But my thoughts are concentrated on the steel colossus which is now coming right at us, its engine screaming. It is firing at everything that moves, and in between the shots its machine gun rattles, spraying the blind spots.

Is there no hope of salvation? In despair I send a quick prayer up to heaven and notice that the others, helpless, are seeking cover. Will the monster miss us this time? Surely we won't be so lucky a second time? Or will we?

I take one last look at the T-34, which is no more than 30 metres away—then I suddenly feel transported from hell to heaven. My fright dissipates, and instead my blood begins to pump in excitement. Everything around me is forgotten—and I see only the tractor pulling the anti-tank gun appear over the hillock. Even before it comes to a halt three men jump down and in no time the gun is detached and swung into position. The gunlayer is already turning his wheel to aim the weapon at the tank. Then the tank notices the ATG. The protagonists are no more than 100 metres apart.

Slowly the tank turret turns around, seeking its target. Who will fire first? It must be the ATG. But will he hit the enemy? That first shot will decide the outcome. I call the others out of the bunker and almost fall over in my excitement. Then a report tears through the charged air. A lightning-like explosion illuminates the surroundings and with it comes the hit—right on the turret of the T-34! Seconds later comes another hit, lifting the turret and moving it sideways off the tank.

'Hurrah!' A yell of delight issues from many a raw throat, the amazing release from the terrible despair of the last few hours. Saved! We were, literally, saved in the last second. Those wonderful fellows with the ATG won the battle with their first shot, cheating the hand of death hovering over us. I feel like giving that crew an enormous hug because of their heroic efforts. Swina, Grommel and Weichert are straightaway back to their old selves.

As if stung by a bee, two Russians now dash out of Döring's bunker; in our jubilation, we hadn't noticed them. They're running for their lives back to where they came from. No shots are fired. Now there is a temporary cease-fire from both sides. We can't stand it in the trenches any longer. We climb out, and with us they all stream like rats out of their holes—dirty, pale, but happy that they have survived. Later we learn that today, in addition to the slightly and seriously wounded, we also have eight dead to mourn. Some were apparently buried alive in their bunker by the tank.

To our dismay and great sorrow, *Unteroffizier* Döring and two of his men also are among the dead. Among us in the trenches, Warias and Seidel remain unscathed. Küpper was wounded in the head and shoulder and was driven down to the village with the other casualties. Meinhard lost his machine gun because he had not managed to snatch it away before the tank tracks crushed it. Wilke survived the nightmare.

Most of the soldiers from the ATG are now in the trenches, and Weichert and I go over to see them and to give them our heartfelt thanks for saving us. The ground between us and the hillock is all churned up and mixed in with snow. A new and peculiar type of odour is in the air. It comes from the mangled human flesh that covers the ground. I have somehow become used to seeing dead bodies, but this is a completely new and frightful experience.

Those who lie here are not just dead bodies, with one wound in them or possibly with one part missing. Here are individual lumps of flesh from arms, legs and buttocks, and in one instance from a head, on to which part of a damaged helmet still clings. These are the remains of the men of the 88mm AA gun and the quad MG, both of which received direct hits from the T-34 and were blown apart, blasted into the air. I feel so miserable as we stumble forward.

The three men from the brave ATG crew are still being thanked by another group of soldiers. The *Geschützführer** is an *Unteroffizier*. On his breast he is wearing the Iron Cross 1st Class and the Silver Wound Badge, proving that he has some experience behind him. In our eyes he is a hero, and had he not already got the Iron Cross 1st Class he would certainly be awarded one now. The faces of the three are dirty, sweaty and unshaven under their steel helmets. The *Unteroffizier* looks familiar: where have I seen him before? I walk towards them, and as he turns round I can recognise who it is.

'Heinz! Heinz Ruhmann!' I yell, startling the men nearby.

The *Unteroffizier* has also recognised me in spite of my dirty face. Surprised and delighted at such an unexpected meeting here in this godforsaken bridgehead outside the Stalingrad pocket, we fall into each other's arms. Still amazed about the coincidence, he wants to know how and since when I have been assigned here to his unit.

I explain the situation to him and reflect what a small world it really is and what chance meetings life often brings. In this vast country of Russia, where there are at the moment a million German soldiers, I happen to meet Heinz Ruhmann, the youngest son of the principal at the primary and middle school in our home town. And on top of that, it is he who saves not only me but all the others from a life-threatening situation, literally at the last second.

* Crew Chief.

Some eight days ago he arrived from Nishne Tschirskaya at the Don bridgehead on the southern bank of the river. Yesterday he had been ordered to give us support with his ATG against tank attacks. From Heinz I also learn for the first time that our forces have established two bridgeheads on the south bank of the Don manned by remnants from several units, and that our unit here is a so-called buffer unit in an advanced 'hedgehog' defensive position—in other words, we are a sort of suicide unit.

Asked about the other three tanks, he tells me that one ran on to a mine at the edge of the village. He caught the second along the railway line, and the one which came from the north-east into the village was destroyed by our last tank, itself immobilised with track damage. We have a lot of news to exchange about our home area, but he has orders to return to his position in the village. As he is leaving he calls back, telling me he will look out for me the next opportunity he has, so that we can catch up on old times.

Unfortunately it never comes to this: I never saw Heinz Ruhmann again. I never did find out whether he was killed on 13 December in the village, whether he was one of those who remained behind at the Don, or whether he fell or was captured during the defensive campaigns on the Don and Tschir. Moreover, his parents, whom I often saw during my next leave, and with whom I discussed our unusual encounter, never discovered what happened to him either.

Meinhard now assumes leadership of the remaining fourteen men, as he is the ranking *Obergefreiter* in our sector. Until the time comes for my guard duty, I sleep like a log. However, when Warias wakes me for my shift I spring up and tear off like a caged animal which has just been freed. I am still half asleep, but it does prove to me that my nerves are not completely up to par. I am reminded just as Meinhard was when he came to us from Stalingrad. God, in the bunker area near Businovka we were all so full of eagerness and the desire to win! And how impatiently we waited for the opportunity to fight at the front! Now, after exactly three weeks in combat, no one talks of heroism or enthusiasm any more. On the contrary, the only wish is to get out of this death trap alive. This is not war as we imagined it would be, and of which we talked. As soldiers, you know that war also can mean death. But to talk about it without experiencing it is like talking about a house on fire without being in it. We have been in the fire for days and experienced the searing heat, and we have lost many of our comrades.

12 December. When Wilke relieves me from guard duty early this morning, there is a pale red strip of light on the horizon to the east.

'It will be a sunny day,' says Wilke, and I agree.

Towards morning it always becomes colder, and I am thoroughly frozen and glad that there is heat in the bunker. Swina is leaning against the wall and is chewing on a piece of bread. Grommel is also awake and has kept the coffee warm for me, even though it came by an hour ago. After a long time without, we now receive a spoonful of marmalade with the square bread.

Grommel is definitely a good friend, but I'm not sure that I can actually understand him. Is he really unable to shoot at the enemy? Why? It can't be because of fright, because during our counter-attacks he didn't hesitate to come with us. But that business yesterday about having his carbine with the safety catch on, when Weichert wanted to use it—that was bad. And it would have become even more obvious if the attackers had been any closer to us. He did make up for things, however, by clearing out the cartridges that had got stuck in the machine-gun barrel. He is an expert at that. We often take minutes to remove a jammed cartridge, but it's no problem for him. That was vital yesterday, and Grommel was a great help.

In the sky we see a twin-tailed German observation plane, flying towards Stalingrad. He runs into a white cloud of anti-aircraft fire. Shortly afterwards he is shot down, leaving a dark smoke trail. Another aircraft flies low overhead and drops some supplies and ammunition boxes over the village. This evening we should be able to have some biscuits again.

Apart from an hour of artillery fire, today must be considered a quiet one. Grommel, who knows every day of the week, tells us that it is Saturday. But what difference does the day of the week make? Today is almost like a holiday. How undemanding we have become! Just because the artillery has shelled us less than usual, we find it peaceful and manageable. But will it be like this tomorrow? We wish it could be! But wishes are like dreams: in reality they melt like snow in the spring sunshine. Therefore it will probably be a day like those before, with little hope and the unasked questions. Who will it be this time? Who will lie cold and stiff on the brutal and terrible Russian soil? Whose death will be witnessed and mourned by close friends?

It's a good job no one knows in advance whether he is the next. For those who are hit, death always comes as a surprise, and much too early. And when it does come, we hope it will be over very quickly. Up till now it was only our enemies who lay badly wounded along our front and whose cries I could hear. I often wake up at night, thinking I can hear them moaning in the dark, with no one able to help them. God protect us from this terrible fate.

13 December. I slept badly last night. When Grommel wants to wake me, I am already awake. I'm not at peace within myself, and I can't explain it. I have a gnawing sensation in my stomach, like an anthill. The cold outside is good for me.

I meet Warias, who is on patrol in our sector. He tells me that the rumour is circulating that *Generaloberst* Hodt, with his tanks, is on his way to break open the pocket around Stalingrad. Is it true or is it, as usual, just gossip? Perhaps it really is the great salvation that all those who are surrounded are so fervently hoping for? But will it also do something for us here in our battered 'hedgehog' position? Again—questions to which no one seems to have any answers.

The wind suddenly carries sounds to us of a sort we've not heard before. They are a bit like trumpet blasts, repeated at various distances. Later we hear the noise of powerful engines approaching through the night, from the direction of Tschir. The trumpet sounds are new, and we can't make head nor tail of them. When I meet up with Meinhard, he says that he has noticed searchlights being turned on over there now and then.

'Looks like he is assembling troops over there,' he says to himself and then adds: 'Ivan definitely is up to something! If we only knew what!'

The air around us becomes electric. The entire sector is now awake. Soldiers are emerging from the trenches and are walking nervously back and forth. Everyone is looking towards the front, but it is still too dark to make anything out. When I go to wake Weichert at 5 o'clock he is already standing in front of the bunker gazing towards Tschir. The nervous feeling in my stomach is now stronger. I remember that this same feeling of unease would also come to me at home, most often when I was about to start an important sports event. Here, however, it is much stronger: it is a concentrated excitement, brought about by the knowledge that something threatening is approaching and we don't know what it is.

A stifling situation! But we have to wait—wait until the grey of the morning. Little Grommel is the only one left in the bunker. I go inside to warm up my drink over the last bit of heat left in the oven. The drink is a left-over from the supply container dropped earlier. Grommel is sleeping, but his breathing is irregular. He is lying with his face towards the wall and every so often his body gives a twitch. Just as I am about to pour my hot drink from my mess kit into my canteen cup, he suddenly leaps up with a yell and rushes, still half asleep, to the bunker entrance. I drop my cup in astonishment and grab him by the sleeve. He flails his arms wildly and yells, 'Swina! Swina! I'm coming! Help him! Help him!' I grab him around his midriff and hold his arms tight. Then I see that he is once again calm.

Weichert stands beside us and asks in a quiet voice, 'What was the matter, Squirt? Did you have a bad dream? You know that Swina is with Meinhard in his bunker.' Then we go out into the frosty morning air. In the east a narrow strip of light is announcing the dawn of a new day. Grommel is still a bit groggy and is searching for words to explain his dream, but what he says is lost in the infernal racket which is going on.

It comes at us with such a force that there must be a thousand devils in the air, and the earth around us is being consumed like a boiling hell. Before we rush back into the bunker, Wilke, who is standing guard outside, comes dashing over and falls to the ground right in front of us. We look at each other with disturbed, white faces. Nobody says a word, but fear is obvious in every wrinkle of our skin. Our eyes gleam feverishly. Hell is fuming! Fire and glowing steel fall from the sky all around us. If we didn't know that the devastating shellfire was coming from the Soviets, we could be forgiven for thinking that here, on 13 December, the end of the world had begun.

I can't stand it in the bunker any more: I want to see this hell in which we will all perish. When I raise my head just a little above the edge of the bunker, I am paralysed with fear. The surface of the ground is dancing all the way up to the hillock in a hellish turmoil. Not a single square foot seems to be still. Fountains of earth mixed with cold snow and glowing splinters of metal churn over the area being peppered with shell fragments. Nobody, but nobody, could take even a couple of steps without being caught up in this cauldron. The bursting thunderous noise, and the screaming in the air, are so loud that we can no longer make ourselves heard. On top of our bunker there are already a number of shallow craters caused by mortar fire, *Stalinorgeln* and light infantry weapons. But so far the roof, which we only reinforced two days ago, has held up.

The hellish inferno ebbs somewhat after about half an hour, but it seems to us like an eternity. The communication trench and our position have been almost filled. It's a wonder we're still alive. What does the enemy have in mind now? We know that this crazy shelling can only be preparatory to an attack, but the enemy is still hidden by the morning mist.

Somebody calls out my name! Then we see Warias. He comes rushing with long strides between the mortar explosions, and falls almost to his knees in front of us. He is so out of breath that he can't speak straight away. His dirty face is sweaty and caked, but where we can see his skin he is as white as a sheet.

Then he shrieks. 'Döring's bunker has been hit again! Meinhard, Swina and the rest have been killed. The chap on the outside is only slightly wounded, and I have already bandaged him up. But Seidel and two others have also been hit. I need more bandages so I can attend to them.'

Weichert presses two packs of bandages into his hand and he dashes back, zigzagging to avoid the incoming mortar rounds.

The deaths of Meinhard and Swina hit us heavily; my tears are caused not only by the acrid powder fumes. Fright increasingly grips me, my throat is parched and I feel as if I am being strangled. I follow Warias with my eyes and see that he jumps into the trench unharmed.

Then Wilke yells hysterically, 'Tanks are coming! In great masses—swarms of them!' His last words are drowned out by the noise of the explosions from the shells the tanks are firing at us.

Then I see them too! First it's like a wall of fire advancing on us, then a horde of brown beetles slowly approaches across the white steppe. A tank attack! Weichert hurriedly counts fifty, but there must be more. So this is what the Soviets have prepared—a colossal tank attack against our desolate, poorly equipped outpost here, which has been holding him back and has inflicted far too many losses on him for far too long!

Belching a threatening ripple of fire, the T-34s advance parallel with the railway line towards the village. Within the next quarter of an hour they will have reached it and will be able to roll up or cut off our position from the rear. We know that our time here has run out, and that the time of terror without end, the terrible end, has come. The question is, is there still a chance for us to escape this fate?

We are standing in the protection of the bunker and are staring with sweaty faces now at the oncoming tanks, now at the fiery explosions on the churned-up field, up towards the safety of the hillock. A number of men near the hillock are now jumping out of their trenches and running up towards its protection. They want to reach the village before the tanks do, so that they then can escape over the frozen River Don. The sappers have also left their positions and are running towards the hillock. More and more men do likewise. They are running through a rain of shell fire and splinters. The further they have to run, the less chance they have of making it alive. The ground in between is littered with weapons, coats, equipment and other items, discarded so that the men can run faster. Many of them are struck down and remain lying on the ground; others manage to get up again and run on, bleeding. What should we do?

Grommel and Wilke run like caged animals into and out of the bunker. Weichert ducks down beside me ready to run. But he has still not decided. He points at two figures jumping out of the trench and now bounding through the deadly fire towards safety. I recognise the tall Warias and also Seidel, who has a bandage around his head. Seidel falls, but springs up again and carries on. Wilke excitedly indicates to us that the first tanks have already reached the village. What should we do? Rush after the pair of them? We are furthest from the hillock. And if we are lucky enough to reach it, what awaits us behind it?

Obviously we can't stay here in the bunker—that means death or imprisonment. Then rather death. To be taken prisoner by the Soviets? That I would never live through.

'They have all gone!' yells Wilke, surprised and agitated.

'No, not all of them yet—there are still some in that position there!' replies Weichert.

But Wilke has already taken off his webbing and is running into the seething cauldron. I can see him throwing away his heavy overcoat as he runs along, then I lift Weichert and Grommel up over the edge of the trench. They have already stripped off all unnecessary baggage and are running for their lives. Now it's my turn! Am I the last one? No, I can still see a couple of men waiting. What for? There are but two possibilities—run or stay. It calls for just as much daring to stay in the bunker and wait for the Soviets as it does to run through the explosions.

What a perfect soldier I am! Instead of freeing myself of all extraneous weight, I want to take along my belt and all my equipment. As I run I notice very quickly that I am not getting away fast enough, so as I run I tear off my overcoat and loosen my belt. The whole lot falls to the ground, and I keep only my 08 pistol in my hand.

I dash over the shell craters and stumble over the items which the fleeing soldiers have discarded. All around me grenades and shells are bursting. It is a run for life or death. Many have not made it to the hillock. They are lying silently or moaning on the ground; others are calling for help. How can I help them? I could be lying there beside them any moment. The fear of death or a serious injury blanks out every other thought, and I see only the chance of saving my own skin. As I reach the hillock and disappear behind it, coughing and drenched in sweat, I have long since lost sight of my friends. I stumble over a dead body and fall in the snow, which here is still white and almost virgin. The body I have just stumbled over is that of *Unteroffizier* Schwarz, lying in a pool of blood from several wounds. Judging from the colour in his face, he can only recently have died.

Then I see a new danger in front of me. Several T-34s have turned in front of the village and are now blocking the path of the escaping soldiers. They are driving several men before them, and the latter are

105

running for their lives, trying to escape by zigzagging like rabbits. But the tanks are firing with their machine guns. Some of the men fall and are ground up by the tank tracks. I have to get through! It hammers away in my head—I have to stay in the blind spot of the tank. In spite of this the bullets spray around my head, and then I sense a hit against the left side of my chest. Am I wounded? I don't feel anything which slows me down or weakens me, so I continue in my headlong rush.

Suddenly Wilke is beside me. He buckles at the knees and coughs. 'Shit! I can't go on! It's murderous!'

I grab him by the arm and pull him up, but after a couple of paces his legs give out again. Has he been hit? Horrified I see a T-34 tank bearing down on us. With my last ounce of strength I jump aside, but Wilke can no longer get up. The tank track is already over his body and his terrified yell is swallowed up by the gunfire of the T-34. It never noticed the human being it just ran over. The tank is now firing at individual soldiers. Nothing restrains me any more: I run and run until my lungs wheeze like a pair of old bellows. Finally I reach the railings and vault over them. I fall down on some hard ground on the other side. For a moment I remain lying there. The sweat is running down my forehead into my eyes. When I wipe my forehead with the back of my hand it is bloody, but it is only a small graze from falling on the stone. Then I notice a ruined hut. That would give me some cover—I must get over there! And with a couple of strides I make it.

The broken-down door lies on the floor. Too late do I discover that lurking behind the remains of a wall is a T-34, its turret hatch open. A thunderous shot almost bursts my eardrums. Suddenly a Soviet soldier jumps over the remains of the wall into the house and becomes glued to the spot. We are both surprised and stare at each other. He is unarmed, and I am holding my 08 pistol in my hand, aimed at him. The Russian is young, just like me, and is staring with concern at my pistol. If he attacks me I will shoot, but he doesn't move: he just stands there and lets his hands fall to his sides.

106

Slowly I move backwards, until my back hits a beam. Then I turn and run away to the protection of some bushes close to the river bank. There I meet up with a group of soldiers who, like me, are completely exhausted and who, after a short pause to catch their breath, throw themselves on to the snow-covered ice of the Don. Under the terrifying machine-gun and heavy fire from the many tanks which have assembled at the river bank, they are trying to make it across the river to the safety of the other side, joining the ranks of all the other German soldiers who, in a state of sheer panic, are now engaged in a life-or-death struggle. In order to avoid falling into the hands of a merciless enemy, they choose to take the lesser risk of running over the deadly ice, which minutes earlier stretched away peacefully. I also clutch at this straw of hope and race off.

The ice is too thin for the tanks, which therefore line themselves up on the high ground along the banks and fire at us as if at a shooting range. The shells explode without let-up. Men are falling on to the snow left and right. The white covering is now colouring itself blood red. The dead are lying in heaps, and the wounded are groaning and calling for help. In many places the ice has cracked open from the shellfire and fountains of water are erupting high into the air. Many of the bodies lying on the snow disappear in the gurgling water as the ice breaks up. I run, stumbling over dead and wounded, hearing only explosions and aware that the snow is becoming stained red with blood. Then, finally, I reach the safety of the other bank.

There aren't many of us who can manage to reach the far river bank and seek the protection of the birch forest there. But even here we are not safe. The tank shells are exploding in the tree tops, and splinters and branches are constantly raining down. Many who thought they were safe here have been injured.

There are lots of bunkers in the forest. As we are running past one, an *Unteroffizier* waves us in. I stumble through the entrance and need some minutes before I can breathe normally again, and talk. I send a 'thank you' prayer to heaven, grateful that I've been able to survive the death run across the Don.

The bunkers are in surprisingly good condition, clean, and all professionally constructed with birch trunks of the same length. They must have been built to last. But who knows how long they have been standing empty? One soldier reckons that they were occupied by an artillery unit at one time. He has seen the prepared artillery positions on the banks of the Don. I should think it's possible to hold out here for some time.

The *Unteroffizier* offers me a cigarette. When I reach into my left breast pocket to take out my lighter, my fingers grip a piece of iron, deformed by a bullet or a splinter. The material is broken and my fingers run through it. I can smell the gas which has leaked out in my uniform. Now I remember the hit I felt in the left side of my chest as I reached the hillock. The solid lighter that *Stabsgefreiter* Gralla gave me in Stalingrad probably saved my life. I wonder what became of him and the others? But this is not the time to reminisce—we have to go on! One soldier among the last to make it through the terrible ordeal on the Don splutters that enemy infantry with mortar units are coming over the ice and will soon be here.

We can't hold them up; we have no weapons. The *Unteroffizier* hasn't even got his sub-machine gun, and I am the only one who still has a pistol. We follow the *Unteroffizier*, who runs ahead of us through the forest underbrush. Terror remains deep in the bones of us all. Overhead we can hear the mortar rounds exploding in the tree tops, raining splinters down upon us. Our helmets would have come in handy now, but we threw them away because they hindered us during our headlong rush to get away.

At the edge of the forest we emerge on to the snow-covered steppe. An icy wind drives the powdery snow into small mounds which then form into drifts. My body is slowly recovering; the sweat on my skin is slowly drying up. But now I begin to freeze. The same is happening to the others. Collars are pulled up and those who still have caps are pulling the flaps down over their ears.

We seek cover from the icy wind in a *Rachel*, where we find another group of exhausted soldiers who belonged to our unit. They have dug themselves holes in the snow to protect themselves from the icy wind. In one of these holes, to my great delight, I come across my friends Warias and Grommel. They both made it safely over the Don, but now they are really freezing. Warias does not even have a cap on his head, while Grommel is sitting in the snow hole shivering.

Cold can be deadly, particularly when the body is emaciated like ours. And there is not a house nor a barn to be seen—nowhere to crawl for some warmth. So we must go on, until we can find some of our own men. But where are they? Have they gone so far south that we won't be able to find them? Walking and pressing against the wind are very tiresome, although the exercise does keep the bones moving.

Some of the wounded soldiers can't make it any further. We rest in the next *Rachel* and dig holes in the snow. But to stay there too long will give us frostbite, so I force myself to get out and run up and down from time to time, so that the stiffness in my body loosens.

14 December. In the early hours of the morning we are driven from the *Rachel* by heavy fire: the Soviets have noticed us and have trained their mortars on us. We run like frightened chickens. The biting wind whips cold snowflakes into our hot faces, immediately converting the snow into small streams of water which freeze solid into small clumps hanging from the stubble on our unshaven faces. When we regroup, we hear fire being exchanged to the right, then German soldiers suddenly appear running towards us out of the mass of whirling snow, calling out that the Russians are right behind them. We join them and run along together. Behind us a Russian machine gun is rattling away and rifle shots snap. One man turns around and yells like crazy. He holds his rifle

in front of him and blazes away at the enemy, but after a few paces he falls, hit, to the snow. One more has lost the battle.

We race on. The shooting behind us increases. Amongst the firing we hear the Soviets in their forward charge, yelling. Their 'hurrahs' are right behind us and make us run even faster. Suddenly three tanks appear in front of us—German assault guns! They wait until we have passed them, then open fire. The cries and the firing behind us are silenced. The assault guns move slowly forward and fire at maximum rate. Then we suddenly find ourselves in the middle of a combat unit, moving forward with the tanks in a counter-attack to throw the enemy back. But for how long?

Following the counter-attack, we join up with this combat force and return with them to their jump-off point. The *Leutnant* in charge decides to integrate our unit—about thirty men—into his one. The men are lying in the protection of a *kolkhoz* and some farm buildings. Even though we get something to eat after going without for two days, I still feel totally miserable. Or is this cowardice? After all, what can you expect from a soldier who has just passed through the scorching heat of hell, and looks as though he has succumbed to the miseries there, like virtually all his friends and comrades have. Should he accept their deaths simply as the soldier's fate, without question, and keep on fighting? Dammit! I would do it if we were launching an attack and had some chance of winning. But here we are, running scared. Is it cowardice when you no longer have anything in your hands with which you can defend yourself?

This rabble—the one with which we three have ended up—has done nothing, God knows, to improve our will to fight. They're stragglers like the ones who came over to us near Rytschov, but their combat morale is so low that we are forever having to put up with them going on about how best they can get the hell out of it. We're told how the leaders have had to use their guns to keep the men obedient—they'd bolted once, before the enemy was even seen. Some even shot themselves in their arms or legs. They would hold a loaf of bread in front of the muzzle to make sure there would be no powder burns or singe marks. Those found out will be court-martialled, and can expect to be executed.

An *Obergefreiter* will be court-martialled because he is supposed to have deliberately allowed both his feet to get frozen. Before they brought him to the medics he told us that following a Russian attack he had saved himself by playing dead. In order to avoid being detected by the enemy, he had spent the entire night in a snow drift. When another combat unit freed him the next morning during a counter-attack, his feet were two blocks of ice. It was his tough luck that no one in this combat unit knew him.

We are given a carbine and ammunition from our new unit. In addition, I'm able to get hold of a second-hand and originally white camouflage suit with a quilted jacket and trousers. There are no more helmets. The few houses are all full up. Our squad is led to a shed, which has gaps between each vertical plank in the walls so large that the wind blows the ice-cold snowflakes through. We cover them as best we can with ground sheets. There is only wet straw to sleep on. But even this is better than camping outside in the icy steppe. The next morning we receive a hot liquid which is passed off as coffee. But at least it warms our insides.

15 December. My spirits have hit rock bottom. We learn that a group of soldiers has actually disappeared with a truck, and we are now left with three assault guns and two trucks. It is said that the men who left belonged to a penal company before they came here. How rumours fly!

We march off, always forward and somewhere in the direction of the front. The snow is falling more heavily, and soon we can only see a white surface in front of us, interrupted only by the occasional bush. Where are the positions supposed to be? If they do exist, they must have

111

been covered by the snow. The houses behind us have long since disappeared behind the curtains of snow, and the *Feldwebel* seems to be ill at ease in this winter wasteland. He decides to halt in front of a wide *Rachel*.

Suddenly, coming from somewhere or other, rifle shots can be heard. Out of the whirling snow several figures appear and run with us into the *Rachel*. They are German soldiers fleeing from the enemy. They tell us that they've been lost in the snowy waste since yesterday, and only by good fortune have been able to get away from the Soviets, who seem to be everywhere. They belonged to a combat group that was in position on the frozen River Tschir and which yesterday was overrun by a pack of T-34 tanks with mounted infantry. The survivors had bolted and are now wandering around somewhere in the steppe. One soldier was shot during the last exchange of fire—he could not run any further as he had fallen asleep last night and both his legs had frozen. The Soviets in front of us were working on getting their four mortars ready to fire.

The *Feldwebel* is undecided. He sends a runner back to request that the three assault guns be moved up. As soon as they get here we'll attack the mortar position. We wait—and because of the cold we dig ourselves into the snow. For a while we are warm, because of the recent movement, but as the wind increases it whistles through our clothing to our very bones, causing them to tremble. Warias raps his hands intermittently on his calves, arms and shoulders. The winter coat with which he was issued is much too short, and his legs are stuck into a couple of slit-open felt boots that were removed from a dead soldier. Grommel, too, wears second-hand felt boots, and his coat is only a thin, ragged Army type. But he says that he has a warm (and probably lice-infested) lambswool vest underneath which another soldier tried on in the *kolkhoz* and found to be too tight. On his head he wears a Russian fur cap, given to him by one of the assault gun crewmen. He therefore looks like a Russian, and some of our men are already calling him 'Ivan'.

With my camouflage outfit, I am definitely the best off, but nevertheless I still freeze horribly here in this bloody country, where Napoleon and his entire army perished. Everything I have read about this episode in the history books I am now experiencing for myself. I shudder when I think about being wounded here in this snowy wasteland and lying helplessly, until my body slowly turns into a lump of ice.

Why don't the assault guns come? We wait and wait, and then—too late! We hear the mortar shells rushing in. In spite of the fact that they hit the ground some distance away, splinters do zip through the air and pass close to our heads. It doesn't particularly upset us: we're used to much worse. I even decide to stand up, so that I can keep my feet moving. Then a shell explodes on the slope across from us . We can see the splinters fizzing in the snow. A soldier calls out, and I feel a slight pain underneath my left knee cap. They are calling for the medic, who is in our group. He is taking care of the wounded man, whose thigh has been torn open by a splinter and who as a result is bleeding heavily. He is an *Obergefreiter* wearing the blue uniform of a *Luftwaffe* field division. He came to this group with three others when his own unit was decimated.

After the medic has taken care of the man, I show him the place where I felt a hit. Directly under my kneecap there is a small hole, about the size of a pea. It doesn't hurt, and I can move my leg okay, but a thin trickle of blood, almost black in colour, is running down my shin.

The medic attaches a plaster. 'Too bad,' he says almost apologetically and shrugs his shoulders.

I know what he means. He is trying to tell me that unfortunately it does not qualify me for a *Heimatschuss*.* I feel the disappointment—a hope has been dashed. And then I think how quickly human feelings and attitudes can change. It is only a matter of weeks since I was dreaming of glory and heroism and was so full of élan that I was almost bursting. Now I long for a *Heimatschuss*—because it appears to me to be the only

---

* Literally, 'home shot', i.e. leave of absence to return home for convalescence.

113

way that I can, with any sort of honour, say goodbye to this soul-destroying environment and, for at least a few weeks, get away from this awful country and its gruesome winter.

Is it cowardice to think like this, to start comparing our war here with trying to stop a full-blown avalanche merely by using human bodies? With human beings who, full of despair and freezing to death, shiver in icy holes in the snow and each morning thank God that their bones have not frozen solid because they are still needed to help you get away to safety from the attacking enemy? I don't think that this rabble of soldiers, thrown together, and without proper heavy weapons, will be able to hold back the Russians here on the Don and Tschir this winter. Anyone who can escape from this situation with just an injury really can talk about his luck.

But thinking that you might fall into this category isn't being realistic: it's a dream. And when does a dream ever come true? The path of a splinter or bullet does not conform to the wishes of the ordinary soldier. Splinters and bullets are hard, hot and nasty. They search out life hiding in dirty rags and try to extinguish it with one blow.

The wind gets stronger. It howls through the *Rachel* and swirls around us in our hole in the snow. It drives the powdery snow into our faces and melts on the warm skin. When I move my left leg, I can feel a painful pulling sensation and a slight swelling.

Late in the afternoon the three assault guns arrive. Because of the heavy driving snow, they want to wait until they attack. But the enemy pre-empts us: for the Soviets, this is attack weather. We first notice them as they draw close to our *Rachel*.

The assault guns are using anti-personnel shells. We fire blindly into the snowy haze. The flakes drive into us, gluing up our faces and our eyes. Then the phantom disappears! We have hardly put down any counter-fire.

'It was only a reconnaissance squad,' says a *Gefreiter* who belongs to the *Feldwebel*'s circle. He tells us that the enemy attacked here yesterday

114

morning and that a number of dead soldiers are lying covered up by the recent snow.

Then we hear a firefight on one of our flanks. The assault guns are ordered to return to the *kolkhoz*. How will things develop now? We stay in our snow holes and wait. I want to stand up again but find that I can't—it's as though I have a wooden leg. The left knee is completely stiff. If the enemy attacks now, I'm afraid I am finished. I'm not able to walk, let alone run. Oh no! In my anxiety I call for the medic. He taps my swollen knee, which has come up like a balloon. The skin is stretched taut, as if it has been brushed with dope, and is dark blue.

'Haemorrhage,' says the medic. The massive internal bleeding came about because the little hole was stopped up with the plaster and the blood could not therefore escape but instead built up inside my leg.

'I can't do anything with it. The leg has to be placed in a cast and immobilised. But before the medics in Nishne Tschirskaya put your leg in a cast, you should show the splinter to a doctor, because otherwise it could easily cause blood poisoning.'

Nishne Tschirskaya?

'How do I get there?' I ask, surprised, but also happy that I now perhaps can get out of this mess.

The medic shrugs his shoulders. 'I don't know that either.'

'But I can't walk!' Then I feel a tension in my guts, which I always feel when anxiety suddenly overtakes me.

'I know,' nods the medic. 'I've also got the wounded *Obergefreiter*. I wanted to send him along with the assault guns, but they had no room for a stretcher case.'

Damn! Now I've got the opportunity to get away from here and I'm not able to. How unlucky can you get? But I again get a glimmer of hope as the medic returns and tells me that we are to stay here in the *Rachel* tonight and will receive our provisions here. Then we should be able to return to the *kolkhoz* with the supply vehicle. When that supply vehicle is due, he doesn't know. We'll just have to wait.

Well, what does that mean? How long? Two or three hours? It really doesn't matter because I know that I'll soon be on my way to safety. But I'm not there yet! I spend the next few hours in two minds. I can't yet believe that I'll be able to get out of here—out of this snowbound steppe, which has no feelings for anybody and which only intensifies my fear of being wounded or suffering a terrible death through freezing. But the next enemy attack—which we cannot possibly withstand—could alter everything. I can't walk, and I'd have to stay here in this lousy hole in the snow and wait for the end. I can only pray that it won't happen.

My prayers must have been heard, because the supply truck comes earlier than expected. He also brings orders for the entire force to depart immediately, as the enemy is reported to have already broken through the defences on the flank of the *kolkhoz*. The truck driver is in a hurry to return. Warias and Grommel carry me to the truck; the *Obergefreiter*'s three friends do the same for him. We lie on the bare truck bed, leaning our backs on the sides. The *Obergefreiter* is in great pain. He groans as he says his goodbyes to his friends.

The thought that Warias and Grommel will remain here puts a damper on my excitement to be getting out of here. Something wells up in my throat, further and further until my eyes water. It's as if I'm abandoning them. We three were, among the many unknown and foreign soldiers, like brothers. We stuck together through thick and thin and helped each other whenever we could. As they give me their hand in farewell, Grommel wipes his eyes with his arm and Warias tries to hide his feelings by overplaying his mood, boldly announcing: 'Don't forget to say hello to the blonde waitress in the Tivoli. Tell her that I'll soon be there to arrange a date with her.' I force myself to laugh and assure him that I will tell her. Then the truck drives off into the darkness.

In spite of the truck's tarpaulin, the wind blows from all sides, chilling me through to the marrow. The truck follows the tracks which the assault guns have made. Every time the vehicle goes over a bump we feel the truck bed shake. The *Obergefreiter* groans softly; he appears to be in considerable pain. Apart from putting on a bandage, the medic was unable to do anything for him. He feels in his pocket and gives me an *Aktive*. That's what we call a ready-made cigarette you get in a packet as opposed to one you roll yourself.

I am thankful, for I've got only a couple of flakes of coarse curly-cut tobacco for my pipe left in my pouch. We inhale the smoke in silence. The truck jolts and makes a sharp turn. I can feel my knee! The wounded man suppresses a cry of pain and groans: 'Damn and shit! First you wait day and night for a *Heimatschuss* and then everything changes! You can't even be happy about it, because you have to slink away from your mates. Which of those poor devils will ever see home again?'

It's a good thing he can't see my face in the dark, nor taste the bitterness I've felt in my throat ever since we left. Not even the sharp flavour of the tobacco can drive away this sensation.

As we come to the settlement by the *kolkhoz* there is a general atmosphere of breaking camp. They have been waiting for the truck. Away to the west we can hear intermittent tank-fire. An officer allows some clothing be packed on the truck. An *Unteroffizier* and a couple of men sit down among the packages. One of them has a headband. I can't see his face in the darkness, but I recognise him by his voice.

'Kurt Seidel!' I call out, surprised and delighted.

It is him! We have quite a lot to tell each other—the death run over the frozen Don and everything thereafter. He tells me that he was waiting with the others at the river bank for too long. When he did finally start running the first Russians were right behind him. By then the tanks had eased off. He managed to get away from the Russians with three others and later ran into another group of stragglers who were being chased by the Russians. They didn't come across this larger combat unit until today.

I point to his headband. Seidel tells me that it's just a small wound which has almost completely healed, but because he hasn't got a cap he has left the bandage on to help keep his head warm. He does not belong to the fortunate ones with *Heimatschüsse* but must remain here and continue to look after himself.

We haven't seen each other since that time. By the time I was being loaded into an ambulance with many other wounded, just before we got to Nishne Tschirskaya, Seidel had jumped off the truck with the others. Only later, when I was with the convalescent company, did I learn that he had been killed.

The ambulance pulls up in front of a large building. The slightly wounded get out, while I and two others are carried in on stretchers. In the room it smells of ether and carbolic. Everywhere there are wounded lying around; some of them are groaning. From outside comes the sound of commands being given. Tractors and tanks rumble by. I can hear artillery fire in the distance.

I am no longer concerned about all this—I feel safe here. But am I really safe here? One chap tells me that he was wounded just two hours ago not far from here, up north. The Soviets are attacking all the time, and, according to him, we won't be able to hold them back for very long. In spite of this, I sleep quite well on the straw bed because I am dog tired. The unaccustomed heat in the room and the knowledge that I don't have to go out tonight have relaxed my body.

16 December. As two medics lift me up on a stretcher, I rise sleepily and immediately fall back on the stretcher with a groan. For the first time I feel a really stinging pain in my knee. They bring me into a well-lit room. Someone is just about to collect together some amputated, blood-soaked body parts in a ground sheet. Later another man comes over to me dressed in a blood-stained rubber apron. The sergeant accompanying him addresses him as '*Herr Oberstabsartzt*'.* He cuts my left trouser leg with a pair of scissors, as well as my two pairs of long

* Regimental Medical Officer.

johns. He examines my knee. My leg is dark blue from my thigh all the way down to the calf, and as thick as an inflated inner tube. He gives me an injection and tells an assistant to put my leg in a splint and cover it in a plaster cast.

'There is nothing more we can do,' he says before he moves on to the next patient.

The medic cuts off the rest of my trousers and underwear all the way up to my thigh, lays the leg in a splint and covers it expertly with the wetted plaster-of-Paris bandages. The gypsum sets quickly. After I receive a wound receipt with the appropriate dates stamped on it, duly fastened to my chest, I am transferred into a special room where other patients in care are resting. From some of the wounded I learn that those who can be moved will be transferred to Morosovskaya, where there is a larger medical assembly station. A day later I am again loaded into an ambulance.

CHAPTER SIX

A Temporary Lull

DECEMBER 17. The ambulance frequently has to take detours en route to Morosovskaya. In the north the Soviets are said to have broken through another front line, this one manned by the Italians. They are reportedly on their way south. Gunfire can still be heard in the distance. I am not particularly concerned as I'm not in action and I consider my surroundings only from the viewpoint of someone who is bedridden. If no one disturbs me, I'll be asleep either in the ambulance or, later on, in Morosovskaya. I'm catching up on the sleep I missed out on over the last several weeks. Because my leg, in its cast, doesn't need any particular medical attention, I'm only woken up when they serve me my meals or when I have to take a tablet . . .

18 December. I don't count the days any more, so I don't know how long I've been in Morosovskaya in this blissful sleep when I'm suddenly rattled by high fever. I am given several injections and I hazily seem to understand that I am being loaded into an ambulance train together with several other wounded. The fever increases and terrible pictures form in front of my eyes, causing me to cry out, whimper and shudder.

Slowly my surroundings come into focus and I recognise that I am lying on the top of a two-tiered white bed in an ambulance train. A young blonde nurse with a red cross on her cap is standing next to my bed and is softly singing Christmas carols. Some of the wounded are accompanying her in their raw voices.

The rhythm of the wheels is changing and is being converted into a hard, threatening hammering. The sound reverberates painfully in my head. I close my eyes and press my forehead on to the frosty window. It does not cool me down but instead causes the frost patterns on the window to melt.

A cool hand is laid across my hot temple, wet with perspiration, and a soft voice says a few calming words. As if coming through a veil, I recognise the young nurse. She gives me two tablets and helps me to swallow them. Thereafter I fall asleep exhausted, but I don't have any dreams.

26 December. During the afternoon of the second day of Christmas I am once more able to think straight. On my bed are my Christmas presents, still unopened. I'm surprised at the generous contents of the gifts they are the sorts of things which we for months had to do without. Plenty of cigarettes are included. I light one and discover that it tastes good; this is a sign that I am more myself again. But it is still a while before I can really understand where I am and that I have also survived the blood poisoning which the medic back at the *kolkhoz* told me I could expect.

My neighbour, who lies in the top bunk across the aisle from me, has just awoken and greets me with a friendly remark: 'Ah, just risen from the dead? I'm glad you're finally awake, my friend!'

I smile at him and see that he is holding his right arm out like a wing. Later I learn that the soldiers call it a 'Stuka', because the arm is held in a track, in plaster and at an angle which resembles that of the wings of a Stuka dive bomber. This treatment is generally used when the arm has suffered a break caused by a gunshot wound. I assume my new friend has such a break.

He tells me that we stopped in Stalino yesterday and that we offloaded some slightly wounded soldiers. Only the seriously wounded and fever-stricken were left in the beds. The empty beds are, however, already filled up again.

'We are now travelling homewards,' he tells me happily. 'Over Krakau to Schlesien, and from there I will soon be home.'

'Where is home?' I ask him.

'In Marienbad, in Sudetenland,' he tells me with obvious pride. Then he describes the place for me, making it sound as if it were the most beautiful speck of dirt in the world, and I feel an urge to pay a visit some time. I have no idea that, at the close of the war, I would actually be drawn to this idyllic health resort. This conversation with my bunk-mate undoubtedly influenced my ending up in a military hospital there, after my sixth and last injury.

'Where were you wounded?' I ask.

'In Stalingrad, on 10 December,' he says, and I can see how his face twitches. The word 'Stalingrad' suddenly hangs heavily in the room. Most of the wounded come from Stalingrad or, like me, from the edge of the Don or Tschir pocket.

'Was really just lucky to get out of there. Now it's supposed to be bloody difficult.'

'Why's that?' I ask, as I've not heard anything about the situation there for days.

'Because the prospects for those left in the pocket have now become very black,' remarks another patient lying in a bunk somewhere beneath us. 'The last hope—that Hoht with his tanks was going to break through the pocket—has now gone up in smoke as well. They need him elsewhere.'

Others now decide to get involved. They complain bitterly about the top brass. One says angrily that they should all go to hell. No one disagrees, because everyone senses that he didn't say this without good reason. He and some of the others were in the pocket themselves and experienced first-hand how they were given hope and had promises made to them that they would be got out—that is, until it was too late and they realised that the Sixth Army in Stalingrad was, in fact, to be sacrificed.

Only a very small number of them had the good fortune to be flown out in the nick of time because of their injuries. This is now supposed to be pretty nearly impossible, they say. One soldier with a bandage round his head, and who only can see out of one eye, ridicules the latest Army radio report, which plays down the disaster in Stalingrad and refers to the defeat of the Sixth Army in a highly stylised propaganda report about the willingness of the German soldier to make a heroic stand.

Not everyone is as strong, and many are unable to hide even their everyday fears. The chap under my bunk must come into this category, because ever since I woke up he has been whimpering non-stop. Out of curiosity I lean over the edge of the bunk and see that his left arm and shoulder are bound into a sort of a 'Stuka' cast. I can't recognise his face. His whimpering is incessant and never ends. It really gets on everyone's nerves—in particular, it disturbs the seriously wounded men who are trying to get some sleep.

Finally it gets too much for the soldier with the headband and one eye. He turns to the whimperer and angrily tells him off: 'For God's sake stop that bloody whimpering! You're driving us all mad with your constant groaning!'

The fellow does not react in the least: on the contrary, he seems to get worse. We manage to get rid of him in Krakow when he is offloaded with some other men.

28 December. As soon as the beds have been freshly made up, others are carried in. The following day I arrive at my destination. I am offloaded in Bad Salzbrunn, near Hirschberg, at the foot of the

Riesengebirge. I say my goodbyes to my bunk-mates, who are being taken further on.

29 December–20 January 1943. After we are led through the delousing chamber we are laid on clean beds in a newly established military hospital. The rest of my stay here passed so quietly and uneventfully that I hardly have any memory of it. It went out of sight about as fast as the over-ripe Harz cheese that they placed in our dish on the night stand as our ration every other day.

My notes were reduced to comments about the head doctor with the pointed head and protruding frog eyes. After cutting up my plaster cast he told me he suspected me of shirking my duty and pretending to be wounded. Old Frog Eyes even asked me how come I had the leg placed in a cast. He messed around with my louse-bitten and dirty leg for a long time and brusquely ordered me to stand up and not to pretend to be wounded. He even threatened to write a report to the court martial and growled something about malingering, cowardice in the face of the enemy and so on.

But it was very odd—even I couldn't find any traces of my wound, and I couldn't locate the exact point where the splinter had entered my leg. The pea-sized, light red scar could just as easily have been taken for one of the many abrasions caused by the lice and which covered the entire leg.

The x-ray photographs finally exonerated me. I watched how the frog-eyed military doctor stared at the clearly visible jagged splinter in total disbelief, looking as though his goggle eyes would pop out of his head at any moment. A head doctor had absolutely no need to apologise to a mere *Landser*, but he mumbled something about the fact that there were always some among the wounded who would deliberately injure themselves or think up all sorts of other tricks to get themselves out of front-line duty. During the ensuing therapy I discover that the splinter doesn't cause me any problems, so I consider it to have been a lucky *Heimatschuss*, and one which, with God's help, saved me from an awful fate.

Here in the hospital we learned that supplies for Stalingrad could no longer be got through by air, neither could the wounded be flown out. Thus the fate of the Sixth Army was as good as sealed. We just could not grasp the fact that there really was no way of bringing out the men Adolf Hitler had stationed there to create 'Fortress Stalingrad'. We wondered whether we would ever find out how and why this catastrophe came about in the first place.

21 January. I am discharged from the hospital and get my convalescent leave. I'm going home at last! But inside I'm not as free and un-encumbered as before. I can't wipe away what I have experienced with a mere wave of the hand: my skin is simply not thick enough.

As I walk through the streets of our village I am barely noticed. Well, why should I be? There are soldiers all over the place and there are many among them that I don't know. An ordinary soldier with a Bronze Wound Badge is too unobtrusive to be of interest. You get one even for a small splinter under the knee.

It's only a few acquaintances who ask about front-line duty. When I tell them about it, they become curious, but not one of them believes what I say. The truth would devastate them, because, as far as they are concerned, German soldiers conform to what they hear every day in the Army reports—they are heroes who only storm forward! If they fall, it is only during an attack or through defending. They never give up an inch ground unless for tactical reasons they are given orders to fall back. Just look at Stalingrad—there's the proof!

The problem with leave is that it passes far too quickly. Now I have to return to the camp at Insterburg, first to the convalescent company.

14 February. I have arrived at Insterburg. On the way to the orderly room I run into the relaxed atmosphere of the company in the shape of several inebriated soldiers. They welcome me as a newcomer with a 'Hello', although we don't actually know each other. The *Obergefreiter*, or 'Head Snorter' as he is called here, slaps me on the shoulder and offers me a slug of juniper brandy, which I down while holding my breath.

As I leave the orderly room where I reported in, I accidentally bump into a large aluminium urn filled with coffee that a soldier is carrying. The boiling hot liquid splashes over my neat leave uniform. I stare angrily at the steaming wet spot on my trousers while the man who was carrying it yells at me, 'You silly sod! Are you blind?'

I am absolutely dumbfounded! The ever-hungry Hans Weichert is standing in front of me, large as life! I haven't seen him since Rytschov, and I'd felt certain he was either missing or dead. Before I can say anything he slaps me on the shoulder.

'Welcome to the land of the living!' he says.

I can still remember him as a skeleton when, on 13 December, he leapt up and ran out in front of me over to the hill under violent tank fire.

I learn how Warias and Weichert are still on convalescent leave, having just left hospital. They both begin their leave tomorrow. We have a lot to catch up on, but it is too noisy here and we look for a table in the canteen.

In the canteen Warias, as if by magic, produces a bottle of East Prussian 'Bear Catcher'. It is a tasty drink made from honey and alcohol, like a liqueur, which I prefer to the unpleasant juniper brandy.

'Where do you think I got that from?' he asks, suppressing a grin in his freckled face.

'I suspect that you will tell me in a minute.'

'I got it from the blonde waitress in the Tivoli!' he smiles proudly. I'm surprised.

'Then I assume that I don't need to pass on your regards, like you asked me to when I was injured? And I reckon you will not want to buy me a round like you promised?'

'No, no! What do you take me for? What Helmut Warias promises, he delivers!' The tall Warias taps himself on the chest. 'But first you must allow me to go on leave.'

We change the subject and talk about our experiences. I go first, and explain about my wound and about the incident with Old Frog Eyes, the doctor in the military hospital. Then Weichert relates how, after a terrible dash across the Don with two others, he got lost in the snow haze and first thing the next day bumped into a retreating group made up of supply personnel from a *Luftwaffe* unit. After other men from various decimated units joined up with them it was 'Stop', and they were sent into the trenches. He was wounded somewhere south of Tschir at the beginning of January—'Shot through the thigh, with bone damage,' says Weichert. The convalescence took a long time owing to complications caused by the wound constantly festering. Warias tells us that he was with a combat group until the middle of January. The group had slowly been retreating south, at the same time delaying the enemy. On 17 January 1943 he was wounded near Konstantinovka on the Don when a grenade splinter caught him in the throat. We can see a deep scar under his left ear.

'And what has happened to Grommel and Seidel?' I ask.

Well, yes, he was with Seidel for a while, he says. But at the end of December a grenade ripped away both his feet. 'He slowly bled to death before our eyes.' Warias tells us quietly. Then he is silent. We give him time to recover, but after he has had a chance to drink two more glasses of 'Bear Catcher' I raise the question of Grommel again. My guess is that he also has fallen.

Warias nods and closes his eyes.

'When and how did it happen?

'A couple of days after you were wounded. Near Nishne Tschirskaya.'

127

I can see little Grommel with his pale face and sad eyes in front of me. He couldn't open fire on the enemy, and as I watched him he would simply close his eyes when he pulled the trigger. Why he acted like this I will probably never know.

Warias must have been reading my mind. He lays his hand on my arm. 'Yes, I knew about that as well. But a few hours before he died he confessed to me that his religion forbade him to shoot people. In front of God we are all brothers, he said to me.'

'But he was no coward: he saved my life and those of others before he died,' Warias continued. 'I will never forget that.'

'It was during the fighting west of Nishne Tschirskaya, where the day before we had fought back an enemy attack. During the night the weather changed, and we were exposed to a heavy snowstorm. So we didn't realise the Russians were attacking until they actually stormed our positions. Thank goodness we had some tanks in support, which immediately fired on the attackers. But some of the Russians had already reached our trenches, and one big bull of a bloke sprayed us with his Kalashnikov like a madman. Suddenly he bent over and aimed his sub-machine gun directly at me and the others. I could already feel the hot rounds pumping into my body, then some chap standing next to him jumped up and walloped him in the chest with his rifle butt. The Russian keeled over and his Kalashnikov started to go off. The entire string went into this man's body and he immediately fell back into the trench.

'We immediately shot the big Russian bully, but, since the fighting was still going on, no one could concern himself about the fallen. We couldn't make out who it was because of the driving snow. It was only after we had beaten off the attack that we saw that it was our own little Grommel who had saved our lives. His body was literally riddled with bullets, and he was of course stone dead. When we pulled back we carried all the dead bodies with us. Our little friend was buried with a lot of others in Nishne Tschirskaya at the same time.'

We all went quiet after this, each man left with his own memories. Pictures keep appearing in front of my eyes showing the many dead at the bridgehead on the Don and most of the comrades I knew closely and who were important to me. But death takes no account of friendship, nor of the feelings of the survivors.

15 March. I've been with the convalescent company for four weeks now. Warias's and Weichert's leave begins tomorrow, and so I'll go with them to the railway station to bid them farewell. Months will pass before we meet again.

2 May. Before I begin my travels I can sew on a Gefreiter's stripe, along with which I receive a small increase in pay—although you can't buy much these days. I spend the summer holidays in an Army convalescent home in Radom, Poland. The time passes pleasantly and I recuperate well. Before long it is the beginning of June 1943. The weather is beautiful, and at the end of it I have a fresh and healthy tan.

3 June. The numbers of personnel in the convalescent company have gone down significantly during the last few weeks. Those who have been here the longest are slowly but surely being sent back to their units in northern France. The remaining units from our division in Russia are also stationed in France, so that they can be rebuilt with new recruits and those returning from convalescence.

CHAPTER SEVEN

Hunting Italian Partisans

I T IS 11 JULY. Back in the convalescent company orders await me to report to the 1st Company of the 1st Battalion of the newly reconstituted division. Our company is currently stationed in Flers, in Normandy. I am one of a group of fourteen soldiers, and we are being taken by truck to the railway station.

30 July. During the next few weeks we learn discipline. The main part of the work is to do with weapons and field training. Instead of the old MG 34, we now receive the brand new MG 42, which has the much higher rate of fire—1,000 rounds a minute—and is far less susceptible to cold, wet conditions and dirt. Because of our earlier training, my friends and I are assigned to the company's heavy weapons platoon, and the company is again up to strength. While Otto Kruppka (a good friend of mine from the convalescent company in Insterburg), Weichert and I get further training on the heavy machine gun, Warias has been assigned to mortars. Our instructors—from the *Oberwachtmeister* as *Zugführer*,* to the *Unteroffiziere*—are almost all experienced front-line soldiers, many of them decorated. The training is hard but not vindictive.

As I always accept and carry out to the best of my ability the hard but very worthwhile training on the HMG—which apart from the

---

* Equivalent to Sergeant-Major. *Zugführer* means Platoon Leader.

firing exercises includes building gun positions and carting around the heavy mounting and the ammunition boxes—I do not feel any real desire to go out in the evenings. I know from experience how vitally important it is, during an emergency, to have a trained body and to be able to control your weapon perfectly. I'm convinced that these two things—plus my good luck and God's help—have helped me survive the war so far in one piece.

15 August. It's time to say '*au revoir*' to France. No doubt many of the *mademoiselles* are weeping hot tears through their long eyelashes, but they will probably hanker after one of the many communications stallions and are quite prepared to expand their families! The departing soldier, on the other hand, sticks out his chest so that his medals rattle— assuming there *are* any to rattle—and reflects that a hot-blooded Mediterranean girl wouldn't be so bad after all. Although our destination is top secret, the rumour mill points in the direction of Italy. General Badoglio has assumed control of the government there and has arrested Mussolini, and there are concerns that he will pull out of the German-Italian Axis.

This is exactly what happens. First we go by rail to Landeck in the Tyrol, and from there by truck to Meran. The welcome given to us by the local population is indescribable—it's as if everyone is having a party. The tarpaulin over the back of our truck bed is rolled up because of the heat. We wave from the vehicles and are nearly drenched in sweets, chocolate, fruit, wine and huge quantities of flowers. We can only advance at walking pace, and hundreds of people are running alongside us, stretching their hands up to touch ours. Otto even lifts one beauty into the truck and she goes from one to the other of us, kissing us intimately. She tells us that we are the very first German troops seen in Southern Tyrol for twenty-five years. They fear the threatening storm clouds, and we gather that the population in Southern Tyrol

131

would be happy to be annexed to Germany. We stop overnight in Meran and join the population feasting well into the night.

31 August. The situation here in Italy becomes more and more critical every day. We're constantly on alert, but we carry on all the time with our field exercises. We sweat like pigs in our field grey uniforms. The Italian population is openly criticising Mussolini, who has apparently done everything wrong. The word is that Badoglio has opened peace negotiations with the Allies and wants to dissolve the pact Italy had with us.

3 September. We get our tropical uniforms at last, and we feel like holidaymakers. The light uniforms look good—khaki coloured shirts and shorts, to help us cope with the unusually hot conditions. British troops are said to have landed in southern Italy and to be moving north from Sicily. There are rumours going around that we might be transferred to Naples.

8 September. The Italian population is told that a peace treaty is in place between Badoglio and the Allies. The war is over for them. Most of the population is jubilant, and as of now we find ourselves at war with former friends. Our orders are to disarm the Italian troops as quickly as possible.

9–13 September. Our first objective is the barracks in Modena. In the early morning hours our company commander, with the help of a tank, is able to confuse the Italian commander of the barracks so completely that we are able to take possession of the place, without resistance, in one bold move. We take most of the soldiers by surprise while they are still in their beds. We are amazed that the Italian soldiers sleep in such huge rooms—an advantage from our point of view because we can win control over them quite easily. After they have been disarmed, they are turned over to an escort unit for onward transport. Then we're off to Bologna, and the next day to the barracks at Pistola, where the operation is repeated. Another rumour says that the Allied invasion can be expected in the Leghorn–Viareggio area. We've been told nothing officially.

14 September. We set off in a westerly direction and take up a position in a forest between Pisa and Leghorn. We hear that Mussolini has been rescued by German airborne troops and that he has been sent to the Führer's main headquarters. The expected invasion does not materialise; instead we are strafed continuously by enemy aircraft, although they cause no damage.

The following days are quite pleasant. From the point of view of supplies, we are living a life of luxury. The supply depots which we captured during the disarming of the Italian Army are filled to overflowing with all type of foodstuffs. Every day we get quite adequate rations of delightfully tasting grape marmalade, fresh butter and real mortadella.*What's more, we eat crusty Italian white bread and drink delightful wine. Over the following weekends we visit the Piazza della Signoria in nearby Florence and the Leaning Tower of Pisa, or drive with our *Schwadron* commander down to the beach of Leghorn to go swimming.

20 September. Unfortunately, we're being transferred again. First we drive in a northerly direction over the Apennines, then north-east over

---

* A type of salt pork.

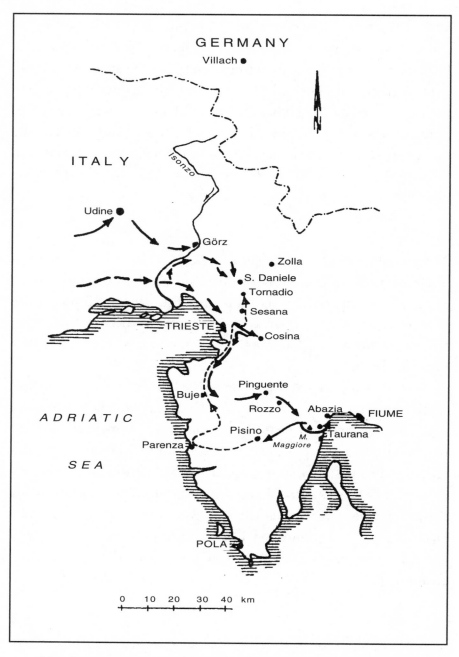

Hunting partisans in Istria: 21st Panzergrenadier Regiment,
5 September–11 October 1943.

Ferrara and Padua and then along the Adriatic coast towards Trieste. On the way there are some incidents with partisans, but we suffer only very minor losses. Our motor sergeant has problems with the captured Italian vehicles, so, because I hold all the Army drivers' licences, I am pressed into service. First I take over a heavy Italian motorcycle and sidecar, though I do not have the pleasure of riding it for long. I quickly get used to the weight of the machine, even though, unlike our motorcycle combinations, it has the sidecar on the left-hand side. During the zigzagging drive through the Apennines I suddenly have engine trouble and almost disappear into oblivion down a mountain gorge. The problem must have been due to either the carburettor or the ignition, because while sweeping round the bends the engine would suddenly cut out and as a result I would get left behind. When I then, in my annoyance, revved up, the engine suddenly kicked in and the machine took a giant leap forward. Although I normally would get the runaway motorbike quickly under control, on one very tight right-handed bend I'm no longer able to control it. The machine accelerates over to a retaining wall on the left-hand side of the road, coming to a halt half way over the edge of the abyss. The *Schirrmeister* helps me push the machine completely over the edge into the gorge so that it will not fall into the hands of the partisans.

I then take over a VW jeep, which initially gives me a lot of trouble. When I drive it, the lightweight vehicle weaves all over the road and I am just thankful that no one is coming towards me. I'm behind the wheel of a passenger car for the first time. My military driver's licences, Class I and II, were gained on a five-ton Henschel diesel truck, with rough double-declutching and steering which could only be done by brute force. So I spend the next quarter of an hour working hard to get used to the foibles of this lightweight 'go-kart' with its sensitive steering wheel and eventually manage to drive along with the rest of the convoy to the satisfaction of the motor sergeant.

23 September. We've reached our destination and are spending the whole day in the assembly area. I have to give up my VW jeep as I'm considered much more important as a machine gunner.

25 September. Our unit and others are hunting down partisans on the Istrian peninsula. Members of Badoglio's partisan movement have holed themselves up in very difficult and rough terrain, in many cases in caves. Thus we have a physically demanding job to do, most of the time on foot since our vehicles can get around only with difficulty.

27 September. We capture two armed partisans and a woman in the houses; they couldn't get away in time. A *Feldwebel* I do not know wants to shoot them at once, and along with them the few remaining residents of the houses, who insist that they were forced by the partisans to let them use their homes. After a discussion with two other *Feldwebeln* he agrees to let the residents go free and takes the prisoners along.

As we continue on our way, Fritz Hamann and I are the last two in the group. The *Feldwebel* waits with the prisoners for us to catch up. Then he orders us to take them behind the rocks and shoot them. We're totally shocked, and we tell him to find someone else to do job.

He gets extremely angry and yells, 'That is an official order! Those swine have fired on us and wounded our comrades; they could even have killed them. And we can't drag that riff-raff along!' He points to the rocks behind us with his sub-machine gun. 'You can do it over there, in the gorge!'

Fritz Hamann now shouts so loudly that his voice echoes from the mountainsides: 'Get going, you swine!'

We force the prisoners off the road and back into the rocky gorge. I look them over as we are walking. In spite of their tans, they look very pale. Perspiration is streaming down their grubby faces and their eyes have a terrified stare. They're afraid because they can sense what our *Feldwebel* has ordered us to do. I know terror in its many variations from my fighting in Russia, but his must be worse, because they can see no escape.

The youngest is trembling like a leaf and talking to us non-stop, although he knows that we don't understand him. I reckon the woman can be no more than about twenty-five. She has a narrow, hard face, with a strong nose. She slowly goes ahead of us, turning sideways with every step. She wants to look at our faces, but instead stares into the barrels of our carbines, which are relentlessly driving the prisoners forward.

I've already agreed with Fritz Hamann what to do next. We force the Italians further into the gorge. As no one can now see us from the road, we yell, as if giving orders, 'Avanti, avanti! Presto!'—these are the only words of Italian which come to mind at the moment—then fire into the air several times. The three prisoners immediately get the picture and scuttle away like rabbits. We hurry back to the rest of our unit. The shots reverberating from the mountainsides must have been proof enough to the *Feldwebel* that we have carried out his orders, and he doesn't mention the subject again after we confirm that we have indeed done as we were instructed.

Although we have disobeyed a direct order and the three partisans have lived to fight another day, neither of us are bothered by our consciences. On the contrary, we are glad that we could extricate ourselves from the affair so successfully. Who knows how it could have ended otherwise? The *Feldwebel* certainly felt that his command was an acceptable one in time of war—though, I have to ask myself, would he personally have carried out the executions? In any case, Fritz Hamann, like me, is one of those people who could never kill in cold blood. Heaven forbid that I should ever become obsessed by such blind hatred that all feeling for fellow human beings is lost and I could slaughter defenceless men and women.

I tell Fritz about my meeting with *Unteroffizier* Schwarz and how, at the Rytschov bridgehead, he executed wounded Russian soldiers by shooting them in the head. He explains to me that people who kill the defenceless must have sadistic leanings, and that war provides them with the excuse to satisfy this inhuman trait under the pretext of benefiting the rest of your men. After this period in Italy we would again be fighting together in Russia for a time and would kill many of our enemies. But, even though war may sometimes cause normal human beings to become insensitive, we would never slay the helpless.

10 October. The search for partisans is over. Although we have suffered some casualties, compared to the experiences at the Russian front this has been little more than a hunting expedition. From the Gulf of Riyeka we drive along the coastal highway by the Adriatic Sea, with a wonderful view over the turquoise blue water, until we arrive at our destination north of Trieste.

11 October. *Arrivederci Italia! Molto grazia!* Many thanks for your beauty and for your wonderful ancient buildings which we admire so much. And many thanks for your sparkling sunshine, lifting the sweat out of our pores, and the sea which shone such a wonderful blue colour. We all want to come back another day. Thank you for your fantastic wine, tasting exquisite and quenching our thirsts—even though our heads sometimes got a bit confused due to excessive consumption! It all fits in so wonderfully well in this sun-drenched land with its temperamental people whose melodic voices bubble all around us like a cascading waterfall.

All that remains for us now as a memory of this country—and it is a poor consolation—are a few barrels of wine and a dozen bottles of Aquavit which we managed to salvage from a ruined factory on the

Dalmatian coast during the last days of our stay. This souvenir helps many of us to overcome our departure from Italy and even manages to take away gloomy thoughts about our inevitable return to the horrific situation in Russia. Word has quickly spread that an advance command unit is already on the way there.

16 October. After a few days of relaxation, during which the older company members have indulged in some really heavy drinking, we travel on to a place near Lyublyana, into prepared quarters. Here we still have a chance to send packages home. I'm wrapping up a box of good wine and some sheets of soft boot leather that I just managed to snatch away from a burning leather factory.

17 October. We are loaded on to a goods train, with our vehicles, at the station in Lyublyana. It is cold and rainy, and we are freezing cold in our thin tropical uniforms.

19 October. We reach Vienna in the early hours of the morning, where we exchange our light uniforms for the regular Army issue. Then we travel east—to an unknown destination.

CHAPTER EIGHT

Return to the Russian Inferno

T HE TRAIN has been rattling along towards the east for two days now. Those of us who are not busy writing a letter, or playing cards with someone, or engrossed in some other activity, are perhaps, like me, thinking about things. Many memories come to mind, and I ruminate about what happened last time in Russia and what might be waiting for us there now. But, compared to those days, everything is different. It's not just to do with the fact that I now know what war is all about, unlike the first time I came to Russia, full of euphoria and not expecting the terrible disillusionment that came about because of our inconsistent policies there. It has much more to do with the knowledge that I now belong to a hard-hitting combat unit, with well trained personnel and the necessary heavy weapons, which can take on the strongest enemy and overcome him.

I wonder why the negative attitude that I had only a few months ago has changed so quickly into a positive one? The continuous drip-drip of propaganda, with its slogans like 'duty to the Fatherland' and an 'honourable contribution' for a 'Greater German Reich', has had its effect on me. I'm quite convinced that I'm fighting for a good cause.

22 October. We were supposed to disembark today, but after a short stop we carry on. We can hear booming and thunder all around us. We

soldiers don't know anything: we can only guess where we're supposed to be going. We do know that the Russians, after their August offensive, advanced across Charkov towards the west, and are now somewhere between Krementschug and Dyepropetrovsk. The newly reconstituted Sixth Army, to which we belong, is supposed to be involved in combat in this area.

A few hours later we get down from the train on to an open stretch of track and we move off in our vehicles, in the general direction of the gunfire. We drive through arid steppeland and through cornfields not yet harvested. The debris of war lies all around us—Russian tanks and artillery pieces, as well as German weapons—providing ample evidence of the to-and-fro movement of combat over the last few weeks. Where is the front line? It is reported to be completely fragmented, and our *Rittmeister** has to feel his way forward carefully.

23 October. We take a rest at the edge of a cornfield, having dispersed the vehicles. We dismount to get circulation back in our feet. The cornfield shimmers like gold in the last rays of the setting sun, the fog is slowly rising from the ground and I can sense the approach of the Russian winter. The shadows thrown by our vehicles become less harsh. The noise from the artillery fire in front of us becomes louder, and we can already make out tank fire to our flank. The front line is flexing like a headless snake. Although the noise of combat is far away, forward elements of the enemy may actually be behind us. This is what the pilot of a 'Sewing Machine' must be thinking: suddenly, out of a clear sky, he is rattling away right overhead. He must have come out of the hollow in front of the cornfield.

We stare amazed at the Russian biplane, which skims over us, flies up in a spiral and then, with its engine cut, dives down at us at a steep angle. Has the bloke gone nuts?

---

* Captain.

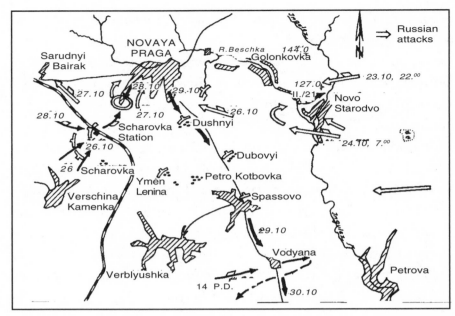

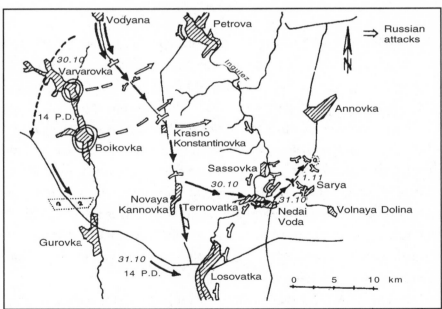

The first battle after the return to the Russian inferno.
Top: 24–29 October 1943; bottom: 30 October–1 November 1943.

The pilot leans right out of the cockpit and we hear him yell in a loud voice: 'Ruski? Germanski?'

We are speechless. Have you ever heard anything like it? The chap didn't know who it was below him and yet he dared to fly his unreliable old crock that low. He would have come to no harm had he promptly turned round and gone away. We just gape in astonishment; it doesn't occur to us to fire at him.

But the pilot is not satisfied. Because of his thick goggles and the fading light—and because he has not been shot at—he must think the figures beneath him are 'Ruskis'. He makes a tight right-hand turn and comes in at us again at a shallow angle. This time he is greeted with a fusillade of rifle shots. The bullets penetrate the thin skin of the aircraft and hit the engine. The plane falls into the cornfield like a stone from about 30 feet and quickly bursts into fire.

Men rush over to the plane and help the pilot out. First he curses like a drunken Cossack, but as he takes off his metal-rimmed goggles and recognises us as 'Germanskis' he does not look amused. Then, however, he acknowledges his stupid mistake with a roar of laughter. *Gefreiter* Rudnik, from the *Schwadronstrupp*, offers him a cigarette, which he quickly lights. He has a pack of Papirossa filter tips in his pocket, and these apparently taste better because he throws away our half-smoked cigarette in favour of his own brand.

'Even after the shooting you thought we were your friends, eh?' Rudnik grins at him and relieves him of a leather case which he has around his neck containing maps and other valuable documents. Rudnik passes the case to the *Rittmeister*. The pilot was injured by a glancing bullet on his thigh; he is attended to by the medic and is later put on board the ambulance.

In the meantime the sun has set: on the western horizon only a reddish strip is to be seen, and it is growing paler by the minute.

'It'll be a nice day tomorrow,' says Fritz Koschinski, who is the last to climb on board.

We set off slowly on in the dark and drive on until a motorcycle courier, who has reconnoitred the situation in his armoured reconnaissance vehicle, gives the drivers the signal to stop. There is supposed to be a village ahead of us, occupied by Russians. They are securing an MSR which leads by the village, but this is very little used.

'Dismount!'

The vehicles disperse and we stand and wait. I can hear our company commander asking the driver of the reconnaissance vehicle about the strength of the Russians in the village and if there are any tanks nearby. He doesn't know. Then a motorcycle courier turns up with orders for us to remain in an assembly position until tomorrow morning, until other parts of our outfit can link up with us. Our sector will get some assault-gun support in the morning.

24 October. The weather is sunny, but it is cold and windy. The entire regiment is now in the assembly area, ready for action. As we launch our attack on the village we make our first contact with the enemy. It is different for me this time, compared to Kalatsch. Here we are the stronger side, and we are able to drive the enemy back. This certainly gives a lift to the ordinary soldier. The village wasn't heavily manned and the road wasn't used much. However, we capture a lot of weapons, and these are blown up by our engineers. About sixty prisoners are taken and are sent to the rear. The front is here quite confusing: in many places Russian tanks have already broken through German lines and are now behind us.

29 October. We drive out of Novaya Praga at daybreak and arrive at our armoured units during the morning. With them we attack the enemy. During our attack we are constantly bombarded by artillery and *Stalinorgeln*. We suffer casualties and must constantly dig ourselves in.

A fellow in our unit, Heinz Bartsch, one of our ammunition carriers, is severely wounded in the head and shortly afterwards our Italian volunteer, whom we call 'Marco', has his shoulder ripped open by shrapnel. Kilometre after kilometre we push the enemy back, and when it gets dark, some of us soldiers, including me, suddenly find ourselves in the middle of some men who start talking to us in Russian. There are ten of them, and in the darkness they have been unable to retreat quickly enough. They surrender without a fight.

We continue to advance with the tanks in the darkness, stopping now and then, dismounting and continuing on foot. We have strict orders from the *Schwadronschef* that at each long stop we are to dig ourselves in. Fritz Koschinski, who belongs to our group, has got hold of a long-handled shovel from one of the vehicles, enabling us to dig a hole in the ground much more quickly than with the small folding field shovels. During our advance there are quite a number of these stops. I reckon that in the last few days I have dug more holes in Russian soil than I have ever dug in my entire life in our garden at home.

I've got burst blisters on my hands and I curse this confounded digging on more than one occasion. But I appreciate how important it is to have a foxhole when we find ourselves in the open fields during an artillery barrage or if we are surprised by Soviet aircraft.

30 October. Today we are attacking the enemy west of the River Ingulez, near Ternovatka. In spite of heavy enemy fire we succeed, with the help of other companies and an anti-tank gun platoon, to establish a small bridgehead on the east side of the river. At the start of the action we lose a 20mm anti-aircraft gun and a tank destroyer to tank fire. Both vehicles are completely burnt out. The AAG crew are dead and the tank destroyer personnel have severe burns all over their bodies.

Notwithstanding the darkness, our *Rittmeister* wants to reconnoitre the small village of Nedai Voda forward of our position. A reconnaissance platoon reports that the houses in the village are in rows either side of a small stream. In the village itself they have detected only light enemy units, although alongside a hedge they have discovered a T-34 securing one of the streets, which is not much used.

'Good! We'll get the tank first!' I hear our chief say. Our vehicles remain under cover while we advance towards the village in small groups. The *Schwadronstrupp*, with our *Rittmeister* in front, is accompanied by a 75mm self-propelled anti-tank gun. We creep forward very carefully, and when the guide gives the signal the engine of the ATG is immediately cut.

The closer we get to the tank, the more circumspect we are. We can often hear low engine noises, and every now and then hushed calls, in the night. Gingerly, we feel our way forward. The engine on the ATG runs quietly, and the tracks move easily over the ground. It is almost completely dark, but every now and then the area is bathed in pale moonlight as the clouds waft across the sky. In front of us we can see the shadows of the bushes and houses. Orders are whispered. We fan out in a line.

'Keep in touch! Advance slowly and more carefully—we have time! Orders from the *Rittmeister!*'

The ATG is now advancing at a snail's pace. There, in front of us, is the hedge. The tank is supposed to be standing there somewhere. If we are spotted, we will have lost the element of surprise and he will open fire on us at point-blank range. We advance along the hedge very carefully. The twigs snag on our ammunition pouches, and we stop immediately and melt into the shadows of the hedge. The ATG edges forward a yard at a time. Where is the tank?

As if in answer, a diesel engine suddenly starts up. The noise comes from the right, in front of us—there, where the hedge makes an angle with the houses and the street curves away. Has he discovered us?

The excitement frays our nerves. If a flare goes up the excitement is over, but then all hell will break loose. We hold our breath and the

ATG cuts its engine. But the gunner cranks down the barrel and swings it over to aim it at the spot where the diesel engine noise came from. We soldiers press ourselves flat on the ground and stare into the darkness. The tank noise sounds loud and nervous. But nothing happens.

'We have to move closer,' I hear the *Rittmeister* whisper. 'He can't hear us because of his engine.'

The ATG moves ahead very carefully, its crew ready to open up at a second's notice. We walk along bent double in the cover of the houses. Then, suddenly, the tank engine is cut. The ATG immediately does likewise. It is so nerve-racking!

The Russian tank crew is probably staring into the darkness just like us, uncertain exactly what to do. It's probably not a good idea to send up a flare with the enemy right under their noses. The best thing would be to get away out of here as quickly as possible so as to gain a little distance.

That must have been what the tank crew were thinking when they discovered us, because at that point the engine roars into life and we can hear the tracks move across the ground. Our eyes have got so used to the darkness that we can clearly see the outline of the vehicle. Just as the recce unit reported, it had been sitting right by the hedge, and it is now moving away under cover of the bushes. The ATG gunner aims at the dark mass. The moon appears again, causing the matt silver gun barrel to glint.

'Ready!'

A voice breaks the tension. There is a dull report and a bolt of white lightning streaks through the night, bathing everything around us in brightness. Blinded, we look at the T-34, which is no more than 30 metres away and broadside-on. Along the hedge we see some figures running for cover. A shot rents the air, and the almost instantaneous explosion of the ATG round tears a hole the size of a man's fist in the side of the tank. Seconds later another round finds the target, and in the light of a tracer we see black smoke billowing out of the tank's turret

147

hatch. The hatch is ripped open and, holding one hand against a bleeding head wound, a Russian jumps out and hurries down to the stream.

We are lying in the hedge firing at the Russians, who appear between the houses and fire back at us, but within a short time we have either inflicted casualties or forced the enemy to flee. We don't have time to search through all the houses, but instead we take up our positions in front of the village—which we assume the enemy will make an effort to retake.

31 October. During the next few hours a hard and bitter firefight develops, but we are able to hold the enemy back. Our ATG destroys five T-34s. Later, another seven are captured, having run out of fuel and been abandoned by their crews. The enemy infantry, pushed back, have dug in only a few hundred metres from our positions, but most of them can avoid our fire by staying hidden in a hollow just 100 metres away. We selected this hillock at the edge of the village for our HMGs because of the excellent view it commands, but there is this shallow depression with tall grass growing in it offering concealment. It is also impossible for us to control the banks of the stream to the right of us, where our light platoons are stationed, because of the bushes there.

As a result, the enemy attack from the bank of the stream comes as a surprise. We get our first sight of the attackers when their earth-coloured helmets appear out of the shallow depression. The first waves are mown down by the murderous fire from our two heavy machine guns and those behind now fall back down into the hollow. And then something happens that makes our hair stand on end: we witness, first-hand and close-up, the inhuman treatment meted out to Soviet soldiers by their leaders, and we have real sympathy for the poor devils.

Because of the fire power from our two MG 42s, at a range of about 50 metres, the attackers have little chance of getting out of the hollow and certainly none at all of storming up the hillock to our positions. We have heard how the commissar forces his men forward with a shrill whistle, as if he were controlling a pack of mad dogs. We fire as soon as we can see their torsos; anyone who manages to come up over the edge of the hollow can't get further than one or at best two paces forward before he is hit. Those who fall back still alive are cursed and sworn at as if they were animals.

Is this Russian commissar or officer crazy? Or is he only worried about his own life and is therefore sacrificing his men? It can't have escaped his notice that he is caught in a trap, and that when daylight comes that he'll have no chance to get away. Does he intend to sacrifice his troops until evening comes, to tie us down so that he can secretly make a getaway under the cover of darkness? But the death that awaits him, and unfortunately also the other poor devils, is worse than death from a bullet.

The tanks move up, two of them on the right flank peeling off from the others and moving towards the hollow. I note their fat barrels, which, unlike the other tank guns, are pointed down towards the ground.

Fritz Koschinski knows his equipment. 'Flame-throwers!' he says in a voice so loud that we can all hear him.

I've heard about their effect, and my spine starts to shiver. I wouldn't like to be one of those chaps in the hollow, and the crazy bastard will probably lose the whistle he keeps blowing. There is now no chance of anyone getting out of the hollow alive. I ask myself if the slavish obedience of the Russian soldiers goes so far, even in this situation, as to prevent them from liquidating an inhuman superior officer.

Even before the flame-thrower has disappeared into the hollow, we can see the long jet of flame as it spews out of the barrel and burns everything in its path to a crisp. Panic erupts in the hollow—we can hear all the yelling. And with the thick black smoke comes an unbelievable stench of burnt flesh and clothing. Some of the men are running up and out of the hollow, crying and ablaze. Panic-stricken, they run past us and throw themselves on the ground, rolling over and over. Many have jumped into the stream in order to save themselves. The heat is so intense that we can feel it from here. It is a truly terrible sight. We climb out of our foxholes and follow the advancing tanks. We have to go on: the destruction of the enemy has not been accomplished yet.

After a kilometre we receive strong counter-fire: the enemy has dug himself in. When we're unable to advance any further, four more flame-thrower tanks attack from the flank. This is a terrible weapon! I'm experiencing its destructive power for the first time, and I won't easily forget the terrible stench that takes my breath away and threatens to suffocate me.

1 November. We have many dead and wounded in our unit on this day. Later, our successful engagement for the bridgehead near Ternovatka will be mentioned in the German Army rolls of honour, under the name of our *Rittmeister*. This kind of special award is used to try and get units motivated.

2 November. We are travelling at high speed to a new sector. We, the ordinary soldiers, are left in ignorance as usual, but rumour has it that we are making for a bridgehead on the Dnieper. We drive through the night and freeze on board the trucks. For the last two days it has been freezing during the night and raining during the day, and the awful strong wind blows right through our limbs. The ground is muddy and the vehicles frequently get bogged down to their axles. When we board the trucks after we have helped to heave them out of the mud, the sticky black Ukrainian clay clings to our boots and our uniforms. Finally we stop in a village and move into quarters, where we receive new felt boots and padded camouflage suits for the winter that is imminent.

5 November. We are back in a defensive position around a large market town called Werchnyy Rogaschik. The main battle line is supposed to be quite near. We can hear gun fire and other noises of battle in the distance. We are told that the Russians have broken through our lines on a wide front. Our regiment, with the support of artillery and tanks, is supposed to attack in the early morning hours to try to re-establish the old front line.

6 November. Following a prolonged bombardment by heavy and medium artillery, we advance on a wide front against the enemy. The Soviets greet us with a huge defensive barrage. As the sun gets up it blinds our tank gunners, so that they frequently have to stop and have a lot of problems getting the targets in their sights. It develops into a murderous attack, with high casualties in both officers and men. We have many dead. Right beside me an *Unteroffizier* has his head blown off by an artillery shell. A grenade splinter rips open the ammunition drum mounted on my machine gun.

In spite of our heavy losses we manage to break through the Russian defences and drive the enemy fleeing before us. The flame-thrower tanks take over the task of mopping up the resistance in the foxholes and trenches. They leave behind a desolate and singed landscape, from which for hours a stinking cloud of smoke rises to pollute the air. This merges with the moving white clouds in the sky, carrying the remains of the burnt corpses over a wide tract of the endless countryside.

Just as we think we might be able to take things a bit easy today, the Russians counter-attack. They take us by surprise with a devastating barrage from their *Stalinorgeln* and field howitzers. Again we suffer a great number of casualties, but as we in the meantime have been backed up by yet another section of Hornisse heavy tank destroyers, and in addition some Hummels with their 150mm howitzers, the enemy has no chance of breaking through in our sector. At about this time our

Stukas start to attack the enemy's assembly areas, and we see the clouds of black smoke rising into the sky, indicating that they have hit their targets.

After we've mopped up the old front-line positions, the 79th Infantry Division reoccupy their previous positions. Tonight we move on to a new sector, this time near Werchnyy Rogatschik again. The Russian defences are weak here. We're told later that we have defeated a Russian Guards artillery division with their guns and other heavy weapons and have also caused heavy casualties in men and equipment among two further Guards divisions.

But our victory has cost us dear. There are more than twenty dead in our section alone, and for our regiment the total losses amount to the strength of an entire company (about 155 men). Along with the many soldiers, *Unteroffiziere* and *Wachtmeistern*, there were also a number of officers killed, among them the commanders of the 1st and 2nd Battalions and three company commanders. In our heavy weapons platoon we lost one mortar and one heavy machine-gun section. To everyone's regret, and to our rage, our beloved *Unteroffizier* Faber was killed by a pistol bullet in his back, fired by a Bolshevik officer who was lying wounded on the ground and whom he had just bandaged. It made me think of *Unteroffizier* Schwarz, who at the bridgehead near Rytschov had done this sort of thing, which I reckoned was inhuman. This time I was not so much concerned, as a *Wachtmeister* from one of the light platoons shot the bastard with a burst from his sub-machine gun. God prevent my anger developing into such an intense hatred that I will ever become like Schwarz.

7 November. Days later we miss our highly respected *Rittmeister*, who could always be found in the very first of our front lines. Our *Zugführer* tells us that he has been ordered by higher command to take over the decimated battalion, and we are to get another company commander.

In the meantime word has spread that we are, with the entire division, now at the strategically important bridgehead of Nikopol on the Dnieper. The weather has changed. Although it is freezing throughout the night, during the morning it begins to rain. The ground has become nothing but slime—even tracked vehicles have problems trying to make it through. Most of the time we wade through the sludge pushing our vehicles.

After hours of exhausting work we reach Dnyeprovka, a large village at the eastern end of the bridgehead. We are soaked through and completely covered in mud and slime. The staffs of an infantry division and a mountain infantry unit are supposed to be stationed in the village, and their fighting elements are reported to be dug in along the MBL, defending it against a continually attacking enemy.

8 November. We occupy the quarters relinquished by the men of an Army tank unit. Our unit moves into a roomy wooden house which we call a Panje hut. Here we find a Russian woman living with her eighteen-year-old daughter Katya. Both live in the front room with the great clay oven, on which, according to Russian custom, both women have their beds. All of us soldiers move into the next room, which is large and is also heated by the clay oven. Outside it is clammy and raw cold, and before we clean up after the other occupants we stoke up the oven.

CHAPTER NINE

Alarm at the Nikopol Bridgehead

WE SPEND the next ten days (9–19 November) in Dnye-provka in anticipation of being ordered to counter-attack. We know that the MBL runs a few kilometres south of the village and that the position on the left side is occupied by the men of the 3rd Mountain Division. Adjoining them on the right are the foxholes and trenches of part of the 258th Infantry Division. Both units are seriously depleted owing to the hard combat during the summer months. They have to defend a wide sector with greatly reduced manpower and weaponry against a very well equipped enemy force. The soldiers in my unit talk about this and pity the poor devils who have been in the front line for so long and still have to live in the wet and muddy foxholes and fight the enemy.

We, as a far better equipped unit, have been upgraded to an elite force, with the mission to attack only when the enemy has broken through our lines. Since we also enjoy the privilege of returning to our quarters after a successful action—unlike the troops manning the front-line positions—we are that much more respected.

After the fighting here at the bridgehead our losses are so high that, of the three light companies, not one could be completely re-formed, despite our having been continuously reinforced with replacements. When the battle at the Nikopol bridgehead was finally over, two full months of hard fighting was behind us.

154

We no longer have a group leader, so our *Zugführer* has assigned the veterans Waldemar Krekel and Fritz Koschinski as squad leaders, giving them sub-machine guns to carry. My second gunner is the strong *Gefreiter* Willi Krause. Fritz Hamann, who up to now had been my second gunner, has himself taken over a heavy machine gun, after *Obergefreiter* Heinz Bartsch was seriously wounded by a direct hit from an ATG. His number two is now *Panzergrenadier* Bittner, one of the younger generation. Two fallen ammunition carriers in our team are being replaced by one volunteer helper and *Panzergrenadier* Mersch.

Our mortar team is also being reorganised. *Unteroffizier* Fender has now taken over from *Wachtmeister* Hauck, who was badly wounded. Besides Warias, the only other people in the team I still know are *Gefreiten* Erich Schuster and Günther Pfeiffer. The team has moved into the neighbouring house, and sometimes the three of them come over to play cards. The others are mostly new arrivals. Otto Kruppka now belongs to the *Zugtrupp* and is also the personal ordnance of our *Oberwachtmeister*, whom we only call '*Ober*' among ourselves.

Spiess is always sets a good example at the front lines, but he is an experienced old-timer and is therefore careful enough to avoid taking major risks. This benefits us in the heavy machine gun team, as, because of our heavy fire power, we are generally given the task of fire support to the light platoons in the attacks and thus are spared any close-combat engagements.

As a replacement for the *Rittmeister*, an *Oberleutnant* took command of our *Schwadron* for a short time. During his command, some of the more enterprising soldiers organised a sauna in an empty house—an excellent idea, and we made good use of it!

Right from the start Weichert and I had a good relationship with Katya, the daughter of Mattka, our 'landlady'. Katya works half a day and her mother works the whole day in the kitchen for the mountain troops. Katya is a slim, blonde Russian girl, a so-called 'Panyenka'. She wears her hair in small braids woven like a wreath around her head. She dresses in a large Russian frock which was once light blue but is now bleached to a grey. Every morning she exudes cleanliness, and when she comes closer she smells of plain military-issue soap. As soon as she sees us she greets us with the usual Russian *Sdrassvitye*, ('Good day') and her eyes light up like cornflowers. I think that were Katya to dress in fashionable clothes, she would be a charming and attractive young lady.

Although we had orders that, because of the risks of espionage and partisan activity, no close contact must be made with the civilian population, it so happens that we have to discuss a number of matters with Mattka and with Katya. Mischa, our volunteer helper, who also comes from the Ukraine, serves as interpreter. Later on I learn a little bit of Russian, and I am able to make myself understood when I or some of the others need something. Weichert is usually the one to take advantage of this—he is always appearing with a chicken from somewhere which he wants Katya and Mattka to prepare. There is even a little flirting between us soldiers and Katya, and she is greatly amused when we pronounce Russian words incorrectly or when she tries to say something in German. However, none of us thinks seriously of trying it on with her: she is definitely off limits in that sense.

Over the days and weeks, Katya becomes, for us, a sort of guardian angel. It all began as we returned to our quarters from combat one day, wet and frozen to the marrow, and found our room pleasantly warm and spotlessly clean. Even our straw beds had been freshly arranged. She continues to look after us in this way day after day, and to show our appreciation we give her lots of pieces of chocolate from our Army rations. She once asked us for a pair of socks for her mother, and immediately received several pairs and also some underclothing. She even got a tropical-issue khaki shirt; she looked quite fetching in it. She was as pleased as Punch and looked herself over in the half-broken mirror hanging on the wall in her room. But when we have to go off to another engagement she looks serious and I often see tears in her eyes.

As we sit in the trucks she always comes up to say goodbye to us and to wave until we are out of sight. On many occasions she has come running up at the last minute because she's been down in the village peeling potatoes when the alarm sounds.

22 November. We had frost again during the night, and during the early morning it starts to drizzle. This rain softens the ground once more and we are soon up to our ankles in mud. Ahead, along the MBL, heavy fighting is under way, but after an hour we are told that the enemy has been forced to fall back to the south. The commander of the 2nd Company has fallen, along with several of the men from his *Schwadronstrupp*. But the successes are played up—the static AAG platoon of the division which inflicted more than fifty casualties among the enemy using their weapon in the ground-support role, and our capture of some T-34s and destruction of sixteen ATGs and a number of field guns.

We're still in the assembly area awaiting orders to engage the enemy. It's been rather quiet during the night, and with Willi Krause, my number two, I've cleaned up our foxhole of clay and mud and covered the base with steppe grass and a couple of planks from an ammunition box. This lifts our spirits, and we now try to get some sleep, standing up in the roughly two metre deep hole.

23 November. Early in the morning we are woken up by a heavy enemy artillery barrage which is concentrated on the infantry positions on our right flank. While we are listening to the barrage and hoping against hope that they will be able to hold out, our thoughts are interrupted by the loudest and most terrifying engine noises we have ever heard. The walls of our foxhole vibrate and the ground shakes as if an earthquake has hit us. The roar increases and then reverberates from the walls.

157

Slowly a huge object hauls itself along the floor of the *Rachel*. It is nearly as big as a house, and it has a long barrel poking out in front of it. Then I count four of the steel monsters—bigger than anything I have ever seen before. They move forward at a walking pace on very wide steel tracks.

All the soldiers get up out of their foxholes and look at these giants; even the old-timers amongst us have no explanation. Then the news spreads like wildfire: these are 'Ferdinands', new 75-ton tank destroyers with an 88mm gun and a special sight which enables them to destroy enemy tanks at unheard-of ranges. An *Unteroffizier* from the crew informs us that the monsters are each powered by two huge diesel motors and two electric motors. They move on extra wide tracks but, even so, still sink into the mud. Rain and mud are their worst enemies, capable of rendering them totally immobile. So the 'Ferdinands' are better suited for positional and defensive combat. For the moment, five of them are being assigned to this sector on a trials basis.

Whilst on the subject of these 'Ferdinand tank' destroyers, I'd like to mention here an incident that took place a few days later, illustrating the effect they had on the enemy. We had stopped an enemy attack and delivered a counter-attack. In support of our advance were four assault guns and four 'Ferdinands'. As the enemy disappeared into a field of sunflowers and we took over his positions, a total of 22 T-34 tanks began to roll towards us; the assault guns and the 'Ferdinands' had moved into a *Rachel* behind us and were well out of sight. They waited until the T-34s had closed to a favourable range, and as soon as they opened fire, six of the enemy tanks were immediately destroyed. All the other T-34s stopped dead, though they returned fire straight away. When the guns behind us roared again, the turrets of three more T-34s were sent flying through the air and two more T-34s were set on fire. The rest of the T-34s turned and ran, halting at a respectful distance and turning around to face us again. Eleven T-34s were now standing at what they believed to be a safe distance, out of range of our tanks and ATGs. But they were mistaken, and what happened next was unbelievable. The 'Ferdinands' moved up a little, out of the *Rachel*, so as to get a better view; the T-34s had in the meantime taken up positions in line on the top of a small hillock to observe us—I could see them better through the telescopic sight of my machine gun. The four 'Ferdinands' then fired almost simultaneously, and I could clearly see the glowing shells explode among the T-34s, two of which began to smoke. Two hits! Quite incredible at this distance! The enemy tanks started to move off, but the 'Ferdinands' continued to fire, and again they hit one of the T-34s. The rest of the enemy tanks were by this time in a great hurry to get behind the hillock.

The Russians must by now have begun to wonder what kind of weapon they were confronted with. We were all convinced that from now on the 'Ferdinand' would be the great nemesis of the T-34. As the enemy infantry was no more than 300 metres in front of us in the sunflower field (which has still not been harvested), we decided to remain in their old positions overnight . . .

For security reasons, every so often we fire off flares. Around midnight a black shadow is suddenly over us, throwing out a bag full of anti-personnel bombs over our positions. After that two 'Sewing Machines' circle overhead, preventing us from illuminating the area towards our front: as soon as they see even a small gleam of light they immediately drop a bomb. To the right of us they have hit a light machine gun, and we can hear people calling for the medics. Because of this, we don't dare light a cigarette, even under cover.

We gaze out in front of us. It is a black night. Willi Krause thinks he can hear a noise. I can't see a thing, and the 'Runway Raider' above prevents us from firing a flare to see what it might be. For a while everything is quiet, but suddenly a light machine gun to our right opens fire. At the same time flares are now sent up, and in an instant the front is wide awake. Machine guns and rifles open up along the entire line. We also send up a flare, and in its light we can see figures in front of us jumping up and trying to run back. Some fall to the ground; others hold up their hands in surrender.

We take six prisoners in front of our position; the neighbouring light infantry unit on our right flank has taken eleven. All are immediately escorted to the Squadron battlefield collection point. The prisoners are a surprise: all of them are old grandfathers with beards—I estimate the youngest to be 50. From the prisoners we learn that thirty men, under the leadership of a commissar, were given the task of breaking into our lines and taking prisoners. They wanted to learn from us what new weapons we were deploying against them. We also discover that they have only recently been drafted and, after very limited training on how to fire a rifle, had duly been given rifles and yesterday found themselves on the front lines.

What is surprising to us is that, under the leadership of the commissar, they were so cautious that they needed almost four hours to crawl the 300 metres from the sunflower field to our position. The work of the 'Sewing Machine' over our positions was all part of the operation. But we have seriously disrupted their plans, and they will just have to continue to guess about what kind of new weapon it is that can destroy their tanks before they have come close enough to our lines even to be within range of their own guns.

Over the course of the next few weeks the new 'Ferdinand' tank destroyer would often be employed at the bridgehead. It soon became appreciated that because of its superior equipment it was without question a magnificent tank destroyer during a defensive operation but that owing to its heavy weight it could seldom be employed to its best advantage because of the quagmires and bottomless mud of the Russian steppes. This is why they would be blown up by a special demolition unit from the engineers when the bridgehead was evacuated and the retreat began through the Ukrainian morass from the Dnieper to the Bug.

24 November. It has been frosty during the night. We are still in our defensive positions between Dnyeprovka and Stachanov. The arrival of the 'Ferdinands' has boosted our morale, although they were withdrawn in the night and moved to another sector.

During the course of the morning the weather changes and the rain teems down. We cover ourselves as best we can with our groundsheets, but it doesn't make much difference. We are soaked to the skin and are wading through mud and water. Then the roar of battle is heard towards our front as the reports from tank guns tear through the air. After two hours the noise starts to die down. Since this is primarily a tank battle, we don't have to get involved.

News gets around very quickly that our 'Ferdinands' have destroyed 40 tanks and fifteen ATGs in the area. Our Hummels and Hornisses—assault guns and tank destroyers—have accounted for fifteen tanks. To the west of us, other units of the division have succeeded in throwing enemy units back to the MBL.

It's quiet now. It is still raining heavily and the sticky mud is gradually filling up our foxholes. The enemy will also have difficulties with the terrain—we are told that he is having problems bringing forward his replacements and weapons as well as other supplies.

25–28 November. We remain in our filthy trenches and foxholes a further four days. The weather is variable, but mostly cold, wet and rainy. Our equipment is dirty and sticky. During the night it is usually freezing and then everything becomes rigid, and many of our weapons don't function any more. They are changed during the night because we are constantly under fire during the day. Because of the atrocious conditions the mess provisions arrive at all sorts of times. On one occasion the delivery vehicle took two hours to cover the eight kilometres from the rear area.

29 November–1 December. The enemy has attacked us three times in battalion strength. He has succeeded in breaking through our main defensive lines here and there, but each time he has been thwarted with the help of assault guns and heavy weapons. He has suffered such heavy losses that he has now had to bring in new reserves.

2 December. We are finally relieved by mountain troops. It is raining hard when their vehicles arrive. The Russians seem to know what we're up to because they open fire on us with their heavy artillery. Again we suffer dead and wounded, and two of the vehicles are hit and become unserviceable. The drivers attempt to get away but the thick mud makes this impossible. Our vehicle gets stuck and we have to get out and push it out of the morass. The distance the driver would normally cover in fifteen or twenty minutes now takes two hours.

Dog-tired, exhausted and depressed over the loss of so many good friends, we drag ourselves into our quarters. The first person to greet us is Katya. She has a surprise for us, because a small gift had been laid on each of our bunks—a couple of cigarettes, some pages of writing paper, a packet of cigarette paper and similar small items. She has probably scrounged these things from the mountain troops. Three bunks are now empty, two because of the wounded and one that was occupied by the tank infantryman Mersch. Katya has placed a small cross made of twigs on his belongings. We wonder how she could have known.

3 December. Many of our men have been killed, and the crosses on the cemetery increase daily. A lot are from the light support troops, whom I knew very well. I remember how happy and full of hope they were in France and later in Italy. Now they are no longer with us. It's particularly sad to learn that just a few hours ago, during the artillery barrage when

162

we were being relieved, the good-humoured *Gefreiter* Rudnick of the *Schwadronstrupp* was unlucky enough to have been struck in the head by shrapnel, killing him. Now we think only of sleep; no one complains about that.

4 December. Yesterday was like a holiday. We were able to wash, shave and dress in clean clothes. The food was excellent. We had goulash with noodles, and for dessert we had semolina pudding. We were also able to take our time washing our dirty uniforms and cleaning our weapons. We were even able to take a short afternoon snooze while it snowed outside. However, the snow didn't last long: it merely added to the slush of the bog. We laid planks along the path to the latrine, so that we could at least get there with clean feet.

Because of the losses we have suffered, individual squads and platoons are being reorganised. My second gunner is now Paul Adam, a tough soldier who was previously assigned to the Rottman heavy weapons section. Willi Krause goes to Fritz Hamann as his second gunner. Our volunteer helpers are transferred to the light supply trains, and in exchange we receive some of the mortar section crew members. These reassignments always bring some uneasiness, but it really doesn't matter much because, as a general rule, whether in quarters or on the line, we are a strongly knit unit.

It's important to me that I keep my heavy machine gun—I would otherwise feel quite naked and unprotected, and would undoubtedly become insecure and unsure of myself. I think our *Ober* has also decided that he can depend upon me—in spite of the fact that, as he told us, a couple of senior *Obergefreiter* are being assigned to us from the 2nd Squadron. They are also heavy machine gunners, but Fritz Hamann and I will keep our weapons, in recognition of our performance over the past weeks.

5–9 December. We have been assigned a new *Schwadronschef*. Because of the reduced sizes of the *Schwadronen* the officer assignments within them often change. Our new commander—we all refer to him as the 'Old Man'—has not, apparently, served in a front-line unit, although he pretends to have done. It is said that now and then he calls in all his subordinates and lectures them on military operations which he learned at some military school or other. Otto, who, as a professional waiter, is often required to serve as a batman to the Old Man, tells us that he has a fad for foreign words. His lectures are delivered primarily in a so-called academic German, which is full of foreign words. Otto says that it makes him laugh when the *Wachtmeister* and other NCOs are asked if they understand and always answer, '*Jawoll, Herr Oberleutnant!*' And afterwards they ask 'Turnip' what was said. Turnip is an *Unteroffizier* in the orderly room who is also an academic. He got his nickname in Italy because instead of eating meat he always ate vegetarian meals.

So Turnip has to explain what the Old Man means by 'preventative attacks', 'proportional engagements', 'divergent front demarcations' and similar gems. The Old Man actually expects his soldiers to understand his posh language: apparently he has lived so long among his own kind that he is no longer able to speak clearly and concisely.

Once, in front of an assembled group, he asked a tank grenadier, who had only been with us three days, if he had been able to 'integrate' himself yet. The young soldier, who came from Upper Silesia, and spoke German in a rather humorous and twisted form, looked at the Old Man in a rather quizzical manner, but then, seemingly having understood, answered, 'I don't know yet, *Herr Oberleitnand!*'

We could see that the Old Man had not expected this answer. He therefore asked: 'Why not? You've been here with us for three days!'

'*Jawoll, Herr Oberleitnand!*' answered the man. 'But I only got my first black crap tablet two hours ago!'

The entire group just howled with laughter! The soldier thought the Old Man had asked him if the charcoal tablets had helped his diarrhoea.

The Old Man laughed with us of course, but he didn't realise that we were laughing over the delightfully down-to-earth answer to the posh way the question was put to him. The Old Man had of course only wanted to know if the soldier had found himself at ease in our group.

After this episode, the Upper Silesian *Panzergrenadier*—his name was Josef Spittka—was the subject of many a joke. We called him 'Peronje': he often used this word because it apparently covered many subjects, but what it actually meant not even he could tell. Peronje soon became a close friend. He was always dependable, and even in the front-line trenches he had such an aggressive nature that we often had to hold him back to keep him out of danger.

14 December. Last night was quite an occasion. You could hear the men laughing out loud, as if someone had just told a terrific joke. In many of the barracks you could hear loud singing throughout the night, intermingled with the sound of an accordion. It reminded me of *Unteroffizier* Döring near Rytschov, who played almost identical tunes. Soldiers' songs—often merry and joyful, but sometimes sad and moving. Everybody then quietened down, becoming immersed in his own thoughts, asking himself if he could join in with the singing next time round. To cope, many turned to the brandy bottle. They carried on drinking until they were legless, then collapsed on to their bunks and fell asleep.

Waldemar Krekel and *Obergefreiter* Koschinski were two of them. Where on earth did they find all that brandy? They seem to have discovered a never-ending supply. Every so often one of them would disappear, only to reappear shortly afterwards with a fresh bottle. Once I sniffed at the bottle and it made me feel quite sick. Fritz Hamann said it was Samagonka, a Russian home-produced brandy of some sort, made out of corn or often beet. You can buy it from the Russian volunteer helpers who work in the kitchen for the infantry. Now I know! They guzzle the wretched stuff here in the barracks area, straight from the source as it were, because they know that when they are up at the front line they can't get more than a sip or two.

15 December. We have had sharp frosts for a few days now and the streets are once again passable. Yesterday it even snowed, and you can feel Christmas in the air. This will be my second Christmas in Russia. Maybe we'll be lucky and can celebrate it here in our quarters.

16 December. Today we covered all available vehicles with white chalk so as to camouflage them. For our next engagement we have turned our camouflage battledress inside out so that the white lining is showing. I'm off with Weichert and Paul Adam for a few minutes to the reorganised mortar section. Warias has told us that they have three new men from another squadron there. They are supposed to be old hands who have quite a bit of experience. Even before we go into their Russian cabin, a pleasant smell of chicken meets our noses—surprisingly, as requisitioning poultry or anything else in the village is strictly prohibited. Nevertheless, a hearty chicken soup is being boiled up. I can see Weichert licking his lips.

As we go into the hut, the men are just lying or sitting around having their soup. Some are holding chicken bones in their hands and gnawing at them feverishly. After a short greeting and introduction Weichert asks curiously: 'Incidentally, Warias, where does this heavenly grub some from?'

Instead of Warias, an *Obergefreiter* who introduces himself as Bernhard Kubat stops eating and says to Weichert: 'Where from? Well, three turkeys suddenly came flying in through the window and perched on Mattka's soup saucepan. The darned things wouldn't go away. See?'

Weichert looks at him dumbfounded and we all laugh.

'The feathered inhabitants around here are very domesticated, you know,' the *Obergefreiter* continues while gnawing away at his chicken. 'Of course, we were really upset because the poor things were freezing cold and just wanted to hang around and warm themselves up.'

The entire group grin in approval, and many of them start chuckling.

The *Obergefreiter* point towards the outside with his half-gnawed chicken bone. 'It was certainly too cold for them outside, what with the snow and ice and all that.'

Kubat shrugs his shoulders. Weichert, who is secretly hoping to get hold of a bit of the prized chicken, plays along and asks, 'Yes—and then?'

The *Obergefreiter* scratches his flushed forehead and says slowly: 'Well, then, I naturally granted them their request for warmth and merely . . .' he pretends to twist their necks with his hands '. . . because I could not of course have put live chickens in the pot. You do see, don't you?'

Weichert grins and says, 'Right, then we shall also have to have the window in our place open, and maybe then a couple of those tender frozen chickens will fly in. I've always had a soft spot for our feathered friends. As soon as they see me they stretch out their necks to be tickled.'

Kubat starts to choke on a chicken bone, and when he can finally talk again he looks over at Weichert for a while and then says firmly, 'You'd better leave that alone, you chicken tickler. You know the rules. If they catch you at it the shit will hit the fan and we might well be blown away with it!' After a short pause he continues: 'In other words, leave the chicken-tickling to those who know all about it—okay? But you can come over now and then and gnaw on a couple of bones with us if you like.'

Weichert doesn't say any more but grins bravely at us and then shows the *Obergefreiter* a wide set of dentures, with his gold cap in the upper row. After that we all get a tender piece of chicken and half a canteen lid full of fat chicken broth. We note of course that Kubat, as well as the *Gruppenunteroffizier*, has the last word here. Warias tells us later that his friends refer to him as 'Scrounger', in recognition of his genius at organising anything edible—and, after all, the 'Scrounger' sounds better than 'Thief'.

In further conversation with the newly arrived soldiers, we get to hear several snippets of news about *Schleiferunteroffizier** Heistermann, whom we know from Insterburg . He is supposed to have arranged things so that he would be the *Geräteunteroffizier*† in his *Schwadron*, so that he could work with the trains and avoid front-line service. However, what Kubat then went on to say about him is disgusting. When the entire unit was on the front line, Heistermann is supposed to have made indecent assaults on Russian women, luring them to his house on the pretext of giving them work. The mountain infantry accused him of having brutally raped two young Russian girls who worked for him. He supposedly lay in wait for them one evening, then took them to his vehicle, where he violated them. I'm sure he's capable of this kind of thing.

Although Heistermann denied the incident, it was investigated by higher authority, according to Scrounger. The investigation was not completed, however, as Heistermann suddenly disappeared: he left on a routine visit to a repair unit in the rear area and didn't come back. It was assumed that, while he was on his way across the Dnieper lowland, he was attacked by partisans, who would often have a go at people if they were on their own. No one knows anything for sure, but as far as I'm concerned the chapter on Heistermann has been closed. Looking back, I can say that I certainly came across other unsavoury types during the war, but none of them was as mean and degenerate as Heistermann.

---

* Literally, 'Slave-Driver Sergeant'.
† Literally, 'Equipment Sergeant'.

17 December. Today has for some of us been a very special day. Because we have continually stuck our necks out, and can still count ourselves among the living, we are being decorated with the Iron Cross 2nd Class and the bronze Close Combat Bar. Fritz Hamann, Warias and I are the ones from our age group. I can't deny that I'm rather proud, less because of the IC II than because I can now be counted among the so-called '*Frontschweine*'.* The business of decorations is a strange matter. First, of course, the leaders are decorated. Well, that goes without saying: how could we carry on if, say, a soldier received the Iron Cross 1st Class and his *Zugführer* didn't? What would happen to the pecking order?

We soldiers know how it is with the handing out of decorations. One for all, they say—and the 'one' is always the chief and the superior. When the chiefs are taken care of, then something can also be dished out to the Indians. For example, if a regular soldier is written up for an IC I, then he really must have risked his neck. As a result, we, the *Frontschweine*, do not rate the decorations awarded to our superiors as highly as those at home do. Officers' decorations are usually awarded on the basis of what their soldiers contribute, when, *en masse*, they manage to save their officers' necks. In general, no one quarrels with this system, as long as the superior has demonstrated his ability to lead. Unfortunately, I have also met those who never remotely deserved their decorations based on their own performance.

Although I would receive a higher decoration few months later, I don't rate military decorations that highly. They are, after all, very much dependent upon luck, and all the brave soldiers who didn't receive any (and, what's more, all our dead comrades) are undervalued. I knew brave soldiers in the close-combat days of Rytschov—and later towards the end of the war—who several times over deserved higher decorations but never received them because their superiors had become casualties in the fighting, or because commanders had come

---

* A slang term for a front-line soldier.

169

and gone, and nobody was left to attest to their bravery. Or commanders who perhaps didn't want to commend their men, in order to reap the glory for themselves. That is the soldier's fate: in the end, it is always down to the opinion of his superior—unless, because of a fortunate combination of circumstances, his contribution is so outstanding that it is drawn to the attention of higher authority. This did happen to one of our friends some months later: he received the Knight's Cross for his actions. I made notes about this incident in the spring of 1944, as we were engaged in the most horrific retreat, dragging our way through the deepest mud and mire which I have ever experienced in my life. We pulled back all the way to the Bug, and from there we were transferred to Romania. This retreat took place over several months, during which many of my good mates were lost for ever or, thank God, were only parted from me because of their injuries.

Today, after I had received my first decoration, I had a few drinks—having kept away from them for some time. In this atmosphere there is always a lot of talking going on, and as a result we got to bed rather late.

18 December. During the night it snowed again. We wash our bodies with fresh snow and afterwards have a snowball fight. In the morning sun the snow sparkles as if diamond splinters have been scattered over it. Everything is unusually quiet. The only noise from the front is the occasional explosion or sound of gunfire—only the normal harassing fire. Yesterday a group in the village was showing films. Part of the *Schwadron* went yesterday and today it's our turn.

When we return to our quarters from the movie, the place smells seductive. Katya and Mattka surprise us with a Russian borsht soup—a sort of hot-pot. It contains sauerkraut, stuffed tomatoes and of course plenty of canned beef, and it tastes superb. The soup makes a real change and is delightful.

Paul Adam is frequently hanging around Katya. They laugh a lot together. I do not begrudge him. As I wander up to them, Katya is showing him some family pictures. A couple of them are painted portraits.

'Who is that?' I ask, and Katya becomes serious. She says something I don't understand. Paul has learned Russian very well, and he tells me that they're paintings of her brothers: they also are in the war. One of them has painted most of the pictures himself; he is reckoned to be a good portrait artist.

Then, suddenly, Katya begins to weep. She curses the war and then raises her rough hands and calls out: '*Woina kaput!*' and, again, '*Woina kaput!*', which means 'The war must end'. Poor Katya! We want the war to end too, but who knows if it ever will?

19 December. Today is different; there is no more peace. Immediately after I wake up, a rolling barrage starts, but as it continues it gets louder and louder. It's the long-awaited major Russian assault. Will the troops in the trenches on the MBL be able to hold the enemy back? No! He breaks through our lines and immediately thereafter the alarm is given. As we sit in the vehicles, Katya comes to us and says her goodbyes. She has tears in her eyes. Does she sense something? This engagement will be one of our heaviest yet, with very many dead and wounded. It's a good thing we don't know about this beforehand.

Katya follows our vehicle for quite a distance, and as we start to pick up speed she waves to us until we disappear round a bend. The vehicles drive to the village exit and then take cover in a natural hollow in the terrain. The noise of combat in front of us gets louder and louder. We jump down from our vehicles and await the order to engage.

Then, suddenly, several T-34s appear in front of us. They are only a few hundred metres away, on top of a ridge, and are firing into the village. Word spreads like wildfire that the enemy has broken through the infantry lines and sections of the mountain infantry and have apparently rolled over the artillery position in the gorge a few kilometres from the village. The Russian troops that are now pouring through the breach in the line are already moving out the German prisoners.

Behind us, our assault guns and tanks drive into position and an aggressive exchange begins between them and the T-34s. The T-34s make very good targets, sitting as they do on the snow-covered high ground. Before long we have taken out over twenty of them, with only two losses on our side. The rest of the T-34s seek safety.

Towards noon, we, the *Panzergrenadiere*, go into action. We have to cross open country without any cover. The enemy has been waiting for this, and he greets us with a furious bombardment using all his heavy weapons. All hell breaks loose around us, and a tumultuous inferno of violence and unceasing destruction comes pouring down. A score of combat aircraft swarm over our heads, raining bombs on us and our tanks. The tanks rapidly make smoke to avoid being seen. In the meantime, we are lying flat on the ground without any cover, wishing that we were moles so that we could crawl to safety.

The ground beneath us shakes with the impacts and explosions. All around us we hear painful cries from the wounded calling out for the medics. We run forward through the thundering hell, with only one thought in mind—to somehow find some kind of cover there in front of us. Even though we make it through the artillery crossfire, death waits for us a thousand times over. The Russian machine-gunners hammer away at us with all barrels and the enemy anti-tank weapons and divisional artillery fire at our every movement.

Bursts of hot bullets swish by me and tear up the thin snow cover around. I can feel a hot burning on my skin and throw myself on the ground again. Unfortunately I hit my chin on the steel jacket of my machine gun, which I have allowed to slide off my shoulder when I hit the ground. For seconds I am knocked out, but I jump up again and bound over towards my right, where I have seen a flat, snow-covered hedge. The bullets are fizzing into the ground. For seconds I am reminded how many times over the last few weeks I have sped through the enemy's rain of fire. Up till now I have been lucky and have, with God's help, always come through. Will I manage it this time?

I do now what I have always done: I run, bent double, driven on by fear that I'll be hit any moment. My body seems as if it's electrically charged, and I feel hot waves running down my back. Sweat pours from my forehead down into my eyes, making them sting. Every now and then I throw myself flat on to the ground and stick my head in between my shoulders like a tortoise. Thinking that a hit low down in my body would not cost me my life, I prefer to cover the distance to the hedge crawling flat on my stomach, feet first. But I jump up again and run on, the machine gun on my shoulder. It seems like an eternity has passed before my assistant and I reach the hedge. Finally we get there and find a little bit of cover.

On the churned-up field behind us the wounded are whimpering, for they can no longer run. They lie amongst the many dead bodies and roll over in pools of blood, often in their death throes. Less than ten paces behind me I can see Willi Krause lying in a pool of blood. Willi is dead, and still has the gun mounting from Fritz Hamann tied to his back. Beside me lies a young *Panzergrenadier* from the group belonging to Dreyer. He is bleeding from his head and is trying to reach the mounting. He can't reach it. I see him hit by a burst of machine-gun fire, and his bullet-riddled body just collapses. Paul Adam, who has also seen it, lies next to me and coughs from wheezing lungs. His eyes flicker. He had untied his mounting during the run and carried it in his right hand, so as to present the enemy with a more difficult target. Behind us, an armoured personnel carrier tries to collect the wounded.

Further along the hedge the Russians are lying in trenches. Machine guns from the light platoons are now firing from the flank into them. Our attack goes on. Our tanks and assault guns advance along a broad front and fire into the Soviet positions. Then the Russian artillery begins to open up again. This time the shells land between us but also on the Russian lines. The Russians hurriedly fire green flares, and the next rounds land only in the area between us. 'Hurry! Fire green tracers!' someone yells, and immediately the lights zip away from our lines into the sky. The trick works! The next shells whine over us into the quagmire beyond

With support from our tanks, we are making pretty good progress. The platoons on our right are already tossing hand grenades into the Russian trenches. I've inserted a fresh magazine in my machine gun and am now storming forward with the others towards the trenches. The Russians are surprised and disorganised. Some of them start to jump out of the trenches and run towards their rear without their rifles. Two of them are still standing behind a heavy machine gun and firing. Still at full pelt, I empty my magazine at the pair of them and hit them. Then I slip on the ice on the rim of the trench and dive headlong into it.

A shining metal point glints in front me and I feel a rip on my right cheek. I hold my machine gun in my right hand and am about to get up just as the Russian in front of me is about to run his bayonet through me. At that moment he crumples from a burst of fire. Fritz Koschinski is standing on the edge of the trench with his sub-machine gun, but before he can join me in the trench he too buckles and sinks to the ground. I grab hold of his camouflage suit and someone helps me pull him into the trench. He moans and grimaces in pain. The other man is a really young medic, his face as white as a sheet. He mumbles something and we both stare at the blood-soaked spot on the Fritz Koschinski's white camouflage battledress.

The medic wants to turn him a little bit on his side, but Fritz presses both hands on his stomach and groans, 'Just leave me! It hurts!'

The medic nods. 'Shot in the stomach,' he remarks.

Fritz tries to support himself. 'I can already feel it running into my stomach.'

174

I want to give him some encouragement and mutter something about sewing him up. Then I give him my hand and say, 'Until then Fritz! We didn't have much time. Good thing you got him.'

He nods and tries to smile.

The fact is, Fritz Koschinski saved my life. Another time it will be someone else, and I'll save others in turn. That is the way of things at the front. Everyone tries as best as he can to save his own life as well as those of his mates. No one talks about it much: it is the natural thing to do.

The attack continues—the enemy trenches are still not all rolled up. I run after the others until I catch up with Paul Adam, who is the last of them. He turns around and says with a worried look, 'Good God! You are bleeding like a pig! Where did you get that?'

For the first time I notice that blood from my cheek is running down my neck. However, I can't feel any pain. Then Waldemar Krekel squeezes through the narrow trench and wipes my cheek with some bandage.

'Lucky for you, it's only a surface wound,' says Waldi and covers the cut with a plaster.

When I tell him his good friend Fritz has been shot in the stomach, he is shaken and says, 'Stomach wounds are very bad. I only hope that Fritz didn't fill his belly before he was hit.'

Everyone knows what Waldi means by that. Although no one orders us not to eat too much before going into action, old hands have warned us never to fill our bellies with food beforehand. If you get shot in the stomach and it is empty, you have a much better chance of surviving than if it's full. No one knows for sure whether it's true, but it sounds plausible. Many soldiers, including me, follow this advice; others can't help themselves and just have to eat. More to the point, they can't resist tucking into their cold rations when they arrive, even just before going into action. Some eat during the drive up to the jump-off point, with comments such as 'What's gone is gone' and 'I can't leave good food behind for Ivan to eat'. I get the impression that many of the men who speak in this way do so to calm their nerves, from which all of us suffer just before combat.

Fervently hoping that Fritz Koschinski will survive his stomach wound, we press onwards in the narrow trench. At one point, there are so many dead Russian soldiers lying on top of each other that we can crawl over them only with difficulty. Poor devils—most of them have faces as young as ours. They were our enemy and they wanted to kill us; now they can harm us no more, and are lying still and silent, like many of our comrades on the snow-covered fields behind us. The only difference is the uniform, and perhaps they are not, as are our dead, given a wooden cross on their graves in Dnyeprovka, but when time permits are buried in a mass grave and incinerated by our rear-echelon troops when we have successfully ejected the enemy from his assembly area.

During darkness we withdraw a short distance and occupy a new line. We're pleased that there are defensive positions all over the place and also shelter from tanks. Digging out new positions in the frozen ground would call for a back-breaking effort. Even now the sweat is pouring from us as we break up blocks of deep-frozen earth to camouflage our machine gun in its new firing position.

During the night we can hear the enemy return and start to dig himself in out there in front of us. We can clearly hear him using picks and other tools to break the ground up. He stops work only when we send a mortar round or two across. Since the Russians are so busy digging in, we are spared further close combat, and so our fresh supplies of food and ammunition arrive unhindered. From the drivers we hear the bad news about the number of dead and wounded this attack has cost us. Apart from the loss of the commander of the 2nd Battalion, we are told that our former *Schwadronschef* and current commander of the 1st Battalion has also been wounded, as have two other officers from the battalion and a senior doctor. The Old Man is also supposed to have taken a hit in the left arm. The leadership of our *Schwadron* is now reported to have been turned over to a *Leutnant* whom nobody knows.

It's said that our *Schwadron* has suffered seven dead and 21 wounded, among them Willi Krause and the young *Panzergrenadier* Hanke, who comes from our heavy weapons section. Two more wounded soldiers are added to the total, and they've only been with us for a couple of days. The mortar section report four wounded. The second *Schwadron* is supposed to have suffered particularly heavy casualties. It now has only nineteen men, with many wounded and twelve dead. This has been a very bad day, and it does not pass unnoticed. It tempers all the feelings of confidence I have—which, as a winner, you often experience—when I think of the high price we have had to pay.

20 December. Paul Adam and I work all night to improve our defences, and as a result can keep ourselves warm. The frost got more severe during the night and we were given a blanket to help. As dawn breaks, there's no sign of the enemy. The Russians are masters of camouflage.

After an hour or so the clouds thicken and it begins to snow. This is fine from our point of view, since the snow covers everything with its white sheet and therefore camouflages our position. Paul, forever peering through the telescopic sight, spots a couple of mounds of snow in the distance, under which, we suspect, the enemy is hiding. However, the Russians are keeping quiet. Towards noon we are subjected to intensive mortar fire, and shortly afterwards, on our right flank, there is some close-range shooting. We can also hear tank and anti-tank guns. But all is quiet directly to our front.

After nightfall we can again hear the picks and shovels at work, and the noise lasts well into the night. The enemy is reinforcing his jump-off positions, and he will again try to throw us out of the MBL. Orders from the regiment are that we stay in our holes until the danger has passed, and the infantry and mountain troops will take over the positions again. Fat chance!

21 December. The day begins with poor visibility, but it doesn't snow. During the night we were supplied with straw, which helps to insulate the frozen ground and keeps the feet a bit warmer. The enemy is firing continuously with his mortars and machine guns. We can't raise our heads, so we keep quiet and don't give him the advantage of discovering our positions—assuming he doesn't attack.

In the evening it's quiet again. Waldi and Dreyer come and see us. They tell us that an enemy deserter has divulged that the Russians are preparing for a major assault. We therefore get together several extra boxes of ammunition for our position. During the night it is really cold, and there is no way we can even think of sleeping. With every breath of air, tiny icicles form on our stubble. I suggest digging out a tunnel at the narrow end of our trench, knee height, so that we can crawl into it for sleeping. Paul is delighted with the idea and so we make a start. After digging straight into the bank for about half a metre, we excavate at a right angle so as to protect us from splinters. The frozen walls give us additional protection against being crushed.

22–23 December. The front has been quiet, and we are asking ourselves if the Soviets are going to be as tolerant over Christmas. It would be nice, but we don't trust them. We are told that the *Spiess* has prepared something special for us at the front line. We hope the Russians won't disturb us on Holy Night.

24 December. It's been freezing cold again during the night, with a heavy frost, but we didn't notice this in our sleeping tunnel. I covered

myself with a blanket and the ground sheet and between shifts I slept really solidly.

Soon the mortar rounds are whining in over us. The Russians are again trying to surprise us with sudden shelling, and sometimes they unfortunately manage to catch us in the open. As I hear the rush in the air overhead, I prick my ears like a fox and listen intently to the sounds. My ears are so well attuned that every type of noise along the front is picked up. In front of me nothing has changed, only the mortars continuing to fire at our positions for another half an hour. When it's all quiet, *Gefreiter* Plischka—whom we all know as 'the Professor' because we respect him for his knowledge— from the other heavy weapons section runs up excitedly and tells me that, sadly, *Stabsgefreiter* Dreyer has been killed by a direct hit from a mortar round. Two young *Panzergrenadiere* were also killed. He has also learned from a medic that Fritz Koschinski died from his stomach wound while at the main dressing station. This is bad news, reminding us how near death is all around us.

Much to our surprise, the day passes without an attack. The clouds are low, and now and again it snows. Often we hear the sharp report of a rifle shot, and shortly afterwards the bullet exploding with a light crack. The Russian snipers are using explosive rounds, which tear large holes in any flesh they hit. When it becomes too much for our machine gunners they answer with a short burst.

We get our rations while it is still dark, and because it's Christmas Eve we receive potato salad and a lump of meat. Instead of coffee the canteens are filled with tea and rum. In addition, each man receives a *Frontkämpferpäckchen*—two packages of cigarettes and Christmas biscuits. Our *Spiess* had held up delivery of the packages from home for several days in order to hand them over to us tonight. Paul and I each receive ours. We place everything on the ground sheet. As well as some sweets—lovingly packaged up by my mother—I discover a small artificial pine tree branch, decorated with silver threads and dotted

179

with small toadstools. A Christmas tree candle and holder are also included.

'Great—now we can celebrate Christmas!' says Paul, holding up the branch.

'Yes, why not?' I agree.

Using the ground sheet weighted down with some ammunition cases, we cover our narrow foxhole. Then we crouch down and light our candle on the branch, which Paul has laid on top of the flattened paper cartons from our packages. We think about our loved ones at home and munch on the biscuits. The tea with the rum goes to our heads a bit.

Then Paul interrupts the silence and says, 'Merry Christmas!'

I nod. 'Merry Christmas, Paul!'

I wonder about him as he suddenly breaks into a carol; he is usually the one who waits until someone else does something. He begins with 'Silent night, holy night . . .', and I mumble along. But our voices sound pathetic, and Paul notices this as well.

After the first few lines he begins another carol. 'O! come all ye faithful, Joyful and triumphant . . .' Paul's voice sounds soft and dejected. Then he stops in the middle and shrugs his shoulders. 'It doesn't work!'

I understand what he means. It is not the best moment to sing Christmas carols: too much has happened recently, and we can't help but think of those of our comrades who can't be here to celebrate with us. Only a few hours ago we lost Dreyer and the two young *Panzergrenadiere*, and three days earlier Willi Krause, Fritz Koschinski and the other young *Grenadier* Hanke, to mention a few. They were looking forward to Christmas back in the barracks as well. We understand that for some of them there are still mail and packages waiting in the orderly room. Those who have written them do not yet know that they will not be reading their mail.

Lost in these thoughts, we suddenly hear the familiar *whoosh!* over us and then the impact of shells. So, Ivan is not going to give us any respite this Christmas Eve after all. We blow the candle out and peer into the darkness. Over the entire front, tracer bullets are rising into the night sky.

'Well, we at least have festive lights on Christmas Eve,' says Paul rather bitterly.

Still nothing moves in front of us, but then we hear the unique noise of incoming rockets.

'*Stalinorgeln!*' yells a soldier from our light platoon.

We duck down into our tunnel in the ground, and the next minute we hear an explosion and a piece of rocket shrapnel hits one of our ammunition crates and tumbles into our foxhole. The Russians play their organ twice more before it becomes quiet again.

25 December. At eight in the morning the Russian drum roll breaks loose over us like a devastating hurricane. We crawl into our tunnel and come up only now and then to check the conditions in front of us. We're ready to defend ourselves, but we know that this will begin only after the enemy has advanced so far that our defensive fire can be effectively directed. Even though I have experienced enemy barrage fire with heavy weapons several times before, I can't help but get anxious all over again; the endless waiting makes me nervous and restless. I know that the barrage will lift sooner or later, and only then will the actual fighting begin. However, until that happens a thousand thoughts swirl around in my head.

With these thoughts come memories of earlier engagements. Images appear before my eyes and I see again the despair and the disaster at Rytschov on the Don—bitter experiences which I thought I'd long forgotten but which now stand again before me. Again I am seized by terror as I was at that time, and I pray quietly and fervently that I will again come through this attack without injury.

The gruelling shelling lasts nearly two hours. Then someone yells loudly, 'They're coming!'

Finally! I take a deep breath. But I am uneasy because I know that, again, some will not survive this battle. It is, however, also my freedom from the grinding barrage, which I'm unable to ignore by willpower alone. As soon as I get behind the heavy machine gun with Paul, my thoughts are all concentrated on the advancing enemy. The Russian artillery has lifted a little, and the heavy rounds now howl over our heads. When we suddenly open fire, we are filled only with the desire to defend ourselves from the enemy in front of us and prevent him from being able to overrun our positions.

The shells from our defensive fire are now screaming over our heads from behind. It is as though a hundred cannon are loosing off their deadly projectiles all at once. In front of our artillery a defensive line of tanks and assault guns has rapidly driven up and is now firing point-blank into the enemy assault waves. The enemy does not have a chance to come even close to our defensive positions: he has already been destroyed before we can attack him with our infantry weapons. In the end our machine guns stop a few small groups which have been able to escape our deadly crossfire and who still attempt to reach our positions.

During the evening we learn that our shells have been fitted with impact fuses, which cause the rounds to burst on striking the target and with their anti-personnel splinter charges cause havoc amongst troops. This results in a terrible massacre for the enemy, and we couldn't help but feel a certain satisfaction. When all's said and done, he had dared to disturb us during our holiday!

During the late afternoon the Soviets try to dislodge us with another barrage and advance. This attempt is just as unsuccessful as the first. Now we know that their intentions were to disturb us during Christmas—which the Russians do not celebrate until the New Year. Our losses were within reason, although we did suffer several dead (and one dead is one too many). We were told that the enemy has lost 35 T-34s throughout the sector. It appears as if he has decided to calm down for a while, because for the next few days we would see no combat.

28 December. The day at the front has passed quietly. We believe that the enemy has enough to do, and can leave us alone.

29 December. The troops who occupied these positions earlier are relieving us. They take over their old foxholes on the main battle line, from which they had been ejected by the Russians in their last major assault. We're delighted to be able to return to our quarters and make ourselves half human again. If any of our friends back at quarters hope to recognise us, they will have to look pretty carefully as we are bearded and covered with dirt.

It is surprising how quickly our attitudes have changed. As we sit in the vehicles and get closer to the barracks we joke and talk about what we will do when we get back. But as soon as we see Katya standing there, waiting for us with tears in her eyes, we become serious. Again she has placed small woven wooden crosses on the bed covers of our fallen comrades. Because she wants to hide her tears from us, she runs quickly away after a brief welcome, calling back as she does so '*Raboty, raboty*', which means something like 'I must work.'

After we have cleaned up, we collapse and sleep until evening. Then we get our rations, in addition to which each man also receives a bottle of brandy. I give my bottle to Waldi, because in his grief over the loss of his friend he is sitting still in the corner pouring alcohol into himself.

In the evening I am again with Paul Adam as well as Katya and her mother. We are learning Russian and enjoying ourselves with our gibberish. Once, when Katya touched Paul's hand, he looked into her shining blue eyes and blushed. Aha, I thought, there is some flirting going on here! When I got tired and left, Paul and Katya stayed behind.

CHAPTER TEN

Fear and Hatred Supplant Tears

I T'S 31 DECEMBER and it has snowed again during the night. The new white mantle is dry and powdery, just as we like it. Weichert reckons that our men up front will manage to hold the enemy back—this subject is the most important topic of conversation right now. Weichert may well be right.

In the meantime, *Unteroffizier* Fender from the mortar section has come over to see us. He doesn't know any more than we do, but he suggests that we should get ready, because orders to mount up could come at any time. We wait and wonder . . .

The artillery barrage recedes after an hour. Then we hear our own artillery fire, from new positions in front of the village. We assume that this fire is aimed at the attackers. Then our *Ober* comes along. I can hear him talking to *Unteroffizier* Fender, telling him that the positions up front were reinforced yesterday, and that it was obvious that the enemy would try to reduce the bridgehead further. He, too, expects that we will be called upon, but this would depend on the situation up at the front line and on the orders from the staffs.

The *Ober* would be proved right: the deployment order comes an hour later. Most of the men have already climbed aboard the vehicles, but we are missing Katya, who never forgets to say goodbye to us before we leave. It's early in the morning, and she's probably busy peeling potatoes in the kitchen used by the mountain troops.

As if reading our thoughts, Katya suddenly comes running out from between the huts, the powdery snow rising in great puffs under her long felt boots. Like all Russian women, she has a warm babushka scarf on her head, which from a distance makes all Russian women look old. It's only when Katya stands in front of us that we recognise her youthful face, which is warm from running and flushed. She is out of breath and says hurriedly, in explanation, 'Soldier says I work in kitchen. I go. Soldier says no. I say it does not matter and come.'

'*Charascho Katya, nye nada*—you don't need to excuse yourself.' I say in my best Russian accent.

My mates, who are already on the truck, stretch out their hands to say goodbye to her as usual. Beside me stand the young *Panzergrenadier* Schröder and Paul Adam. Katya takes Schröder's cap off and strokes his bushy fair hair. He grins happily, but he's blushing. He turns round, and jumps up on to the truck with the others. When she then gives Paul her hands, I can see her fingers twisting nervously. She holds Paul's hand for longer than usual and gazes at him. Then she turns abruptly away, unable to hold back her tears.

I have never seen Katya so broken up. Not quite knowing what to do, I put my arm around her and stutter in German, 'Take it easy, Katya. We will all come back safely. Just you see!'

She doesn't understand, but perhaps she can sense what I am saying. She looks at Paul, who is now climbing aboard the truck. I'm the last to climb up, but she holds me back by the arm and whispers, '*Paschausta*, you will look after Paul and little Schröder?'

I nod. '*Charascho Katya*, I promise you I will.' Then I too jump up on the truck.

The vehicle moves off and we wave as we always do. But Katya doesn't wave back: she stands there with her arms hanging down and with tears running down her cheeks. Then suddenly her body twitches and she clenches her fists. She shakes them towards the sky and we sense rather than hear her desperate call: '*Woina kaput!*' It is a cry of desperation in protest against the murderous war and perhaps also a complaint to the Almighty for permitting such destruction and unending sorrow.

Even as our vehicle pulls to the right after about a hundred metres, Katya is still standing at the same spot staring after us. Nobody says anything. Some are drawing quickly on their cigarettes or, like Waldi, are producing clouds of smoke from their pipes. Each is occupied with his own private thoughts.

My thoughts revolve around Katya and why she is behaving so strangely today. Is it the long period of uncertainty and the build-up of excitement which has made all of us so nervous? Or was it a problem with the kitchen wallahs, who didn't want her to come outside and see us? Her behaviour is really rather odd—as if she knows or senses something.

'Guess what?' The Professor looks at Weichert. 'I found the evidence in the snow in front of the truck.'

'What do you mean?' Weichert looks quizzical.

'Now don't pretend to be so surprised.' The Professor chides him and winks at us. 'You had your lighter between your teeth as you were getting ready to climb up, but when Katya came running you dropped it in your excitement!'

We drive on through the trough of a *Rachel* and listen to the noise of combat, which draws ever closer. Then, suddenly, we are taken under fire by some infantry guns and have to drive back into the *Rachel*. As we dismount, mortar shells are coming in over us and one vehicle is hit. ATG rounds and tank grenades are zipping through the air and are landing amongst our tank unit. The tanks fire back and destroy several enemy tanks, halting the attack.

As we move into a counter-attack our retreating troops from the front line are coming towards us. They are in panic and are carrying their wounded comrades with them. An *Unteroffizier* tells us that the enemy, after a heavy artillery barrage, has stormed their positions with

186

many tanks with mounted infantry. He has inflicted serious casualties, dead and wounded.

We move slowly forward with twenty tanks and heavy weapons in support. At first things go quite well, but then we come within range of the enemy's heavy weapons. There is next to no cover on the open fields, and again we take many casualties, in particular among the light troops. Then we manage to clear the MSR and press the enemy back a considerable distance south. At nightfall we withdraw a little and occupy a line which already has protective foxholes, which we only need to tidy up. Because we have retaken these positions, the HBL has been shortened somewhat.

There is quite a bit of activity during the night. First the enemy bombards the empty positions in front of ours with his heavy guns; then realising that they are empty, he increases his range. A little later, as it begins to snow, Soviet infantry suddenly appear in front of our positions; we see them coming towards us in their snow suits in the light of our tracers. They have no chance of even getting close to our positions, and they suffer heavy losses and their attack is stopped. We continue to hear the calls for help from their seriously wounded, but no one can help them.

Now the Soviets are sitting nervously in their foxholes in front of us. Once in a while they fire off tracers, which climb into the dark night sky and then fall back, flickering for a moment on the snow and casting leaping shadows like the fluttering wings of a dying bird. A few snowflakes sail around in the air. It appears that we now have a bit of peace again.

Someone comes to our foxhole from behind us and asks, 'First gunner?'

'Yes, what's the news?' I reply. I recognise Bittner by his voice.

'Did you get your rations?

'No!'

'Bloody nuisance! What's taking them so long?' Bittner is annoyed.

'That's right,' says Paul Adam. 'The Professor should have been back long ago. The ration truck is not that far away. You can hear the canteen containers clanging.'

Fritz Hamann, who is also kneeling at my foxhole, says: 'I hope the Professor hasn't got lost in the snow. He can't see very well in daylight, let alone in the dark.'

'Don't make a mountain out of a molehill!' I try to reassure them. 'Kramer's with him.'

Another quarter of an hour passes. The men in our neighbouring platoons have neither seen nor heard anything of the two of them. We suspect that they're either in front of us or have got lost in no man's land.

'Should we let loose with some tracer?' suggests Paul.

'I wouldn't,' Waldi counters, correctly. 'If they're in front of us we might hit them. And Ivan would shoot back.'

Waldi has barely finished speaking when, from the Soviet side, flares zoom up into the sky. At the same moment machine-gun and rifle fire interrupt the quiet of the front line. Flares go up from our lines and light up the even snowfield ahead of us. Nothing! There is no movement. Gradually the firing dies down.

What's going on? Is Ivan nervous? This often happens. All that's needed is for someone to shoot into the night and immediately the other side answers and fires a flare. It is now quiet again, but we're wide awake, listening intently. Another half an hour passes, then Paul nudges me and indicates that he has heard some soft crunching noises in the snow ahead of us. Abruptly a muffled voice from the next foxhole interrupts our anxious listening.

'Go ahead, fire a flare, Heinz,' says someone.

A flare chases into the night sky and explodes above with a muffled bang. Immediately a shower of tiny lights rains down over the area in front of us, bathing the field. Didn't some figures throw themselves down in the snow, there in front of us?

188

'One more!' says the same voice as before, and another flare whizzes into the sky. As it explodes we can clearly see some figures in snow suits, throwing themselves on to the ground and merging into the whiteness. I pull my ammunition belt tight and lower the barrel on to the attackers.

'Hold it! Don't shoot! Don't shoot!' yells a voice from the field in front of us.

Waldi yells back: 'Professor! Kramer! Is that you?'

Instead of answering, two figures in white camouflage suits run towards us. Behind them the flash of a sub-machine gun tells of a burst of fire chasing after them. Now the situation is clear. I pull back the trigger guard and fire a few well-aimed bursts in the direction of the flash, and the sub-machine gun is immediately silenced. The Professor and Kramer have already disappeared into our foxholes. In the light of the next flare we can see the Russians lying on the ground. One of our Russian volunteers from the light platoons calls over to them in Russian. Someone answers. As the figures slowly stand up, two of our men go over to them and lead them into our positions. It was a reconnaissance unit of sixteen men. Four of them are dead and some are slightly wounded.

I creep over to the Professor's foxhole; some of the others are already there. The Professor explains that they had got confused over to the right and suddenly found themselves in no man's land, where they lost their orientation.

'God knows how you get around this wasteland, especially at night," he groans wistfully. 'Everything looks the same—a white sheet of death.'

He tells us that they had suddenly heard noises in front of them and thought that they had reached our positions. But they were dumbstruck when a Soviet soldier suddenly loomed up front of them and spoke to them. The Professor managed to knock him over the head with his ration kit, which is when the firing started—the same firing we heard.

189

'We just ran as fast as we could,' Kramer joins in. 'My ration kit and all the grub had to be thrown away. I'm very sorry.'

'Oh, who cares!' says Waldi. 'We won't starve! But how did you end up amongst the Russian reconnaissance unit?"

'We don't know that either,' the Professor replies. 'It was really crazy. The Russians were shooting after us, so of course we ran away from them towards our positions. Then came the next scare as we suddenly found ourselves in the middle of some Russians who were quietly calling out to each other. At first I thought that we'd been running around in circles, until I noticed that they were carefully slithering forward. In the darkness they must have thought that we were their own. I then yelled over to you and we started to run, and they must have been pretty surprised too. The rest you know.'

1 January 1944. A new year has begun. I will no doubt often recall the magic of the fireworks of New Year's Eve. Towards dawn it stops snowing and the visibility is half decent. We know that the enemy is somewhere over there in front of us, but he is well camouflaged. Last night we were told that we might be returning to our quarters tonight, provided nothing in particular changes here on the front. We are sitting in our hole, which we have cleared of ice, and gaze out from time to time towards the front. Many more pairs of eyes are doing exactly the same thing.

The night was so full of activity that we couldn't spare the time to eat, so we catch up on that now. During the attack yesterday we were able to get hold of two cans of American beef which the enemy, in his haste to retreat, had left behind in one of his trenches. As Paul opens one of the cans he remarks that the Russians are living quite well on the rations that are 'Made in the USA'. And besides rations, the Russians have been supplied with vehicles and military equipment, which from time to time we have destroyed or been able to capture.

190

Paul cuts a large piece of pork out of the can which he hands over to me on the point of his knife. I place it in my canteen lid and examine the knife. I have often admired this knife—a hunting knife with a deerhorn handle.

'A very nice knife,' I remark and weigh it in my hand.

'Yes, it belonged to my older brother. He used to go hunting quite often. There are loads of game where I come from in Sauerland. He stayed in Stalingrad last year. You can keep it if you like.'

I am amazed. 'Just because I like it, Paul, doesn't mean that I should have it.'

'I know that, but I'd like to give it to you.'

'What about you? You need the knife yourself.'

'*Bon appétit!* Here we go again!' I hear Paul murmur, and notice that he twitches every time a grenade or shell explodes nearby. Just take it easy, breathe deeply and don't lose your nerve, I tell myself, as I have at least a hundred times before. Sometime our friends on the other side just have to run out of ammunition, for God' sake! But not yet—the terrible firework display goes on for over an hour. The fire dies down after that, but they still open up with mortars and machine guns from time to time.

Every now and then I peer through the telescopic sight and get angry. The Russians are running back and forth, bent double, well within range, but here we are and we can't even raise our heads. They have us in their sights all right—as soon as they see the least bit of movement they fire at us. What's more, out there somewhere, in front of us, a sniper has dug himself in, so well camouflaged that I can't pick him out even with my telescopic sight. I am aware of his presence only because of the dangerous explosions all around our position which have a noticeably higher tone, which continues to ring in the ears. How long will this continue? How long before we can look out again??

Paul comes up behind me from his cramped position in the bottom of our foxhole.

191

'What's the matter?' I ask, concerned.

'I can't squat any more, and I can't kneel any longer. I'll go crazy!' I can understand what he means—I have the same feeling—but I feel responsible for him as he has only been with us since the end of November and is still a bit impetuous.

'Stay down anyway, Paul. They're watching for any little head movement!' I tell him.'

'I wouldn't half like to burn his hide a bit. Then I'd feel better.' He growls angrily and ducks down behind the machine gun.

'Don't do anything stupid! When nothing's happening, don't start anything. It's not worth it!'

Paul looks through the sight, 'Look at those new Ivans, dancing around over there! Let's send a few rounds over!'

'No!' I say firmly. 'No one else is firing.' I wonder why he is so set on opening up. He must know that it doesn't achieve anything in this situation: at best we give away our position and the enemy will fire off another barrage. He continues to watch through the telescopic sight. After a while he gets excited.

'Hell! They are setting up a couple of mortars there in front of us!'

This is interesting. I push him to one side and look through the sight. Okay! The Russians are pulling a mortar forward, out in the open! That's dangerous for all of us. Automatically I aim the machine gun and grasp the trigger. I locate the target through the sight, but at the same moment I spot a fur cap and a rifle behind a snow drift. I dart back and snatch Paul with me down. A piercing explosion nearly rips my eardrum and continues to ring under my helmet. I go white: the explosive round from the sniper has missed me by a hair's breadth. Only slowly does the blood return to my head.

'Damn! That sniper has us in his sights. We can't even get behind the gun!' I curse.

'But at least you know where he is. Just aim there and shoot blindly at him—your height has already been set,' Paul suggests.

192

The Old Market Place, Insterburg.

German reinforcements marching through an occupied Russian town
on their way to join their units.

On the way to Stalingrad through the Kalmuck Steppe,
towards the end of August 1942.

Moving across a broad front to Stalingrad.

A pause on the steppe.

A *Rachel* or *Balka*—a deep, often rectangular trench formed naturally in
the open steppe and used to provide protection for troops and sometimes
entire battalions complete with vehicles and men.

A *kolkhoz* on the Kalmuck Steppe.

A family on the Kalmuck Steppe.

Stalingrad burns: September/October 1942.

Fighting in the ruins of Stalingrad.

Barricades in the streets of Stalingrad.

Receiving supplies in the 'Tennis Racket' area of Stalingrad.

The 24th Tank Regiment Cemetery in Stalingrad.

The *Stalinorgel*—a primitive rocket launcher mounted
on the back of an open truck.

A bridge over the Don built by German engineers.

Travelling through the Tyrol towards Italy.

Farewell to Italy! And back once again to the Russian Front!

A machine-gun team in position.

A Russian officer being interrogated.

Panzergrenadiers in an armoured personnel carrier at the
Nikopol bridgehead, November 1943.

Oberleutnant Prinz Moritz zu Öttingen-Wallerstein (second from right) with his squadron in the Nikopol area.

An attack with the new 75-ton 'Ferdinand' tank destroyer with 88mm gun.

Salute to a fallen comrade.

Infantry preparing for a tank-supported attack.

Many soldiers lost the front entirely in the thick fog.

Waiting in the *Rachel* for the next attack.

Retreat! Vehicles struggle through the thick Ukrainian mud . . .

. . . and even tanks find the going heavy.

Romanian infantry on the road to the front.

The retreat continues.

The author (right) with a companion during their stay at the military hospital.

The author with his sister, New Year 1944.

Well, I could do that I suppose. Then a grenade lands at the very edge of our foxhole. We are glad we are in the bottom, otherwise the splinters would have killed us. We are packed together like two sardines. Clods of earth and snow are falling down on us. We look at each other. Then our mortars wake up and fire into where the enemy is massing. Paul is pushing himself up again.

'Are you tired of living or what?' I yell at him.

'I just want to see what Ivan's up to.'

Paul looks towards the front, but a big explosion hurls him back against the wall of the foxhole and he crumples in a heap, pale-faced. The machine gun has a couple of scratches on the metal.

'I hope you're satisfied!' I grumble to him. It now looks as though we'll have to remain here until dark, with our heads down. Paul soon has the colour back in his cheeks and is taking deep breaths.

'We've got to smoke those bastards out!' he remarks.

'Quite, but how? He has his nose up first and fires instantly. Besides, I don't think he is the only sniper out there.'

We sit hunched together at the bottom of the foxhole and stare at the icy mud walls. Our cigarette butts are piling up on the floor. Our lips are dry and cracked, and when we smoke, small pieces of skin are left hanging on the butt. Paul pulls out an orange coloured butter tin, in which he has a piece of soft cheese and a left-over piece of American pork.

Paul doesn't even notice when I stand up and take a look over the edge. I avoid showing my head on the left-hand side of the machine gun, because I know that at least the one sniper has his weapon aimed right there.

There aren't many Russians to be seen. I can't see the sniper, even through the sight, but I do spot two heads under cover of a snow bank. Looking carefully, I can make out the white camouflaged protective shield of an HMG sticking up above the snow. I let out a low whistle.

'Whatcha got?' asks Paul straight away.

'I've just spotted a heavy machine gun position in front of us!'

'Really?' Paul wants to come up and see.

'Stay down! It's bad enough when one of us looks!' I tell him sharply.

'Maybe the sniper's gone?'

'You don't really believe that, do you? When he's got us in his sights, he won't let go until he's nailed us!'

'But he doesn't shoot at you!'

'I'm on the other side of this gun, or didn't you notice?' What on earth is the matter with Paul? I've never seen him so upset. Again he wants to come up.

'Keep down, damn you!' This is the first time since Paul and I have been together that I have raised my voice to him. I'm angry because he is so *stupid*—and I remember the promise I gave Katya that I'd look after him.

When I again glance over towards the Russian machine-gun position, I notice two figures crawling up towards it and two figures retreating. So—they are changing shifts! If the snipers were not out there I would fire off a few rounds. But at the moment I won't risk anything and would rather bide my time. I lower the entire machine gun on its mounting, to one side, in order to get a wider view, and then there is another sharp *crack!* right in my eardrum. Quick as a flash, I duck down and then freeze. With his eyes wide open, as if struck by lightning, Paul slumps in a heap down at the bottom of the foxhole. He must have popped up behind me in spite of my warning not to.

I stare aghast at the fist-sized hole in Paul's head just above his left eye, from which blood is leaking in dark red streams on to his steel helmet and from there right over his face and into his mouth, which is moving up and down. I am in total panic and try to turn his body over on its side so that the blood in his mouth will drain out. The blood is now streaming out, forming a small pool on the ground. It is pumping out of the wound so fast that I can hear a light 'clucking' sound. The two first-aid bandage packs which I have pressed into his wound don't help

210

and the puddle gets bigger. My hands are trembling, my knees grow weak and shake. I can't do anything more: his face is already as white as a sheet. A shell explodes nearby and makes me jump.

I cup both hands to my mouth and yell to the rear, 'Medic! Medic!'

'What's the matter?' someone replies.

'Paul Adam has been shot in the head. Perhaps he can still be saved!'

'No one can get the bugger out', the voice yells back.

In spite of the danger, I simply can't stay in the foxhole: I have to do something. Panic-stricken, I jump out and bound off to the rear until I tumble into a hole.

'Have you gone mad?' an *Unteroffizier* yells at me. My ears are still ringing from the exploding shell. All around the hole the snow has been churned up by enemy machine-gun fire.

I breathe heavily and cough. 'Maybe, but a medic must come! Perhaps Paul Adam can be saved.'

'Calm down', says the *Unteroffizier*. 'If he's been shot in the head, there's nothing even a medic can do.'

'That's as may be, but we must at least try. He can't stay in the foxhole. If anything happens up front, I can't keep stepping over him. Besides, I need an assistant gunner.'

'I know, and the CO has also been told. He is a bit further back by the mortars. A couple of blokes were killed by the artillery shelling.'

My excitement is slowly beginning to wear off. Why on earth did I run out of the foxhole? Did I want to fetch the medic myself, or was it pure panic because I couldn't bear to look at Paul's face? We had just spoken to each other—and then within seconds he was lying in front of me with this terrible head wound. Everything was instantly different. He was lying there in his own blood, unable to talk. I've never seen so much blood flow from a single wound—it was just like a gurgling spring.

I knew that Paul had been killed instantly the moment he was felled like a tree beside me. His mouth moved up and down only because his

211

nerves were twitching. That bloody sniper! If only I could catch him, it would give me the greatest pleasure to wipe him out—without compunction, even if he were on his knees in front of me and begging for mercy.

During a short lull in the shelling, someone jumps out of a hole and sprints over towards my machine-gun position.

'Stay here!' someone yells after him.

I recognise the runner as being our new *Sanitätsgefreiter*,* and I jump up and run after him. He is a really nice bloke, and I hope nothing happens to him—it would be my fault if it did. The mortar rounds and the machine-gun bullets force us to take cover in a shallow depression in the ground.

'Is Adam still alive?' enquires the medic. I shake my head.

'The explosion ripped open the entire left side of his head,' I tell him.

'I'll check it out myself,' he nods, and dashes the few metres to my foxhole. With a couple of strides I am in there as well, pressing myself hard against the inner wall so as to not step on Paul Adam.

'He's lost an awful lot of blood,' says the medic as he looks at the frozen pool under the corpse. 'There's really nothing more we can do. He must have been killed instantly.'

I nod.

'What can we do? I can hardly move in this position, as you can see.'

The medic looks at me. 'You can, but you would prefer not to have to walk round and over your friend—and I can understand that. Let's see if we can find an empty hole to put him in. I know of one hole where there are two dead already, killed by a direct hit from an artillery shell.'

An hour passed before it became quiet enough for us to risk moving Paul Adams' heavy body into an empty foxhole. Fritz Hamann gave us covering fire with his heavy machine gun, keeping the snipers' and the enemy machine gunners' heads down. But then all hell was let loose. The Russians opened up furiously with mortars. When I managed to

---

* Medical orderly.

212

save myself by diving into my own foxhole, I found *Panzergrenadier* Schröder there, pressed against the frozen mud wall.

'The CO told me I was to report to you as your assistant gunner,' he says.

Good grief! I think. Why on earth did they send me the little fair-haired Schröder. Didn't they have anyone else? I feel like yelling at him, although I don't know why. Then I sit down on a couple of ammunition boxes across from him and light my pipe. Schröder smokes a cigarette.

'You know how Paul Adam died?' I ask him.

'Yes, a shot in the head!'

'Good, then you can imagine what will happen to you if you stick your head up.'

'Well, that doesn't happen to everybody. And besides, we need to keep a look-out now and then—right?'

I wonder whether Paul had a premonition about his death. But Katya! She must have sensed something, because she told me to look after him. She can't blame me for what happened: I did all I could. I even yelled at him—something I'd never done before. And now little Schröder is in my foxhole! I have to watch over him as well, Katya said. My God! Well, I'll do my best, but I can't tie him up!

It is already late afternoon. The air is misty, and this could be an advantage for us—it's more difficult for the snipers. The mortar fire has eased a bit. From time to time I look towards the Russian positions. They are also quiet. Only occasionally do I see a hunched figure slinking across the snow.

It's unpleasant for me, but I have no intention of pulling rank.

'It's for your own good, Schröder,' I explain. He is already up and crouches close behind the machine gun. Perhaps the enemy really can't see us any more.

'There isn't much to see, that's for sure,' he says. After a while he points with his hand at something and asks excitedly, 'What's that over there?' I can only see a thick black line, moving from left to the right.

'Can't we take off the telescopic sight off and look through it?' he asks me.

'That's not a bad idea—then we could stay down more and be better protected. Good, take it off! But be careful.'

Schröder leans forward carefully and unscrews the butterfly nut. The sight doesn't move. It might be frozen. He uses both hands and as he does so raises himself up a little more. Then there is a *crack!* like a whiplash in my ear. Schröder sinks down, just as Paul Adam had done before, and lies at my feet. Even before I bend down over him with the bandage from my kitbag, I call loudly behind me, 'Medic! Schröder's got a head wound!'

The young medic is not far away. With a couple of strides he is back with me in my hole, bending over the wounded man. My face is deathly white and I am shaking at the knees. My mouth dry, I warn him of the sniper and ask, 'Is he dead?' The medic shrugs his shoulders.

'Almost the same injury as Paul Adams',' he decides. 'Only this time the bullet exploded as it exited his head.' Hellish ammunition! This is the second one after Paul Adam.

Schröder has a normal bullet hole over his left eye, but behind the left ear is a large wound, from which blood is just streaming out. The medic bandages him around his head, but the bandage is immediately saturated. So, he winds another one around his head.

'Is he alive?' I ask with concern.

The medic carefully holds Schröder's head, looks into his pale face and feels for the artery in his neck. He can't feel anything, apparently.

'Maybe he is alive, maybe not. I can't tell here in the foxhole. With head wounds like these there's not much more you can do, but I'll try to get him to the main medical station. He may not survive the journey there, even though there might still be a spark of life left in him now.'

According to him, there was not much hope.

Thus Schröder was the second man to die in my blasted foxhole. And for some unknown reason I survive, even though I have been observing from this hole for a lot longer than they had. Fate is terrible and not to be dismissed lightly. I have been fated to experience, close up, how my comrades can be snatched away within the blink of an eye. I am doomed to bear the pain and the sorrow over their loss, and also to bear the fear for my own life even more strongly than before.

'Come on, you take the legs,' I hear the medic saying, and together we lift the lifeless body out of the hole and lay him in the churned-up snow drifts behind us. It is almost quiet, with only the occasional rifle shot. It is already so misty that visibility is very low.

'Let him lie here for a moment. I'll fetch a stretcher from the *Schwadronsgefechtsstand*,'* says the medic, and he disappears to the rear.

He returns after a couple of minutes, with a *Sanitätsunteroffizier*. He bends down over the lifeless Schröder.

'I don't think there's much we can do, but we'll take him with two others to the main dressing station, where the surgeons can take a look at him."

After they have placed him on the stretcher, I take a look at little Schröder one last time and gaze into his pale face. I think I can see his eyelid twitching, but I'm not sure. He really looks like all the other dead men I've seen during combat. And, amazingly enough, I would see Schröder again—ten months later when, after a serious wound, I ended up at a convalescent centre. I will mention this again at the right time. Up until this moment we had all considered Schröder to be dead, and as far as most of the war casualties were concerned, we never had any feedback as to what had become of an individual—except if a known officer was concerned.

With Schröder taken away, several of my friends come to me in my foxhole. In the course of our conversation an awful lot of expletives rise into the frosty winter air, directed at the snipers. In all, five men have fallen victim to them, based on the fact that all these five men had been killed by shots to the head.

---

* Squadron Command Post.

By the time it is dark, everything is over and the enemy has been thrown out of his positions near to our front. The troops relieving us enjoy some respite. But for how long?

When the next day dawns, we are again en route back to our quarters.

2 January. Katya has, as usual, cleaned and organised things, and made sure that they are pleasantly warm when we return. On Paul Adams' bed is a woven wreath, in the middle of which a lighted candle has been placed. Little Schröder has his bunk in the neighbouring hut. I wonder how Katya could have known: no one has come back from the front since yesterday; the ration vehicle was not at the front either, because they knew that we were being relieved; and the first bodies were only brought back this morning. I begin to get an uneasy feeling about Katya's uncanny ability to sense what is going on.

She doesn't welcome us as she usually does. The candle has not been burning for long, so she must have been in here only a short while ago. We do not see Katya until the evening. Her eyes show that she has been crying, and she doesn't talk to us very much.

Nor do we have much time. Our unit has again been reorganised, and Peronje from the light platoons joins us. Later the *Spiess* comes and tells Warias, Fritz Hamann and me that we can now sew the long-overdue second stripe on our arms. This promotion means a bit more pay. Since we now are expected to offer a round to the men, I'm glad I saved a bottle of juniper brandy from the last canteen supply we were given.

3 January. During the evening we suddenly receive our marching orders. We're told to move to another village, not far from Dneprovka. We assume it's a parting gesture from *General* Schörner. Everything

happens so fast that we don't even have time to bid a proper farewell to our lovely Katya. She's in the kitchen, and only her mother is in the house. Her mother tells us that Katya has been crying and praying a lot. Paul's death must have affected her badly. We see Katya when our vehicle has taken up its position in the convoy and we're about to move off. She tries to run after us, but she can't quite manage it and stands waving to us with both arms.

Maybe it's a good thing that it happens so suddenly—a goodbye so quick and sudden, just like death so often is: completely unexpected, from one moment to the next, but final and irrevocable. It's a good thing we don't know about it beforehand. Now it's all behind us—the good days and the bad, which we experienced in Dneprovka. That place is now history. But the war will go on, with a future full of blood, fear and sorrow, from which death will garner a rich harvest.

23 January. During the night we are ordered out of the bridgehead. There is talk about giving it up altogether, but that's in the lap of the gods. The weather has turned: an hour ago it started to rain. As we wait in front of a bridge for traffic to pass from the opposite direction, we recognise the outline of one of our Ferdinands. In conversation we hear that the engineers are busy dismantling it and that it will eventually be blown up.

24–27 January. We reach a small village during the morning hours and take over a couple of empty houses for our quarters. We remain here for two days, and then we travel north-westwards. The roads are now softened up and are becoming seas of mud.

We stop at another village. The houses are nearly all occupied, but we find an empty one at last and move in with twenty men, packed together like sardines. During the night it begins to stink something awful, and the next morning we discover a heap of rotten cabbages and a vat of sauerkraut in a corner.

2–3 February. Tonight we have reached a village called Apostolovo. It is a large place—almost a town, in fact. We hear explosions coming from all over the place. No one seems to know where the front line runs. The Russians have broken through the MBL north of Krivoi Rog and are marching south, driving elements of the German Army before them. The roads are a disaster. Not only wheeled but also tracked vehicles are sinking deep into the mud and clogging up every even halfway passable road.

We are always leaving our quarters to pull our vehicles out of the mud—a never-ending task. When daylight comes, Russian combat aircraft strafe and bomb the vehicles stuck in the mud. Petrol tanks explode, and everywhere vehicles are in flames. During the day the Russian artillery fires into the mêlée. Then we are told that the Soviets are close to the town. Chaos ensues when everyone tries to save himself as best he can. Many of the vehicles from our unit and from others are stuck fast in the mud. Those who can, blow up their vehicles to make sure they don't fall into Russian hands. We run across to ours, which has been standing under cover, and are lucky enough to be able to jump-start it and get away. But a few days later we lose our truck in the mud as well,, and now we have to walk.

8 February. A general retreat towards the west gets under way. While our men try to save as many vehicles and heavy weapons and as much equipment as possible, struggling through the mud or by using the railway, we are employed as rearguard security to prevent the advancing enemy from reaching the main column. The road takes us, with many engagements along the way, over Schirokoye and Mikolayevka to

Ingul, and from there by means of a harrowing march through the sticky mud all the way to the River Bug.

This is a terribly demoralising time—trudging through gluey slime, without sleep and with very little food, our feet blistered and bloody, our ears aching because of the unrelenting yells of 'Hooray' from the pursuing enemy, whom we had to fight off in order to stay alive—and I have neither time nor opportunity to make any notes. However, as soon as my battered body has had a bit of time to recuperate in Vosnessensk, on the Bug, I catch up with recording my never-to-be-forgotten experiences and traumas. I have given up trying to quote the exact dates of the various incidents of the retreat in favour of concentrating on what actually took place during this awful period.

CHAPTER ELEVEN

Through Bottomless Mud

THE WEATHER has calmed down a bit, and during the night there was even a bit of frost again and many of the vehicles had a chance to get back out of the mud. However, the further we retreat, the muddier and more churned up the roads become.

Under the leadership of a young *Leutnant*, our *Schwadron* is more often than not assigned as rearguard, our job being to hold the enemy back for as long as we can and, if possible, mount a counter-attack. But, as a rule, the Soviets attack us in massive force, and without suitable heavy weapons we have nothing to match them. When they charge after us shouting 'Hurrah!', it is often as much as we can do to escape in one piece. As a result, our little band gradually becomes smaller and smaller.

At the start of the retreat between Apostolovo and Schirkoye, we are at least more or less organised. In order to gain time for our baggage trains and heavy weapons to churn their way through the mud, we as the rearguard occupy a former artillery position with a bunker. We are under orders to hold this position until evening and then, after nightfall, move back. As support, our *Schwadron* is reinforced with several men from other units, including a 75mm ATG towed by a tracked vehicle. As the artillery position is located in the middle of the steppe, the conditions are quite good; only the sunflower field off to our right is a bit of a morass.

It is quiet here to begin with: we can neither see nor hear anything of the enemy. But we know he has been advancing relentlessly and can appear at any time. He has realised that there is no continuous front line any more, and he often just leaves us sitting in our trenches when we prove awkward for him and simply bypasses us on our left or right flank. This is apparent from the many fires and clouds of smoke to our left and right which the enemy leaves behind along his route.

Our young *Leutnant* makes the bunker his headquarters. While my HMG goes into position in a narrow foxhole to the right of the bunker, Fritz Hamann is supposed to secure the bunker. The light platoons are to the left The ATG has been left behind the heap of dirt excavated when the bunker was built. *Wachtmeister* Fender's recommendation that the ATG be positioned further to the rear is based on the argument that, if spotted by the tanks, it could endanger both the bunker and the HMG. His suggestion is, however, disregarded.

As I improve the field of fire in front of my HMG with Franz Kramer, the first enemy artillery rounds scream in towards us. The barrage is not directed at anything in particular—'A bit of disruptive fire,' says Waldi, who is standing in a foxhole to my side and behind me and is scanning the rolling hills in front of us with his field glasses.

After a little while I hear him yell, 'Bloody hell! They are coming at us like a swarm of ants!'

I look through the telescopic sight and see them too. The Soviets are moving towards us like an army of termites, hell-bent on destruction. Waldi estimates that the range is still three or four kilometres. They're moving slowly, at an almost leisurely pace, but they are making progress at a constant speed. They could be on us in about an hour's time. After a few minutes, however, we decide that the mass of troops is not moving directly at us, but rather towards our right.

'Looks like they might actually pass by us,' I say.

'I don't think so,' says Waldi. 'We'll probably just catch his right flank.'

In the meantime the Russian guns are firing further ahead, pounding the vacant terrain immediately in front of their slowly moving infantry. Waldi is right: if they continue in this manner, we will brush their right flank. The first thing is that we mustn't move, but when they get dangerously close we should open fire. Waldi agrees. The *Leutnant* sees it differently. He calls over to us and says that both machine guns should open fire now.

'That's crazy! At a range of one and a half kilometres it is a total waste of ammunition—and we will give away our position,' says Waldi, annoyed.

So I wait. But then the other weapon opens up, so I fire off a belt too. The brown mass in front of us doesn't stop for a moment, but continues forward as if nothing has happened. Then my gun jams.

I curse the enamelled steel cartridges: as so often happens, one has got stuck in the barrel. I normally only use this type of ammunition when the enemy is still some way off and needs to be disrupted while he is getting ready, but I always have a few cases of good ammunition in reserve and use this when the enemy makes his frontal assault. I still need one or two spare barrels, in case we go into action here. Josef Spittka, our ammunition carrier, has got at least one reserve barrel. But where is he?

'They must all be in the bunker,' Bittner answers from next door when I ask him if he knows where our assistant is. I need to get over to the bunker and ask Waldi.

'Of course, I'll man the gun in the meantime. The Russians are still a long way away.'

Waldi is saving his ammunition and fires only very short bursts at the Russians. Only Fender and two other men are in the bunker—the *Leutnant* has sent the rest off to the nearby foxhole. I quickly light up a cigarette and am on my way out of the bunker when someone yells 'Tank!' Seconds later rounds hit the top of the bunker. The ATG fires one shot, then the tank destroys it.

I run out of the bunker, trying to get to my machine gun. The tank shells explode all around me. I leap into the next foxhole. Then I see three T-34s, approaching from the left, heading directly towards the bunker. The men in the trenches are already out of their holes and running back.

'They are all running away!' yells Fritz Hamann. Then he too jumps out of the foxhole with Bittner and dashes after the *Leutnant* and the others. Two tanks fire on the fleeing soldiers, while the third is circling the bunker and opening up. One round tears the escaping ATG crew apart, then the turret hatch on the T-34 opens and several hand grenades are thrown into the bunker entrance.

My muscles tighten—I want to jump up and run behind the others. Too late! The tank has just waltzed over Fritz Hamann's HMG and flattened it. Now it is lumbering past me, following the other two. To get up now would mean certain death. I have to stay in my hole and see what happens. Both Waldi and Kramer are still in their foxhole. Fender should still be in the bunker—or has he been hit?

The thread by which my life is hanging continues to be very thin as I look over to Waldi and Kramer. They are not firing, but working on a machine-gun barrel, in which no doubt another cartridge has become stuck. At this moment the attacking Soviets are getting unpleasantly close. Then I hear *Wachtmeister* Fender.

'What's the matter? Why don't you shoot?' Fender is standing by the bunker, holding his left arm close to his body. He must have been wounded.

'Cartridge jams in all barrels!' Waldi yells back, trying desperately to release the jammed cartridges. Finally he manages it. He replaces the barrel in its socket, closes the breech and pulls the ammunition belt tight. The machine gun rattles away and sends off two long bursts. The Soviets in front of us throw themselves down on the ground. Then the gun jams again. It is exasperating—I know the feeling! When the barrel is hot and even the smallest imperfections have built up inside, the

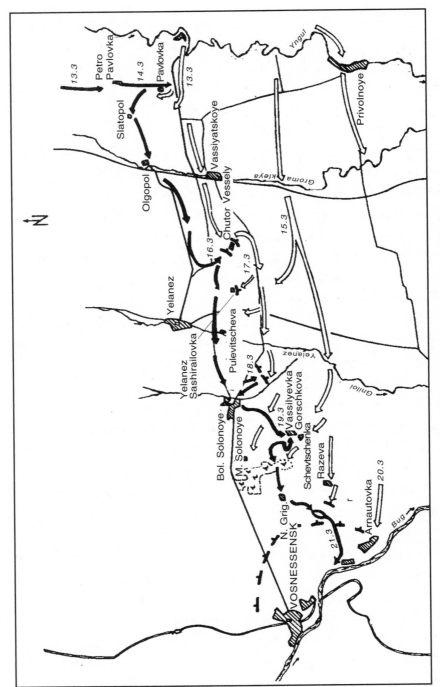

The retreat to the Bug in the Russian mudbath.

problem starts all over again. The only solution is to fit a new barrel and let the others cool off, or use good-quality ammunition.

I hope Waldi realises this, but over the last few months he has only been using his sub-machine gun and doesn't have the routine any more. If that machine gun doesn't fire we'll all be dead men—the Russians will pull us out of our foxholes and then either shoot us or take us prisoner. Waldi and Kramer are keeping their heads down, messing around with the barrels, while rifle bullets are zipping all around them. Waldi is swearing and praying, every now and then glancing up at the Soviets moving ever nearer towards us. I too am panic-stricken and blame myself. Why didn't I stay where I was?

I reckon Waldi and Kramer have been using that lousy ammunition for too long, even though they have at least six cases of good ammunition in their foxhole. I am also much better at getting cartridges out of barrels, as I have had more experience of this than Kramer, who has never really come to terms with it. If both barrels have cartridges stuck, and if they have punched out the bottoms of the cartridges, then getting the rest of the cartridge out is a major problem and would take time.

All these thoughts are racing through my head. But before all is lost I just have to try everything possible to get that machine gun to fire. My God—up until now I've always been able to depend on my machine gun. In panic and fright I yell through the ever increasing inferno of rifle fire: 'I'm coming, but one of you must get out of the foxhole!' The hole is too narrow for three; Waldi knows that too. We leap at the same time, and Waldi disappears in a neighbouring foxhole with two strides. I have much further to run, through the rain of bullets, and feel a hot graze on my left forearm. It's not much, but I can feel blood running out of my sleeve.

With a final leap I land in the hole and start to look at the barrels. Just as I thought—cartridges stuck in both of them, both with their bottoms punched out. Damn! I am going to need more time to clear them out. I see a couple of soldiers at the bunker. 'I need spare barrels!' I yell to them and then try to free the cartridges with a special tool. The brown figures in front of us are now almost so close that we will soon see their faces. By this time I can hear Waldi firing his sub-machine gun, and rifle fire is also coming from the bunker. So there are some riflemen left after all!

However, against this great horde, a few salvos of rifle fire are worthless. Is this, then, the end? That's certainly the way it looks. I never really thought it would finish like this. But why should I be an exception? Now it's death or imprisonment—maybe something worse. We've heard so much about the Red Army, and how they treat their prisoners. A quick death is much to be preferred, then—I'd never survive Russian imprisonment. I try to pray quietly, but because of my churning stomach can't say anything coherent. Quite automatically, I unbutton my holster and feel the cool handle of my 08 pistol in my hand. . .

Then someone behind me coughs. 'Here you are—two barrels from the other machine gun!'

I turn round and recognise our ammunition carrier, who amidst a rain of bullets from the enemy had leapt up from a foxhole and thrown us two barrels in their protective covers, landing about a metre behind us. He can see Franz and I trying to reach the package with our hands, then he jumps up again and runs back. He manages just two strides before he falls silently to the ground and remains motionless. The bullets keep ripping into his dead body, but Josef Spittka, our ammunition carrier, feels them no more. He has given his young life for his comrades.

I am choking with emotion, but I do see a chance to keep all of us alive for a while longer. My hands trembling, I open the sleeves and pull out a new barrel, which I lock into the gun. Franz Kramer has already brought out a new belt of the good brass ammunition. I pull the belt tight and close the breech.

My entire body is shaking like a leaf—the first Soviet soldiers are already running towards us. But then my machine gun starts to chatter! An indescribable feeling of relief comes over me as the belt flows through as if oiled. The attackers at the front start falling like flies to the ground. Franz Kramer has already opened all the ammunition cases and is feeding in new belts with both hands to make sure they will pull through without any stoppages.

How often I have stood behind a machine gun and felt the strength embodied in this mechanical purveyor of death. But never have I used it with such relief as at this moment. I see our enemy falling and dying. I see them bleeding from their wounds, hear their whimpering cries and have, believe me, not a spark of pity or compassion for them. A sort of madness has come over me. It's the bloody revenge for the crazy terror and despair which I experienced just now . . . and it is retaliation for the death of Josef Spittka, the ATG crew and the others who became casualties.

Revenge and retaliation! That inflammatory clarion call for revenge! That's the way all war leaders want their soldiers to be. Remorseless, and with hatred and retaliation in their hearts, men can win battles, and quite ordinary soldiers can be turned into celebrities. Fear is converted into hatred, anger and calls for retribution. In this way you are motivated to fight on—even decorated with medals as a hero. But heroes have to stay alive, so that others can see their medals; they are supposed to inspire the weaker among us. Therefore heroes—like Josef Spittka, at least as far his own comrades are concerned—are an irreplaceable loss. In terms of the war effort, however, they are not worth a jot.

But, as I look at our enemies lying there on the ground, all my pent-up aggression vanishes. I am thinking clearly once more. In the far distance, beyond my firing range, the Soviets continue unconcerned. The mass has not allowed its right flank be affected by my machine gun: there is only a large heap of Russians lying on their stomachs in a shallow depression in front of us. We can only make them out when they raise their heads.

I have fired almost six cases of ammunition so far. The palm of my right hand burns as if on fire because I changed the hot barrels in seconds without taking time to grab the protection of the asbestos rag. Strips of skin are hanging on the barrels.

'We only have half a case of good ammunition left,' Franz Kramer reminds me. His eyes gleam feverishly and his face is soaked with sweat. His lips are cracked and covered with thick crusts of saliva. I probably don't look any better myself.

The Russians in front of us are motionless. They are less than 50 metres away, but in a really tricky situation. They have cover only when they lie prone: the second they move, I shoot. It must be bloody awful for them I reckon.

Franz expresses what I am also thinking.

'At this range, if they all suddenly jump up and charge, things could get pretty awkward,' he remarks nervously.

Interrupting these thoughts is a sudden call from the hollow: '*Pan! Pan!*' At the same time a steel helmet is held up on a rifle and waved back and forth. Again the voice: '*Pan! Pan!* Not shoot—we come!'

I don't trust them. How should I respond? I wrap my hand around the grip with a finger on the trigger. I would of course be delighted if I don't have to shoot and kill any more. But can we rely on them? We are only a handful of men. What if I let them come forward without firing and then they suddenly run us down? What a predicament!

'Throw your guns down!' I call back.

The one who did the talking slowly rises to his feet and speaks to those lying on the ground. I wonder about how much confidence he has in us. Some of them stand up, but they are still holding their rifles.

'Throw away your guns!' Waldi yells at them.

The Russians throw themselves flat again as a result of the shouting, leaving just the fellow who has done the talking standing with his hands stretched out over his head, waving from side to side, and calling out 'Don't shoot, don't shoot!' Then he speaks to the others again, and then slowly, one at a time, they also stand up, this time without their weapons. I don't feel very comfortable seeing so many Russians in front of me, and my finger is still ready to squeeze the trigger.

'Our men are coming back!' Fender calls out to us from the bunker.

I glance back quickly and—thank God—they are no longer far away. That was the reason, then, why they decided to surrender: they thought that we were about to counter-attack and that they would be killed in any case. I breathe more easily in the knowledge that the danger is now finally over.

The Russians now come towards us with their arms in the air and are collected by Fender and three soldiers. There are more than sixty of them, all with good equipment, but they are not youngsters. An officer is among them. I learn that the fifty-year-old Russian who speaks some German is a teacher from Kiev. His former supply unit apparently came to the front only three weeks ago. He had been indoctrinated in the belief that he must never surrender to the Germans, as they were 'known' to mutilate their prisoners before they killed them. In answer to the question why he still surrendered, he tells us that during the last few weeks of the German retreat a number of Russian prisoners had been able to escape, and they had met up with them and been told that they had been put to work by the Germans with the rear echelons. These prisoners hadn't mentioned anything about acts of brutality, although they understood that they'd have to be cautious if they got amongst the SS units. We had no idea what the drill was in the rear areas: on the front line, it was all you could do to stay alive.

I have often heard tales from Russian prisoners about the supposed treatment of POWs by German front-line troops. These stories served their propaganda purpose, making sure that the Russian soldier would prefer to fire his last cartridge and fight to the death rather than surrender. There is no doubt that it was this fear that often persuaded

Russian soldiers to put up unbelievable resistance in completely hopeless situations. But it's the same with us. I have seen atrocities perpetrated on German soldiers, and the fear of similar treatment is greater than the fear of dying in battle. Many incidents involving acts of brutality and murder were committed by the Russians against their own people too, and they definitely tried to blame these on the German troops, especially during the turbulent times of our retreat. I will report on my own personal experiences on this topic later in this chapter.

As the prisoners are transported to the rear, it again becomes quiet. The Professor and Otto Kruppka, who in the meantime had been promoted to *Unteroffizier*, come to see us in our foxhole.

'What's with the tanks?' I ask.

'They were immediately taken out by an anti-tank gun,' says Otto somewhat quietly.

The Professor takes the part of the enthusiast. 'Wow, it was quite something, you seeing off the Russians with one machine gun!' he says in admiration.

'I had no choice but to stay here. You blokes all ran away without saying a word!' complains Waldi.

'We only ran after the *Leutnant*,' Otto protests. 'When the tanks appeared, the entire left flank ran for it. And when the ATG was destroyed, there was no stopping them.'

'No one's blaming you,' I add. 'If we'd noticed them earlier, we would've run with you too. But, as it happened, it was too late.'

'And if it hadn't been for our ammunition carrier, Josef Spittka, we would all have been lying here dead now,' says Franz Kramer, whose nerves are still jumping. .

For our *Leutnant*, the hard-fought defensive close combat was apparently nothing unusual. He probably doesn't talk to us because he can see what we think of him. A responsible superior waits until all of his men have been able to reach safety. He can probably read this from our stares. While other soldiers come up and want to know all the details, the *Leutnant* only talks to Waldi, our section leader. Later we hear that he had been awarded the Iron Cross 1st Class because of his supposed heroism. However, he is quickly forgotten because by the end of February we have our respected *Oberleutnant* Prinz Moritz zu Öttingen-Wallerstein back again as *Schwadron* commander.

Shortly before nightfall, the clouds quickly cover the sky and a light drizzle starts to fall. *Wachtmeister* Fender says that we have to vacate the position by 2100 hours.

A few kilometres further west, the rest of the unit is collected and a new defensive perimeter created. Although the advancing enemy is quickly stopped, we nevertheless have to move off again at once since the Russians have moved forward on both flanks, without meeting any resistance, in an attempt to take us in a pincer movement. Unfortunately not everyone manages to get away. This hopeless situation repeats itself almost daily. During this time we lose Franz Kramer, who, with his heavy gun mount, was apparently unable to get away quickly enough and fell into enemy hands.

We are repeatedly trying to hold the enemy back, but it is a hopeless venture as we are busy running almost all the time. As soon as a soldier is on the retreat, nothing will persuade him to stay in one place to await an onrushing enemy.

We cannot consolidate until we get to Nikolayevke on 28 February, under the leadership of our well-respected *Schwadronschef*, who, following his recovery, has returned to us. We hold the enemy back for quite a while here, and even launch a number of successful counter-attacks, but, as the Soviets quickly begin to envelop us on both sides, we are forced to withdraw again.

Behind the village of Petro Pavlovka we are spread out in all directions when we are suddenly attacked. We've been without sleep for days and are totally exhausted, so we, as the rearguard of our unit, have been looking for quarters in the last houses of the village. After a while the Soviets come storming into the village yelling 'Hurrah!' and mowing down everything in their path. I just have enough time to escape out of a rear window with Otto Kruppka. I can't take my machine gun with me; it wouldn't do me any good in any case—I'm out of ammunition.

Later on in the retreat Otto and I run into some more of our mates from the *Schwadron*. We all haul ourselves through the mud and slime, tired and exhausted. Then one day they too are gone and I am now alone with Otto. We join up with a combat unit made up of personnel from a mish-mash of all types. In the meantime it begins to rain and the mud now becomes even deeper. The ice-cold easterly wind whips through our starved bones; the hunger gnaws at our intestines. During the nights we seek shelter in the Panje huts. They are always mostly full. The men lie stacked up like herrings, helping each other to keep warm. Their faces are dirty and pale. They listen intently to every little noise outside, reacting to anything out of the ordinary. Only a few have got weapons with them.

When each morning breaks—and assuming Ivan hasn't driven us out of the houses with his shouting—we pull ourselves together and stumble on. In every village we come to we meet up with new groups of German soldiers fleeing from the pursuing Soviet Army. Some of them have misjudged the speed of the Russian advance. These men are mostly rear-echelon troops from field bakeries, repair and maintenance shops, etc. and supply troops who have never seen the front line. Once in a while we would even come across so-called *Kriegsverlängerungsräte**
whose uniforms for the first time have come in contact with dirt.

Kriegsverlängerungsräte, or *Schmalspuroffiziere*,† are the administrative managers of the Army. You can pick them out by the narrow epaulettes of their tailored uniforms. They are the finest soldiers of the *Reich*, who manage all the goodies the Army gets—the sort of supplies which the average soldier never even lays eyes on. During the turbulent times of

---

* Literally, 'War Extension Officials'.
† Literally, 'Narrow-Gauge (Railway) Officers'.

the withdrawal, these stuck-up and officious administrators were often done away with if they refused to open the gates of their overfilled supply depots to the angry, starving and tattered common soldiers trying to escape the clutches of the pursuing Soviets. They would quote orders given by their superiors, who themselves were long gone to the rear, to secure the depots and to blow them up or set them ablaze before the Soviet Army could take them over.

One day Otto and I found ourselves standing in front of just such a depot, in front of which a *Kriegsverlängerungsrat* had placed himself together with his assistants, to stop famished soldiers from getting in. In spite of the fact that the Russians were not far from the village, the official stood his ground and denied the soldiers access, saying that he had orders to blow the place apart but not to let it be opened before that. As the crowd of soldiers steadily grew and the official stood his ground, the debate was settled with a sudden burst of fire from a sub-machine gun. The corpse was unceremoniously shoved aside and the starving men went into the depot, egged on by an *Oberfeldwebel* as the charges were set to blow in 20 minutes.

We couldn't believe what we saw. Everyone stuffed his pockets full. 'Take only the best,' Otto suggested. 'When the Russians are after us, you'll throw away half of it.' Otto was right. But what was 'the best'? Everything we saw was of value to us half-starved individuals. Where did all of these goodies come from, these luxuries I had never seen up at the front? Who were these delicious hard salami and smoked hams supposed to be for? At the front we had soft cheese or canned meat at best. In one corner I discovered cases of wonderful chocolate cola in cans; in my entire service career I had been able to get this from the canteen precisely twice.

'Man, look at this golden liquid!' Otto called over as he held up a bottle of French cognac. 'A bit different from that kidney-water juniper brandy which we soldiers always get!' Otto was eagerly tearing open some of the highly sought-after *Frontkämpferpäckchen*, which we seldom

233

had the luck to receive. He only took out the packs of cigarettes, throwing the rest of the goodies away. There was no knowing what treasures were being stored in this warehouse while we at the front had suffered hunger for days on end when our kitchen could not deliver food to the front line.

'Or was this stuff just not meant for us?' I wanted to know.

'Meant, yes, but the best stuff always gets looted on the way. Mostly it goes to the staffs—I've seen that myself,' Otto explains. 'What I've seen would make your eyes pop. I saw it all when I was an orderly. It's always that way when something passes through a lot of hands. It's not even the high-ranking officers who take advantage, but those who want to brown-nose their superiors. It is no different with the kitchen wallahs. The best goes to the person they want to suck up to.' Otto shoved a huge piece of cheese in his mouth which he had taken from another *Unteroffizier* on the blade of a knife.

'We should get a job like that!' interjected his friend, who in the meantime had half-emptied the bottle.

'Well, that'd be okay, but it's not for us old foot sloggers, right?' He grabbed his friend around the shoulder and said heavily, 'We have both been lying in the dirt too long!'

As the *Oberfeldwebel* hurried us out because of the danger from the explosions due any moment, I came across a room with some new jackboots next to some uniforms. As my own boots were soaking wet and swollen up, I quickly tried on a new pair. However, in my haste I decided on some which were one size too large, thinking I could fill out the extra room with an extra pair or socks or foot warmers. I shouldn't have, because in the deep slime the new boots rubbed my feet and made them so bloody that I only could drag myself along in agony, and at times literally got stuck. The only one who stayed with me was Otto. He also had blisters on his feet, but he said he could stand it.

I often wonder how I will be able to manage to run as the Russians beat us back now my feet are raw flesh. As soon as I stop I suffer awful pain. Now I understand what you are prepared to go through when your life depends on it. During the day I go through hell with my feet and at night the yells of the oncoming Soviets rip me out of my deathlike sleep. I recall that for weeks afterwards, on quiet days, I would wake up from nightmares in which a deep voice of a yelling Russian had been following me around. He was for ever on our heels shouting 'Hurrah!' and never giving us any respite. How I would have loved to have given this noisy devil a burst! But only having my pistol— Otto's sub-machine gun was out of ammunition—it would have been suicide. So, in my terror, I preferred to run for my life on raw flesh. Many soldiers did not manage to get away and were shot out of hand or bayoneted. Others were driven crazy and went for the attacking Soviets with their bare hands or fell on their knees and begged for mercy. The Soviet soldiers just laughed as they massacred them. I didn't notice any prisoners being taken.

It was days before the yelling behind us stopped, but instead we can now see the Soviet soldiers marching forward on both sides of us, almost near enough to touch. They do not even bother to get into position to fire on us. We are a sorry sight, tired, and bedraggled. They do take the liberty of taunting us with a victory pose as they pass by on their little wagons, loaded with all kinds of things. This seems to me to be downright grotesque—to see the enemy so near at hand just marching by instead of fighting with him, and to be shown only threatening fists and ridicule.

Occasionally their advance units run into strong German opposition. Then they withdraw and leave behind masses of murdered Russian women and children in the villages, hacked to death along the muddy roads and in the houses. Above all there remains an unremitting hatred towards the Germans and towards all those who have served them during the occupation. They don't ask if those who have served have done so voluntarily or if they have been forced to do it; it's enough that they have lived under German occupation. The Russian Army demands obedience without equivocation to the patriotic slogan 'Rather dead than enslaved!' The same words always come from those on the winning side, the motive always being hatred for all who think differently. If everyone temporarily forced to do something against his will or his convictions had to be struck down, very soon there would be nobody left. These women, murdered by their own forces, were really only normal everyday women. God knows, they didn't want to work for their occupiers: they only wanted to survive.

These terrible pictures send an additional shiver into my body, driving me forward ever more determinedly. I have the feeling that I am wading through blood in my boots. When we arrive at a village in which a group of stout-hearted soldiers has just driven the Russians out, I suffer terrible pains which I simply cannot stand. My feet are burning, as if I've been running over hot coals. For the first time I shout with pain. 'I am finished Otto! Nobody can run on raw flesh all the way to the Bug.'

'You have to!' Otto insists and tries to calm me.

We are about a hundred metres behind the last of the trailing party. Nobody pays any attention to us. And why should they? Everyone's had enough. And what difference would it make anyway if one person stays behind and dies? But I don't want to peg out—not yet! I grit my teeth and drag myself forward once again. The fire in hell can't be worse than this, I think, and at the same time I bite my lip until it oozes blood for having let my willpower slip. But after a short period the pain is so unbelievable that I resign myself to my fate. I am completely finished, and my willpower is paralysed. I can go on no further; I can't take another step. With a groan I let myself fall into the mud. Otto wants to get me going. He even tries the Russian yell and calls me a lazy dog and so on. I don't react; my spirit is broken. The pain almost finishes me at every step.

'It's over, Otto! I can't take any more! I'm going to stay here come what may—I just don't give a damn!' I moan. 'When the Russians come I've got my pistol. But you hurry on, Otto, so you can catch up with the rest.'

Otto is livid. 'Don't talk such nonsense! Let's at least go to the next hut. When you have rested for a bit we might be able to go a little further.'

He takes me under the arm and helps me up. A hot current runs through my body, reaching up into my throat. Is this the end? Damn! I've been on the front lines for months, and have at most been slightly wounded in the many close combats, and now my life is hanging in the balance all because of a couple of lousy army boots which are tearing the skin off my bones! Well, I guess it has to be that way. I could of course have pulled off the boots long ago and run barefoot as so many others are doing. However, when I see what has happened to so many of the men who have done just that, and what infections and other problems they have picked up from the mud, I decide that I would rather keep the boots on. In any case, I would probably never have been able to get the boots back on again due to the swellings.

With Otto's help, I manage to drag myself to the next cabin. It's empty, but we come across a small chunk of bread and a glass jar containing some beets. The food gives us some new energy, but it also makes me dead tired, and while Otto snoops around the cabin and outside I lie down on an iron bedstead with the Army blanket wrapped around me and immediately fall asleep.

Eventually I can hear my name being called as if from far away, so I get up and drag myself to the door. Otto is waving to me from the other side of the street, beckoning me to join him, Beside him are two scruffy looking Russian ponies, two hemp ropes rather than the normal bridles around their necks. He has a broad grin on his face.

'Took me a good half-hour to round up these little beasts. But they're our only chance of getting out of here in a hurry.' With that he presses one rope into my hand and is already on the back of his pony, without even asking me if I can ride.

My pony is not a big animal, and with a single bound I am on his back and pressing my legs around his belly. He immediately stands up on his front legs, raises his hind quarters and starts shaking like a wet cat. I slide forward and am almost thrown off, but at the last moment manage to hold on to his bushy mane.

'Daway! Daway!' yells Otto as he slams his heels into his animal's flanks. The pony trots along and is soon several metres in front of me. Then my one scurries after Otto's, jolting my bones, and only by clinging on to the mane can I manage to stop it unseating me. This riding is good fun, I decide—but only if you know how. I have only ridden once, and that was on a fat old farm horse. It was in the first year of the war, when we were ordered by the school to help bring in the harvest. I remember that riding on that thing was much easier than riding on this spindly creature.

Otto's pony goes too slowly for his liking, so he smacks the nag on the neck and digs his heels into its flanks, but the little horse doesn't move any faster. In return, it tries to snap at his legs. My pony copies what his is doing, just as if they had agreed upon it: he too bends his head back towards me and snaps at my knees. I move backwards and just about manage to cling on to his mane. One foot is already dragging on the ground.

'This devil will be the end of me yet!' I moan, and because of his jerking gait I am rattled from side to side and it sounds as if I am stuttering. I slide from left to right and back again and feel like a bundle of clothes on a old wheelbarrow. I can feel every jolt the blessed thing makes as my backside lands against the animal's bony spine.

'No, Otto! I'd rather get off and walk, even on these bad feet,' I call to him in a stuttering voice.

Otto, who is in front of me, turns around, then ducks suddenly flat alongside the neck of his nag. 'The Russians! he calls, and then rifle salvos rattle off from between the houses and the bullets zip around our ears.

238

My nag makes a leap and stretches his legs in a gallop, with me pressing my chest against his neck and clinging to his mane. We easily overtake Otto, who is also now galloping.

Suddenly I find riding to my liking. I feel as if I am in a cradle and notice with pleasure that we are very quickly putting some distance between ourselves and the enemy fire. Both animals have passed the last of the houses and are now galloping on out on the open steppe. Then mine, out in front, stops suddenly and snorts so heavily that the foam flies into my face.

As I turn around, Otto comes sweeping by. The mane of the little beast waves in the wind and Otto, in his fur cap, looks like a Cossack on the attack. He stops beside me. Even though it is light, we can't see the village behind us.

My pony moves off at a canter and I again start bouncing around like a bundle of rags. Later we come across another village, and he stops and decides not to take another step. Otto's follows its lead, and they both look at us scornfully.

'We have to get down,' says Otto. 'They're in one of their moods. I've seen this before—Panje ponies are unpredictable.'

'Good, we'll walk until they get over it and let them stretch their legs,' I say, glad to be able to dismount. Every bone in my body is aching, it seems, and my rear end has pretty well had it. Nevertheless, thanks to the food and sleep, my feet have had a chance to recover a bit, and I'm not now in so much pain when I walk.

As we approach the village, Otto can see through his field glasses that there are lots of Russians there, so we are forced to skirt round the village using a *Rachel*. By the time we are almost past it, shots are again being fired, from behind and also from the side. We are up on the backs of the animals again like lightning, and fortunately they are already upset and want to get away. They are off at a gallop as if the devil himself was after them. We don't mind. They relax into a trot only when we reach the broad, well-used mud road of the retreating troops.

239

We continue westward through the mud and the hard packed steppe. There are frequent downpours, and the ice-cold wind causes our bodies to stiffen. We give the ponies food and water on the way, but instead of being grateful they continue to be temperamental. Every now and then they stop and stand still, and nothing we can say will cajole them into moving. Even when we try to trick them with a few rounds from Otto's sub-machine gun, the little devils show no reaction. They know full well who it is that's doing the shooting—us, not the enemy. When we go to pat them kindly on their heads, they snap and even try to bite us. They don't react to friendship, the aggressive little buggers; we reckon they must have been very harshly treated in the past. And every time my pony stares at me with his pale yellow eyes after he has been having a go at me, I always get the feeling that the little devil is laughing.

Not until we have organised some old blankets and placed these over their sharp bones do they become a little easier to get along with, allowing us to ride for a bit longer—but again, only until they decide to stop and to go through the old routine about not wanting to move. We're completely dependent upon the mood of these small shaggy beasts, but, even so, we're thankful that they have carried us for days on their backs (although I will frequently think back about my seriously taxed rear end).

Somewhere, far beyond the Ingul and near the Jelanez, our riding days are over. One day, as we are looking around in some houses for quarters, having tied up the ponies at a tree, they suddenly vanish. As the ropes had not been torn away by force, we know full well that they've been stolen, along with their blankets, by other soldiers.

It is the middle of March and the height of the muddy season. From now on we join the retreating masses once more. Resistance is only offered if the enemy comes too close. Superiors are always trying to form combat units out of the demoralised men, but these dissipate after short periods of resistance.

One day we find ourselves at a supply depot. We fill our pockets with chocolate, cigarettes and other items. Just as we are about to down a thick slice of beer sausage, several mortar rounds crash nearby and a soldier on the outside yells, 'The Soviets are coming!' Electrified, everyone jumps up and runs to the exit. An *Unteroffizier* from one of the vehicles has already rolled out several diesel and petrol drums and then set fire to them. The jets of flame just miss his back. The Soviets are at the other end of the depot, and we soldiers run and pile on to the vehicles to get away faster. The crews curse and try to push some of the men away but they cling to the vehicles like blackfly and fight each other for any free space.

We manage just to hang on to a bit of the side cover, mainly to help us to get through the mud a bit faster. A soldier calls out, 'No more space, comrade! Let go, otherwise we'll have to get down!' The damn fellow then stamps on our fingers with the heel of his boot until they bleed. We just have to let go, and we fall into the mud. There are many more like us.

Otto is angry. 'They aren't human any more! They're just animals, and don't give a toss if other people die, just as long as they can save themselves. And they have the cheek to call us "comrade"! "No space any more comrade!" "I am sorry comrade!" They're the ones who are getting away, dammit! I'd like to punch them on the nose! What do the hell do they know about "comrades", and the friendships which exist on the front lines? They spit out the word so easily, without understanding what it really means.' Otto has worked up a real fury, but afterwards he feels a bit better. He has also said exactly what I am thinking.

We clean off the worst of the mud and then run along in the trail left by the half-track. The Soviets are to the side, behind us, and are shooting at individual soldiers who try to take refuge among of the houses.

'Here comes another half-track! Otto yells. 'We've got to get up on this one, otherwise we've had it!'

This vehicle is also full to bursting with soldiers. We run along beside it and wave to the driver. Then a *Stabswachtmeister* sticks his head out and gives the driver a signal. The half-track is now driving at a walking pace. We notice that the man's epaulette piping is the same gold-yellow as ours. He has also noticed that on us, and he stretches out his hands to Otto and me and asks, 'Which *Schwadron*?'

'First of the 21st!' we answer in unison.

'Come on! I'm from the Eighth of the 21st!' he replies, and shoves one soldier from the running board to the front mudguard and pulls another into the driver's cab. We both jump up on to the running board and hold on to the door. That's what you call being saved at the last moment!

We are thankful that the Soviets behind us haven't got any heavy weapons, otherwise we would not have got away so easily. We managed to escape with only a few slightly wounded, me among them: I caught a glancing hit below the knee, a ricochet. It's only a graze though, as were the others earlier. It doesn't cause any problems—at the next stop I need only stick a plaster on it.

Although we lose sight of the other vehicles for several hours, we drive over the bridge on the River Jelanez. There we run into another combat unit, which has a number of men from our own unit. A capable officer has tried to hold up the advancing enemy by counter-attacking and has even managed to push him back for a short while. In one of the recaptured villages I get hold of a German sub-machine gun from a Soviet officer, and with it several magazines of ammunition. He also has two German wrist watches on his arm.

In the village we can see the atrocities that have been committed by the Soviet soldiers against their own people. This bloody war—involving women and children! I think of Katya in Dnyeprovka and her prayer that the war should be over soon. *Woina kaput!* How often she and many others prayed for that! And now, if her own troops move into her village, it will be their death sentence too. The hatred for those who had

242

lived under the Germans has become bestial—the thorn of revenge sits so deep in their flesh that they can't stop killing even their own people. And then they tell us in their propaganda leaflets that they will treat us, their enemies, very well if we surrender!

In the next few days we'll be getting close to the River Bug. This is supposed to be our interim destination. We're told that the enemy will be brought to a standstill here by strong German forces. However, before we reach the Bug, we have to survive a couple of very dangerous days, with our unit scattered in all directions because of the overwhelming strength of an attacking Soviet force. To add to the misery, the rain is teeming down by the bucketful, making the mud and slime deeper and deeper and making walking virtually impossible. We hang on to the frame of the Panje wagons, whose wet tarpaulins are blown about like the sails of a ship by the freezing easterly wind and smack us round our ears. It is a pitiful picture.

The little Panje wagons, along with the tenacious, hardy steppe horses, are in the end the only means of transport for the troops. Tired, beaten and as hungry as wolves, we reach the German reception stations at the Bug. Our unit has already been transferred from Wosnessensk to Kantakusenka, on the west side of the river, where there is another reception station. Here we discover that most of our unit has already been flown by Ju 52 to Kischinev in Romania. Otto and I remain in our quarters for three days, making ourselves more or less human again, then, as it is assumed that the last of stragglers from our unit have already reported in, we and some others are flown in an old Ju 52, without seats, directly to our unit in Kischinev. Although I have flown at the glider school at Sensburg in East Prussia, this is nevertheless my first flight in a motor-driven aircraft. Thinking back, I can say that this flight in the old 'Tante Ju' was really enjoyable, not least because we were finally leaving Russia!

CHAPTER TWELVE

Deadly Intermezzo

T HE CITY of Kischinev looks like a jewel box in comparison with the dirt and mud of Russia. It even has a western character. It's 27 March, and the Russians are said to have already crossed the River Prut and advanced into Moldavia. The city has been cleared of all communications units, so we now only meet up with German and Romanian front-line units in the streets. The spring sun is just beginning to test its strength , allowing us to make the most of several days. We receive, almost daily, delicious golden-yellow Romanian wine in a bowl. After the arduous weeks during the retreat new vigour is again flowing, giving us renewed hope after the retreat.

But it doesn't last long. The enemy, who is also having problems with the deep mud, has brought his tanks and heavy weapons forward and pushed back the Romanian front between Jassy and Roman a considerable distance and occupied the important railway and road links between Kischinev and Jassy. We were ordered to retake these areas, and this we managed to do this with the support of the 'Grossdeutschland' *Panzergrenadierregiment*. This unit was not the Waffen SS outfit of the same name, but a well-equipped combat unit alongside which we had frequently fought in the past.

During this period I've been wounded in the leg again, but I have been able to rest a few days with the trains. Waldi and Gustav Koller have also been having problems. As a result of the earlier wound in his leg, Gustav frequently had difficulty running and so was often left with the supply trains. From the time we got to Romania, he and Warias were assigned to our HMG section. In the meantime, our trains were diverted to Jassy, a city of about 100,000 people.

1 April. Our unit is again being used to drive back an enemy unit which has broken into the Romanian positions. They are fighting near Horlesti. I'm still with the rear trains, and I'm delighted to be able to remain in quarters at the moment! The weather has turned completely. After starting to rain in the morning, it has changed around and developed into a severe snowstorm, as bad as the one I experienced once in 1942 in Russia. Within a very short space of time everything is snowed in and the roads are impassable. Even our weapons are so iced up that every counter-attack is being delayed.

6 April. This snowstorm has lasted for three days, and only today can our men return to their quarters. They had survived some really harsh conditions

7–14 April. The enemy is now only four kilometres from Jassy. He has again overrun the Romanian positions with tanks and infantry and is now marching on the city. While our unit takes care of the security of the northern flank, the 26th Regiment and a few tank battalions are attacking the enemy. We are committed a bit later and are immediately attacked by a swarm of Russian aircraft, which bomb us. Over the following days we are continuously involved in hard fighting and cut the tips off the advancing enemy troops, thus detaching them completely from their main attacking body. As a result, the enemy comes to a standstill. We have lost out on an Easter holiday. On these two days we are storming trenches held by the strong Soviet units and forcing the enemy back towards the north.

15 April. The Romanians are now able to return to their earlier positions, but we wonder how their officers can go into action like men on parade, all spruced up and with well-ironed uniforms. When I have the opportunity to talk to a Romanian soldier who comes from the Banat region and who speaks German well, I learn that their officers frequently leave the positions at night in order to drive into Jassy, to 'amuse themselves' with women. We see in this undisciplined attitude one reason why the Romanians, whenever a strong enemy attack takes place, leave their trenches and go AWOL. There must be an unbelievable relationship between officers and men in their army—something akin to serfdom, I expect. I've often seen officers whipping soldiers or kicking them. (I have, by the way, seen similar behaviour among the Hungarians.) Once, when we were in position next to the Romanians in front of Jassy, we could hear the orgies being indulged in by the officers behind us at night, even though we were in the front trenches. As a prank, but also because we were annoyed, we shot up some flares and tracers with our rifles and threw a couple of hand grenades to make things noisy, and we almost split our sides laughing as they dashed back half-drunk and half-dressed.

18–22 April. Waldemar Krekel and Gustav Koller are being recommended for promotion to *Unteroffizier*, and I am helping them write up their personal statements, to formulate their applications correctly. In the *Schwadron* it is common knowledge that I've no ambition to become a *Gruppenführer*. I have never given the real reason, because I don't want to be misunderstood, or be blamed for wanting to shirk responsibility. In truth, I have become as skilled as I can ever hope to be with my heavy machine gun, and I feel that the best way I can serve my unit is to be the main machine gunner. But I won't hide the fact that I would feel naked without my HMG. The battles are hard, and I put my survival down to God's help and the fact that I am armed with a strong weapon, upon which I can always depend. I'm also proud that, together with Fritz Hamann, I am the last 'first gunner' in the *Schwadron* to have survived since September 1943 without any major injury and as a result have contributed to the successes we have achieved on numerous occasions.

The hardships suffered during the war have left their imprint on me. The continuous stress on the nerves requires longer and longer periods of recovery. These are secured less through regular periods of leave than through a wonderful *Heimatschuss*, but in any event they shouldn't cause any permanent scars.

25 April. During our short rest period, the *Schwadron* is once again honoured with additional decorations. Besides several Iron Crosses 1st Class, two Iron Crosses 2nd Class were awarded, one to a *Feldwebel* from the rifle platoons and one to me. As a result of having participated in the continuous close-combat fighting from the bridgehead in Nikopol until the present time, we, the survivors of our squadron, are now awarded the Silver Close Combat badge. However, I do not think that these decorations make much difference to my morale. I have a sort of spiritual dread, like that I had at Rytschov when the death-run began.

The current situation is, however, different. I therefore think that my uneasiness has been brought about by the many exciting close-combat firefights I've gone through, which sort of left me unscathed but now demand a price from my body. As I began to think about this some days later, it occurs to me that this condition is like seeing a kind of a curtain before going through a bad experience which is to come, although as soon as it is over I feel normal again. In retrospect it occurs to me that

247

this inner turmoil always comes along before I get wounded, even though this might involve only a minor injury.

28 April. Since our *Oberleutnant* is commanding the *Schwadron*, even we 'old ones' who have grown tired of the many engagements have sensed something like a rebirth of the will to fight. Because of his calm way and sure manner—particularly during these hard weeks in Romania—he gives us the strength and the momentum always to carry our close combats to a successful conclusion. He is always leading from the front during the attacks, and I know that we are, all of us, prepared to go through hell for him. But he is too reckless at times. For example, I have never seen him with a helmet on his head, even during heavy artillery or mortar fire. He always wears his lightweight officer's cap over his dark, somewhat wiry hair, giving him a youthful, dashing appearance. Even though he has suffered several injuries, he believes, as all of us do, that he will survive. And since he's come through many a hot situation unscathed, he's become a symbol of invulnerability. It therefore hits us all that much harder when, during an attack, his exemplary, irreplaceable life is brutally snuffed out when his head is split open by a shell.

So as not to anticipate my notes on his death, I would like to follow the right sequence of events and begin with how we, on a beautiful spring day, are in position outside a Romanian village and letting the sun really warm us through. Although we can't detect any enemy movement in the village, we know that the Russians have occupied it. Everything appears quiet, almost serene. The spring sunshine is playing on the fresh green grass all around us. The heat makes us tired and lazy, and even I doze off a bit at the edge of my foxhole. I look over at my chief, who is sitting on the ground in a hollow nearby. He is whittling a new shape in his knotted stick. All the soldiers are enjoying the sun, and the peace and quiet an interlude between the bloody combats of this brutal war provides. No shells are screaming through the clear air which separates the two front lines; only once in a while does a drunken cacophony or the high-pitched yell of a Romanian woman show that Ivan is busy in the village.

Just a few days ago I pitched a completely drunken Ivan out of the bed of a shrieking Romanian woman in a village we had just occupied. He was so legless that he did not even realise that he was fighting a war and that we were his enemies. As he was not even in a condition to be taken away with the other prisoners, we decided to pull all of his clothes off and throw them down a well. Then we tossed him amongst some cackling chickens on a dung heap. Unfortunately we couldn't hang around for him to wake up; we just hoped that the Romanian women would not let him escape his just desserts.

We were just at discussing this incident of a few days ago with Warias and Fritz Hamann, and imagining Ivan waking up, when we hear the chief calling out in a surprised voice, 'What is the matter with those Ivans over there?' He then runs over to me in the foxhole and looks through his field glasses towards the village.

'They must be struck with the tropical frenzy, those creeps!' he mumbles to himself and begins to laugh. As I look through the field glasses I break out in laughter too.

'Must be drunk, *Herr Oberleutnant*! They're dancing around like lunatics,' I remark, amused.

In the meantime the entire unit is doubled up with laughter, the soldiers arguing about why the Russians are dancing like crazy in front of the village, going through all sorts of madcap routines. I imagine that Red Indian war dances must have looked like a bit this, having read about them in the cowboy novels of 'Alaska Jim'. Then some of the soldiers in the foxholes in front of the village also get up and intermingle with the other dancers, at the same time waving their arms about. We can hear their yells all the way over to our lines. What is happening? Are they so drunk that they have fallen into a sort of trance? We are speculating on what the matter is.

249

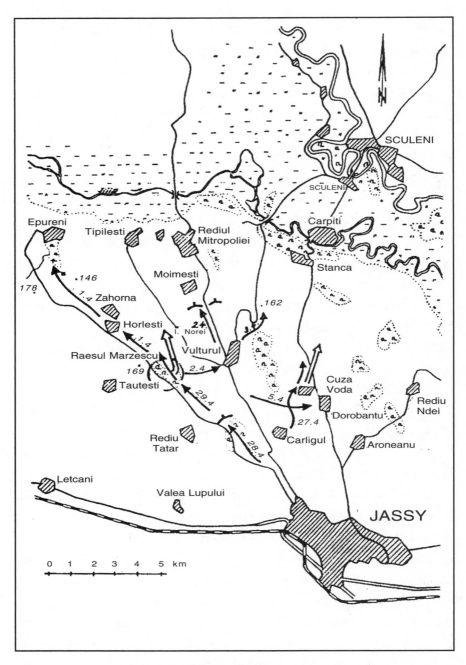

The retreat in Romania near Jassy
21st Pz Gren Regt, 1–29 April 1944

Warias, standing in the next foxhole, calls over to us.

'Wow, they must have sunstroke. They're actually running over here!'

Right! We can see it now. A bunch of Russians are running directly towards us, as if they are chased by the very devil. As they're running they're flapping their arms all about, as if trying to fly.

What is this—a new tactic by the Russians? I'm already behind my machine gun and keeping a careful watching the oncoming enemy, just in case. I reckon there are about twenty of them rushing towards us. Soon they'll have reached the rifle platoons on our right flank. The *Oberleutnant*, who has been keeping them under observation through his field glasses, lays his hand gently on my shoulder.

'Don't shoot! They're unarmed!'

I immediately take my finger off the trigger and watch the Russians, one after the other, leap over our foxholes and keep on running. Our men crouch right down and let them tear on past.

'What the devil's going on?' I hear our chief calling.

Then someone replies, 'Bees! A great swarm of mad bees!'

Some of our men get up out of their foxholes and run after the Russians.

So, a swarm of bees is the answer to the riddle! They caused such panic that the Russians even threw away their weapons and rushed over towards the enemy! To us it was an interesting spectacle, full of comic entertainment, although we're thankful the Russians didn't run across our foxhole. God knows, it's no fun being attacked by a swarm of bees!

The Russian soldiers who ran over to our lines, and many of our own, have been badly stung, but then someone comes up with the idea of setting fire to bundles of straw from a stack and dispersing the bees with smoke. We took nineteen Russians prisoner in this manner! However, they first had to be treated. Two of our soldiers had heads which looked more like balloons, which rendered them *hors de combat* for a short time.

29 April. In the grey of the morning, our tanks are moving forward gingerly. They are so silent that we only realise they're there when they're almost upon us. As our artillery opens fire we follow immediately behind and take the enemy so completely by surprise that he leaves everything where it is and flees the village. We even surprise some of the Russians in their sleep. The confiscated Panje wagons are brim full with food and wine casks. The successful Soviet Army are living like kings. Their motto is 'Eat, drink and, with animal lust, rape the Romanian women'. Following us come the Romanian troops, and they reoccupy the village. Our fighting has just begun for this day. After a short break we drive on in a north-westerly direction towards the city of Horlesti.

With support from Romanian artillery as well as from our own assault guns, we force the enemy back, in spite of his determined defence. Above us, vigorous dogfights are developing between our pilots and the Russians. When, after some time, we reach a new Soviet trench system, we are met with murderous artillery and mortar fire. The enemy doesn't intend to pull back any further, and our forward momentum is stopped. We crouch in the protective holes which Ivan has left behind all over the place.

'Bring the gun into position and hang on!' says the chief, watching through his field glasses the forest to our left in front of us, from which we are getting heavy machine-gun fire.

With Warias's help—for the time being he is my assistant gunner— we set the machine gun up as close to the ground as possible and aim it at the point where the fire is coming from. The Soviets are sitting firmly in their positions in front of us and apparently also have mortars with them in the forest. They are hammering us with them so hard that the splinters are zinging around our heads, and we have to crouch down after each burst. Warias, beside me, complains, 'Damn! Now we could really use our pots—and like idiots we had to forget them and leave them back on the trucks!'

He's right—I too have just been thinking about our helmets back on the truck, which we've exchanged for our peaked caps. Whoever would have thought that the Soviets would employ this many heavy weapons? But we had actually become quite lax as regards our helmets during the last few weeks: as soon as we put them on we changed our minds, saying that the heat had made wearing them too unpleasant. The real reason was, however, our indifference, and the belief that nothing could happen to us old-timers. And until now everything had gone well. Besides, the chief never wears a steel helmet, even though his runner, *Obergefreiter* Kluge, always had it on his belt.

As the splinters fizz around us at an ever-increasing rate, Kluge takes the helmet off his belt and hands it the chief. The latter looks at it for a moment, then across to us. 'Does one of you want to put it on?' he asks.

Warias and I look at each other and shake our heads.

'Well, okay!' He shrugs his shoulders and looks through the field glasses in order to observe the enemy again. To him the matter is settled, but his runner is still standing by, looking uncertain. We know that Kluge would have preferred to have slapped the helmet on his chief's head out of sheer concern. He idolises him and is more worried about his safety than he is about his own. But he can't force the matter, and he fastens the helmet back on his belt. Kluge and most of my other friends are smarter, and donned their helmets at the start of this attack.

Quite routinely, I fire off one belt after another into the enemy position. Then I discover two Russian machine-gun positions at the edge of the forest which have already caused several injuries among the soldiers of the rifle platoons on our right flank.

With a loud explosion, a mortar round lands just in front of us. The iron splinters whirl around and dig into the ground. One hits the steel jacket of the machine gun and the *Oberleutnant* quickly withdraws his hand. Blood starts to flow over his fingers from a wound at the base of the hand. *Obergefreiter* Kluge, who has seen what's happened from the

253

other foxhole, is frightened and yells towards the rear. 'Medic! The *Oberleutnant* has been wounded!'

The chief has already taken out his handkerchief and is pressing it against the wound. More surprised than angry, he calls over to his runner, 'Are you crazy Kluge? Fancy calling the medic here on my account!'

Kluge yells again: 'We don't need a medic, it's only a gash in the hand!' Then he waits until the chief is back in his foxhole, where he attends to the injury with gauze and some first-aid plaster.

I settle again behind my machine gun and fire away at every Russian head I can see. Then another mortar round explodes in front of us and I feel a pain on my upper lip. A small splinter has penetrated beneath my nose. The blood flows over the lip into my mouth. I spit it out and press my handkerchief against it. My upper lip and nose swells up.

'Let the medic bandage you and go to the rear. Warias can take over the machine gun!' the chief says, concerned.

I shake my head. 'It looks worse than it is, chief. It's only a little splinter, sticking in just under my nose."

He looks at me briefly then returns to watch through his field glasses.

I have the feeling that he expected nothing less of me. I am to him a dependable type, not to be upset by a slight injury. He'll probably be disappointed if I go to the rear now, although for this type of injury I would have every right to do so. I'm also honest enough to admit that if I'd had another chief at this time I would have gone to the rear to get myself bandaged by the medic, and thus get out of the firefight that is taking place. My nerves are probably not strong enough after this long period of front-line duty to withstand this combat while suffering from a painful injury. I am not a coward—as I have already proved—but neither have I ever tried to play the role of the hero.

But it now looks as if I am trying to be one, because my comrades, who can see my swollen face, are wondering why I am not already at the rear. It's the *Oberleutnant* who gives me strength, so I don't go back, but rather choose to remain with him. I feel tied to him and would go through hell with him. After you have spent some time at the front, like I have, you no longer fight for *Führer, Volk und Vaterland*. These ideals have long gone. And no one talks about National Socialism or similar political matters. From all our conversations, it's quite obvious that the primary reason we fight is to stay alive and help our front-line comrades to do the same. But we often also fight for a superior, such as our *Oberleutnant*, who through his exemplary attitude manages to instil spirit into even dog-tired and almost indifferent warriors.

What does he fight for? As an officer, first of all because of duty and honour. However, I know him, and the main reason is his responsibility towards his soldiers, and, through personal leadership and example at the front, to take away some of the feelings that they are mere cannon fodder. When he speaks of his unit, he means the unity and the camaraderie of the *Schwadron*. For me, and others, this is something still worth fighting for, particularly in the absence of any other ideals. In all the months he has been with us, I have never heard him mention politics nor heard him speak about National Socialism. I have the feeling that he stands way above these things and that he is not carrying on this war with any political agenda.

The *Schwadron* cannot move another pace forward because of the heavy enemy counter-fire, and the *Leutnant* makes a decision. Watching the edge of the forest to our left, he says, 'We've got to get into that forest, then we can roll up his positions from the flank.'

That could be very difficult indeed, we reckon, because there are lots of Soviet soldiers in the forest.

Obergefreiter Kluge expresses our feelings: 'Shouldn't our artillery give them a pasting first, *Herr Oberleutnant*?'

'What on earth for? We'll manage without it, Kluge! Tell the troops from the *Schwadronstrupp* and the 1st Platoon to follow up as soon as I've gone.'

He then turns to Fritz Hamann and me. 'You give us covering fire with both machine guns until we reach the forest. Then come after us and wait for further orders.'

'We understand, *Herr Oberleutnant!*'

Minutes later he runs in front of his men along a shallow depression hidden by undergrowth towards the edge of the forest. We give continuous cover from both machine guns. As the Soviets see our men coming towards them, they jump up and run in groups towards the rear into the undergrowth. The chief reaches the forest, the others follow him, and they all disappear into the trees.

'Go! After them!'

I grab the mounting by the two rear legs while Warias gets hold of the front two. We run at the double towards the edge of the forest, and a few metres to the side come Fritz Hamann and Klemm, the latter recently returned from leave. Spluttering, we reach the edge of the forest and take a quick breather. Then incoming mortar fire rushes towards us and explodes in the tree tops. Ivan is pouring crossfire into the forest.

Heavy grenades explode in the tree tops and broken branches crash down on us, hitting the tree trunks and undergrowth. We hear the *Oberleutnant*'s orders reverberating through the forest and hear the firing of the light machine gun and sub-machine gun. In the roaring and exploding hell we take cover behind a tree trunk that has been felled in a storm, and await further orders.

A figure emerges from the cloud of black powder in front of us.

'Heavy Machine Gun Section?' someone calls.

'Here! What's up?' I reply.

'The *Oberleutnant* wants the second HMG to move about 100 metres to the right edge of the forest, to secure our flank. The first HMG is to follow me!'

Fritz Hamann is already up and running with Klemm through the undergrowth to the right flank. We stumble over roots and fallen branches and rush after the runner. Above us the mortar rounds are howling and exploding in the trees. Warias coughs and curses. I can hear his voice, but in the hellish din I can't understand a word he is saying. He's probably thinking, as I am, that we'd be prepared to give it everything if only we had our helmets on. But we haven't got them! The only thing I can do is tuck my head down between my shoulders and pray that no splinter will hit me, although at the moment they are raining down all around us. I can feel goose-pimples over my head, and I can literally feel my hair standing up.

At last we catch up with the men of the rifle platoons. They already have a few slightly wounded; a medic is currently attending to them or sending them to the rear.

'Where is the *Oberleutnant*?' the runner asks an *Unteroffizier*.

'Further up front!'

We hurry between the trees towards the front. Suddenly our chief is standing beside us.

'Hurry up, men!' he says. 'You've got to get your machine gun into position on the edge of the forest! The *Oberleutnant* is there!' Then he disappears with some men in the same direction.

We run over tree trunks and splintered branches to the edge of the forest. The legs of the mounting keep getting caught up in shrubs and we stumble and fall. As we get close to the edge of the forest, we are met with a yell from Kluge which hits us like a bullet: 'Medic! The *Oberleutnant* has been badly wounded!'

We run the few paces over to Kluge. Then we see the *Oberleutnant*. He is lying with eyes closed and an ashen face on the forest floor. Beside him are his ornately carved knotted stick and his sub-machine gun. His runner, Kluge, is crouched beside him and is applying a compressed bandage to a head wound, caused by a mortar splinter from the tree tops. Kluge is sobbing like a child, his tears drawing light furrows in his grubby face. Warias and I are deeply touched and my throat is dry. Others join us, their expressions pained. We are all lying around on the

257

ground staring speechlessly at our *Schwadronschef*, whom we all thought invulnerable.

I can only imagine each man's thoughts, because in spite of the fury and thunder all around us we are at this moment quite numb: if the world had suddenly come to an end, none of us would have moved. Only when the *Sanitätsunteroffizier* has bandaged him do we loosen up.

The anxious question which can be read in our faces is answered by the medic while he continues with his bandaging.

'The *Oberleutnant* is still alive!' he says. 'But the splinter has penetrated into his head. He must be taken back to the main medical station as quickly as possible and be seen by a doctor.'

Then the medic points to the helmet, carried as usual on Kluge's web belt. 'If he had worn that, the splinter may not have gone in.'

We know that Kluge mustn't blame himself: he had done his duty many times by offering his superior his helmet.

Our *Oberwachtmeister*, who was also affected by the chief's condition, reminds us that we were in the middle of an attack.

'Okay—everybody up to the edge of the forest, in position!' he calls out to us.

Only minutes have passed since this painful incident, and we can already hear the rattling of Fritz Hamann's heavy machine gun. We grab the HMG by the legs once more and run towards the edge of the forest. My throat is still tied up in knots and my knees are shaking. But we are at war, and no one's interested in how an individual soldier is feeling.

I fire my weapon like an automaton and, with the others, rake the enemy flank from the edge of the forest. Stukas appear in the sky a little later to bomb the enemy, and as a result we are able to push him back several kilometres. The example set by the *Oberleutnant* has been a major factor in our victory. But it has been a temporary, indeed meaningless victory, won and paid for with high losses. Apart from the serious injury to our chief, we have several dead and many wounded.

After we reach the MBL at the north end of the edge of the forest and settle down a bit, we miss Waldi and *Obergefreiter* Krekel, who during the attack had held the link to the rifle platoons together with Gustav Koller. Gustav reports that Waldi has been wounded by a mortar splinter in his hand and his thigh. He has been taken back to the rear with the rest of the wounded. He had just had time to call over to Gustav, to send us his greetings and tell us that we'd soon be following him. It might sound macabre, but I didn't envy or begrudge Waldi his wounds in any way. He and a few others of us had held out for a long time, and it would have been awful if Waldi had been fatally wounded.

30 April. In recent weeks we have often discussed when we might suffer a wound that would take us out of the combat zone. That it will happen is inevitable. But even so, each of us believes that it will pass without serious consequences—Waldi, Fritz Hamann, the tall chap Warias, the Professor, Gustav Koller, Klemm (who after his leave has somehow changed) and I. All of us are 'old-timers', still left from the heavy weapons platoon from October 1943. In the rifle platoons there are only a handful from that time, even though some of them did return after being wounded at the Nikopol bridgehead.

With only three gashes, I have come away from it all relatively unscathed. But these small splinter wounds are still considered injuries and are written up, and now I, like Klemm and Gustav Koller, can wear the Silver Wound Badge. Because of the splinter in my upper lip, I was able to rest in the rear trains for three days until the swelling went down. The Regimental Surgeon didn't want to cut open my lip to remove it, and so it has stayed put, under my nose, to this day.

CHAPTER THIRTEEN

From Knight's Cross to Wooden Cross

MAY 10. Following the hard battles of the last few days, we finally have time to worry about personal matters. The bad and unsettling news that our highly respected *Schwadronschef* had died as a result of his serious head wound reached us a week ago. He apparently never came out of his coma.

We are reminded about his exemplary qualities as our leader and also as a human being. Fritz Hamann and I knew that he hated the war but nevertheless would fight as a model for us to emulate, and that he contributed more than most. He would shoot at the enemy when we were threatened or when we were launching a counter-attack. But he was also glad when many of them surrendered and thus stayed alive. And many a prisoner must have been surprised to be offered a cigarette and a light from a German officer. Because of these humane thoughts and deeds he placed himself above and beyond the growing avalanche of hatred that is now characterising the war. However, none of these qualities enabled him to escape death: it took him just as mercilessly, and tore him away from the camaraderie of his squadron—which was never as strong as under his leadership.

11 May. Today I have received leave papers for three weeks from the orderly room. Early tomorrow morning I am supposed to leave with

two other soldiers from our Schwadron. Gustav Koller does not let the chance slip by to give me a good haircut. He even refuses payment. In return I am to take with me a bunch of letters and mail them from Germany, because this way they can be delivered faster than if they are mailed from our field unit.

Even though I realise that my home leave is due, the news still comes as a surprise. Now, when the chance to escape the dirt and the danger for a couple of weeks becomes a reality, I really ought to enjoy myself. But it is not that way at all. I've got mixed feelings. On the one hand I am glad to be able to see my loved ones again and to be able to sleep in a real bed, but on the other hand it makes me sad to have to leave my comrades behind. For too long we gone through thick and thin, bonded together in success and in adversity. It's like leaving my family in danger. Will I find them all in good health when I return? Including the time spent travelling, I'll be away for over three weeks and, for us in the front lines, much can happen in that time. It's only after we have drunk considerable quantities of Romanian wine, which makes everyone a bit tipsy, that am I able to forget the sadness of tomorrow's farewell for a while.

12 May. Our driver, *Obergefreiter* Jost, wakes me up at four o'clock. Half an hour later the three of us who are going on leave are sitting in the wagon on the way to the railway station. I was only able to say my goodbyes to Fritz Hamann and Warias—all the others are still sleeping off their binge.

When you go on leave, you have to allow plenty of time—so I am told. The trains don't run to the old timetable any more, and you have to find out about the new one at the stationmaster's office. But we do manage get out of Romania without too much trouble. Most of the soldiers in the passenger coach are from the front lines and, like me, don't feel like talking and, rather tired, quickly fall asleep to the rhythm of the train. Only after we reach Vienna, and after some of them had got off, does it become more lively in the carriage. I notice from their uniforms that they are rear-area soldiers, discussing their amorous affairs in Austria and Hungary.

13 May. During the journey I am checked by the so-called 'chain dogs' at least five times in the train and at the railway stations. This is the name we give the unloved military police, because as their symbol of authority they wear a shining metallic shield on their chests, hanging from a chain around their necks. Once in a while they lead someone away. They are specifically checking all leave and travel papers, as well as the remarks written into each soldier's identity book. They do this in order to see if anyone has written themselves up for an extra decoration or if they have added a false promotion. Military policemen are no doubt necessary within units, to keep order.

In my compartment they take away a *Feldwebel*, decorated with the Knight's Cross 1st Class and also the Silver Close Combat Badge, but who in spite of this doesn't have all the right documents. From what I can hear, he doesn't have all his papers with him, so it's possible he might be AWOL. In conversations with other soldiers I find that morale among the troops is not of the best. There are apparently a number of deserters and dissenters. These are bad times! They are called traitors to the fatherland, because they don't do what we all must do, even though we don't like it. Nobody can be himself during a war—we all belong to the people and the state. The latter at least sounds good, because it means that everything that's done is done in the name of the people—in other words in our name.

14 May. It takes exactly two days to reach my home village. The pleasure of again seeing my mother and my older sister, who is on a

visit, is tempered by the news of the death of some friends. Our usually quiet and empty little village has developed into a hectic, over-populated city. There are soldiers and a lot of mothers and children from Berlin and other major cities on the streets, trying to escape the bombing. But for how long can they do that?

15 May. I feel that, bearing in mind all the mixed feelings, my leave will not pass as pleasantly as expected. On the front lines we have other things on our mind. Our thoughts are more to do with our survival and that of our friends and comrades. Even though we have long since got used to the danger, the anxiety always comes back and eats away at the nerves. It makes young faces look old. I have some signs of this too: next month I will be twenty-one, but I feel much older, not least because I have outlived many younger colleagues.

Even with my five minor injuries I have come away from the war relatively unscathed. During combat my nerves are somewhat flaky, but I do at least have them under control. I have often noticed over the last few months that younger and older men have turned grey overnight; their nerves fail and in an hour-long barrage they break down. And all of this is supposed to be in vain? God forbid that it will ever come to that!

16 May–2 June. I am trying hard to enjoy my leave and to let myself be distracted. My favourite occupation . . . sleep! In the afternoon I get on my racing bike and tour the area or go over to the lake and do some fishing. I often spend the evenings with friends in a restaurant or with a girlfriend I knew before I left for the front. But things are not the same as when there was no unrest about—not like now, when I detect anxiety and discontent among the population. They all have something on their minds, but they don't dare express their opinions.

I often get to hear that they have arrested someone and hauled them off to a concentration camp. People say that this is a labour camp, whose guards are SS men. They place dissidents and those who oppose the Third Reich in the concentration camps. But no one knows anything for sure, as no one has ever come out of them.

3 June. I haven't been able to get to sleep lately. Too many things are running through my mind and I am always thinking about my friends. I have the feeling that I won't see all of them again. If they are only wounded they will, one day, come back; only the dead do not return. And in every new firefight, there are always some to whom fate gives no chance. The closer I come to the end of my leave, the more I am affected, proving how close I feel to my friends at the front.

4 June. I've been in a rattling train for hours, en route to my unit. The farewell from my mother was very difficult; she had made my leave as comfortable as she could. The work in her store had been very demanding, so she couldn't do as much for me as she would have liked. My father has been called up for service in a *Volkssturmeinheit*,* which had been formed for deployment in the border area.

The train is filled to capacity with Army personnel from all different branches. My compartment is so crowded that I have to sit on a duffel bag in the corridor.

5 June. We travel through the whole night. Twice we have air raid warnings, the train stopping out on the open track, but we aren't disturbed very much and most of the soldiers sleep on. They are lying all over the floor of the train and many have even made themselves

---

* Literally, 'People's Storm Unit'—a home defence unit consisting of elderly men.

comfortable in the baggage nets. It is absolutely pitch dark in the compartments, as no lights are allowed. But, once in a while, the beam of a flashlight cuts through the darkness, or someone flips a cigarette lighter, in order to warn that others that he needs to take a leak and doesn't want to step on anybody's head.

As dawn breaks we are close to Vienna. However, the train can't get in, and it's lunch time when we pull into the station and can get off. The train is needed for taking front-line replacements, we are told. At the stationmaster's office I meet up with an *Unteroffizier* from our 26th Armoured Regiment who, just like me, is returning from leave and is going to the same place as I am. We discover that our units are still in the same area as before. We wait until evening before we can travel on. It takes another two days before we reach our destination, having to change trains several times.

6 June. Our regiments are next to each other, around Jassy-Monesti. Heavy losses in the last few months and weeks have meant that they have had to be reorganised into combat groups. The *Unteroffizier* is whisked away very quickly in a vehicle to his regiment, and shortly afterwards I'm able to hitch a ride with a supply truck from our battalion to our *Schwadron*. As we part company we agree to keep in contact from time to time. Unfortunately, nothing will come of it: this would be the only time we were to meet, and, like so many other meetings that have taken place during the war, they remain only for a brief period although I often reflect on them.

8 June. This morning I reached my *Schwadron* by means of a supply truck from the battalion. In the orderly room, I notice straightaway that *Unteroffizier* Todtenhaupt—'Turnip'—is missing; nor is the *Spiess* present. A *Obergefreiter* whom I don't know tells me that Todtenhaupt

was wounded in an aerial attack two weeks ago, while he was in his vehicle, and ended up in hospital.

I meet up with Fritz Hamann and Warias, the tall chap, in our quarters, and they're delighted to see me again. A lot has happened in the *Schwadron*. Some of the news surprises and amazes me, and some of it touches me painfully. Two of the worst pieces of news are that Klemm fell last week and that the Professor lost his right arm to a grenade splinter, causing him to bleed to death. *Gefreiter* Halbach, who had not been with us for very long, is reported to have been so seriously wounded that he will probably not make it. These bad tidings remind me once again how terrible the war is here on the front. I can't see Gustav Koller so I ask after him, and I learn something surprising. Both of them let me wait for a moment then Fritz blurts out: 'Gustav got the Knight's Cross!

'What? What did he get it for? What happened?'

'Not much more than what normally happens in our attacks,' Fritz tells me, 'the only difference being that our dear Gustav, who in your absence took over the command of the machine guns, lost contact with the rifle platoons to the left of us. We continued following his lead further into the little forest. As I and my assistant gunner were almost out of it the other end, three T-34s were standing in the edge of the forest with their crews outside. They were talking in an agitated manner with an officer. We immediately brought both machine guns into position among the tees and Gustav and I fired on the Russians. Two died right away and the rest we took prisoner. After one of our men guarded the prisoners we realised that the tanks were securing the Russians' flank and that even an artillery observer with a communications link was there, connecting up the Russian crossfire.

'What happened then was a real party. We were able to fire into the trenches from the edge of the forest, just as hard as we could. So the attack by our lot—which had been stopped—could get moving again and our regiment could roll up the Russian trenches with very few losses on our side. That was about all there was to it—well, at least, all there was to report. As a result of the three captured tanks and the firing into the trenches, Gustav received the Knight's Cross and Warias and I got the Iron Cross 1st Class.'

'Hey, that was great!' I was happy. 'But actually it was an accident, because, well, Gustav lost the connection—right?'

'Right!' confirms Warias. 'But no one asks questions afterwards— its results that count.'

'Where is Gustav now?'

'No idea. Since he came to the regimental headquarters yesterday to get his Knight's Cross, no one's heard of him. They say he was promoted to *Unteroffizier* and will have to go on a course. Nothing more has been heard about him.'

To my great regret, I would never see Gustav again. We all know how it is when a fellow is awarded the Knight's Cross: he is no longer his old self, but becomes a sort of a celebrity, to be paraded around all over the place. I knew Gustav, and I don't believe he will have felt particularly happy being shown off as some big hero. He knew full well that he was no more a daredevil than any of the rest of us. As Fritz Hamann says, they did the right thing when they lost the connection to the rifle platoons. They did the right thing when they fired at the tank crew before they could get back into their tank and blow them to kingdom come. Then they had the good fortune to find themselves right on the flank of the enemy so that they could fire into them, and thus enable the regiment to take the enemy positions while suffering only minor casualties.

Poor Gustav! When those at the top have used you enough for their purposes as a shining example of a soldier-hero, you will certainly be sent right back to the front lines. But your chances of surviving this time will be greatly diminished compared with before, because all your superior officers will use you as a hero precisely there—where the action is hottest and where they can get the most out of you. That is,

267

perhaps, the reason why, in the end, only a handful of ordinary soldiers survive their awards of the Knight's Cross.

Gustav Koller didn't survive. Just months later I would learn of his fate, when, after my serious injury, I am for some weeks assigned temporary duty training recruits. Quite by coincidence I meet up with an *Obergefreiter* who had been with Gustav in combat in Hungary. He tells me that Sergeant Koller was part of every suicide squad, and on 10 November 1944 he was killed with his men while storming an enemy position.

Poor devil! Your glory with the Knight's Cross lasted only a few months, until the fate decided that the proud Knight's Cross should be converted into a simple wooden cross. All that remains are the memories of a good friend and treasured comrade, who accidentally became a hero and possibly, therefore, had to die sooner than those who fought on without getting any official recognition.

CHAPTER FOURTEEN

Condemned to Death

I T IS 9 JUNE and I am back in action once more. Aerial reconnaissance has reportedly found a large number of Soviet tanks in an assembly area. The assumption that the Soviets are starting a large offensive does not prove correct, however, and we are involved only in some minor combats, which result in two wounded.

15 June. Today we are between Jassy and Targul-Frumos, dug in on high ground, with good observation over a flat green area. Behind us several farm buildings are burning, set ablaze by enemy mortar fire. The wind often blows black smoke into our faces; it has a terrible smell and interferes with our breathing. The houses have long been evacuated by their owners, but when they went they didn't always have time to get the cattle out of the buildings and to take them along. If the creatures didn't die from starvation, they will have been killed by the shelling or by the fires. Carcasses are lying all over the place, in various stages of decay, giving off a horrible stench.

16 June. After the onset of darkness we notice enemy movements on the wide, flat expanse in front of us. The expected attack has still not materialised, but we are bombarded throughout the night with high-

269

explosive shells: the enemy can see where we are because we are silhouetted against the flames constantly rising up behind us.

17 June. In the grey of the dawn there is a dense fog, which appears to be slowly moving towards us, driven by the wind. I've never seen it like this. It may be that the enemy is taking advantage of this morning fog and moving towards us under its cover.

The milky wall of fog is approaching us and seems to get even thicker. Then, through my sigh, I spot what appears to be the outline of a bent figure, with what looks like a kitbag or something on his back. I take aim, and at a range of at least a kilometre I fire a short burst at it. The effect is so amazing that we all burst out laughing. Ivan must have been carrying smoke grenades—which apparently also caused the 'fog'! Immediately after I fire, a great cloud of white smoke comes out of his kitbag. He in turn, instead of getting rid of it, races away, zigzagging as if somebody is chasing him. Eventually all the smoke grenades in his kitbag go off, and it looks for all the world as if he is rocket-propelled!

Immediately we open up with our heavy weapons into the fog and halt the enemy attack before it even gets under way. As the fog clears, large numbers of bodies and several mortars and other weapons are spread out on the field below us.

20 June. Although the action over these days is primarily defensive in nature, we do suffer a number of dead and several wounded. Among the latter is our *Ober*,* in charge once more of our depleted *Schwadron*. No one knows for certain how many times he's really been wounded: he was wearing the Gold Wounded Badge (which you get after five injuries) at the bridgehead at Nikopol. If he suffered only minor

---

* Abbreviation for *Oberwachtmeister*, equivalent to Sergeant-Major.

injuries, he always stayed at headquarters to convalesce, but this time his injuries seem to be more serious and he will therefore have to be taken to the regimental medical station and later, probably, transferred to a military hospital back home.

27 June. The regiment was taken off front-line duty on 21 June and we're now at a rest area near Popesti. Despite the fact that we are talking about a regiment, our actual combat strength is only equivalent two *Schwadronen*. Besides one *Unteroffizier*, there are now only seven men left of the original force which made up our *Schwadron*. Even among the replacements which have come to us from time to time, very few are now left, since many have been killed or wounded. So we are now being replenished with new recruits from Insterburg. We've got a mixed bag of young and old men, among whom are many East Europeans of German ethnic background and also a lot of Russian volunteers. Instead of re-arming us with urgently needed weapons, they want to bolster our strength with hastily trained cannon fodder! It's madness!

14 July. A couple of rumours are circulating. One says that our unit is supposed to be going to East Prussia, to secure our border there. We ask ourselves if the government,—and that means Hitler—really believes that the enemy will soon be there. It is also said that so-called *Volksgrenadiere** have been assembled, in order to increase the fighting power of the unit. We have no idea what kind of units these are supposed to be. Many soldiers are joking about it, suggesting that this would mean that our grandfathers are being called up as the last reserve. Some of the newcomers who have arrived over recent few days are talking about a new 'revenge weapon' which is about to be deployed. We wonder when this is supposed to take place—when our cities have been

---

* People's Grenadiers, a sort of Home Guard.

flattened and occupied by the enemy? I'd heard about this wonder weapon during my leave, and I reckon it's a rumour put about to give the population new hope.

15 July. Some days ago were assigned a *Leutnant* as our new *Schwadrons-chef*. I can't even begin to count how many officers we have had since October 1943. He doesn't seem too bad, but he doesn't have the gift of imparting to the *Schwadron* the feeling of belonging and comradeship that is necessary. Somehow, something is missing—something we old hands can feel. Too many new faces have come along, and we have to get used to them.

We old-timers have formed our own clique. The newcomers admire us for our decorations and for our long experience of the front line, but we don't warm to them. It's the same with the new leaders—they don't know us and they can't judge us correctly, and so they don't know how best to deploy us to the unit's advantage. We'll have to wait and see when we are back on the line. On the front line, where you're dependent on one another, the feeling of unity and comradeship comes about almost by itself.

18 July. The rest and relaxation period is over. We drive to Roman and then march the rest of the way to entrain. We are actually destined for East Prussia, though en route our orders are changed and we're redirected to Poland. The Soviets are said to have crossed the River Bug and are marching west.

20 July. There has been an attempt on Hitler's life. None of us know anything about the reasons for this. There is talk of a conspiracy among high-ranking officers, who are now going to be executed. We're also

surprised to learn that from now on, instead of the normal military salute, we must use the German salute with the outstretched hand—just like the SS, we think. But orders are orders. I don't really think this ruling will do anything to improve *esprit de corps*. On the contrary, we're wondering why they think they ought to move us soldiers closer to the party bigwigs. Anyway, they are hangers-on, and we shall find ways of taking care of them. They're supposed to have assigned political officers even on the staffs, and they are to bring us, the fighting men, closer to National Socialist ideals. What utter nonsense! As if it will help us survive! Thank goodness I've never met up with this type face to face. Anyway, I doubt they'd have the guts to join us in the trenches.

21 July. We're in Poland, given the mission to hold the front line near Jaroslav on the River San. The enemy has already tried to cross the river at several points. During day one we meet up with German troops cut off from their own units, generally panic-stricken and wandering aimlessly around in the lowlands along the banks of the river. They tell us that many of their comrades have been shot by Polish partisans. During the night we are involved in heavy fighting and manage to prevent the enemy from crossing the river.

25 July. While it is still dark, a formation of tanks with mounted infantry launches an attack. We have no anti-tank weapons and have to evacuate our positions. Everyone runs back in panic, seeking protection in a cornfield. The tanks chase us and overtake us. The mounted Soviets attack and many of us are killed in hand-to-hand fighting. Warias and I manage to hide under some straw that has been flattened by the rain. Because of the dark we are very lucky and don't get discovered.

After an hour, as some of the tanks have been destroyed and the enemy is again forced back, we risk pulling out of the cornfield.

273

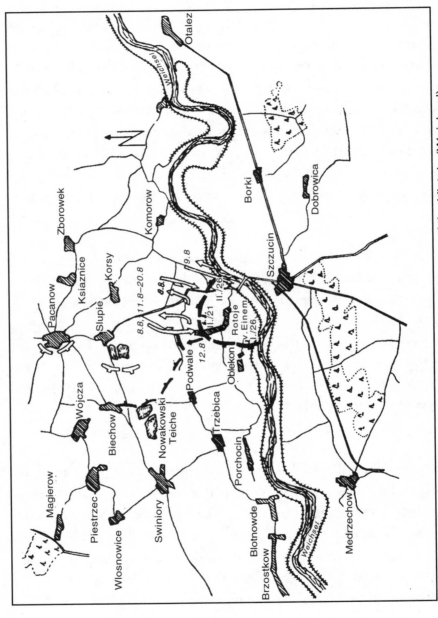

The fighting in Poland: early August 1944 around the Vistula (Weichsel)

Nothing has happened to us, and we have even been able to save our heavy machine gun.

It's been a bloody day, with heavy losses. Many of the men have been butchered in close combat with enemy infantry. They lie there with crushed heads and slit stomachs. Many have been flattened by the tanks. Since our flight through the cornfield our commander, the *Leutnant*, has gone missing. He was last seen with a tank catching him in the field, and he was running back with some soldiers. No one knows whether he is wounded, was killed, or fell into enemy hands. Judging by the massacre, the enemy hasn't taken any prisoners. The word 'missing' gives hope to families, although people who have experienced the war in Russia wouldn't give a farthing for such a hope. Such is the pent-up hatred of the enemy that anyone who falls into their hands doesn't have a chance of surviving, and any hope melts like snow in the spring sunshine.

Even though we didn't know our *Leutnant* well, we regret his loss very much. He may have had only limited experience, but he had a strong sense of duty and was an exemplary officer. Fritz Hamann lost his assistant gunner and with him also the mounting for the heavy machine gun. Now the only operational HMG is my one.

26 July. An *Oberleutnant* has been appointed as our new *Schwadronschef*, and he is taking over our small band and the remains of the 7th Squadron. The enemy keeps attacking our position near Wola Pelkinska. Our losses mount steadily, and the number of dead rises and rises. Between the firefights we're told that our new *Chef* has also fallen. The speed with which blossoming human life is snuffed out is an indication of how hard and terrible the fighting is. And it gets even worse—one leader relieves another. All through this savage butchery the new men in our *Schwadron* become more and more anxious. They are only fighting because of the sense of duty which has been drummed into

them. When there is fighting, more and more of them only go forward reluctantly, trying to stay back under cover for as long as possible.

If I need more ammunition while fighting is going on I often have to yell my head off because the ammo carriers are sitting in some foxhole or other and daren't come up front to us. As a result, Warias or I have to run back to the rear ourselves in order to get it. Our carriers, some of them volunteers, claim they haven't heard our calls because of the racket going on. So we're in even greater danger, and the outcome is that not long afterwards my old pal Warias gets wounded in the shoulder and has to be evacuated to the medical facility.

Now Warias isn't here, I am definitely missing something! A great feeling of despondency has come over me, and I'd love to crawl into a hole somewhere. But I sense that my resignation has caused a further lowering of morale in our replacements, since they look upon us old hands as the fearless, combat-experienced men. I therefore feel obliged to give at least the outward impression of a brave soldier. I am helped in this by my routine attitude and my somewhat stubborn commitment during combat.

27 July. The enemy has crossed the River Wislok in the north with strong forces and is fighting his way forward. We're trying to hold him back between Landshut and Reichshof, but we only partly succeed. My new number two is *Obergefreiter* Dorka, who was formerly with the 7th *Schwadron*. Dorka is an old-timer who, having convalesced after getting wounded at the Nikopol bridgehead, was returned to his *Schwadron* in Romania.

After a heavy day of fighting we pull into quarters in Reichshof, where we are again reorganised. No one knows any longer what belongs to whom. The rest of the *Schwadron* is revamped and forms a kind of a battle group, led by a battalion staff, and we get a trickle of men from the replacement depot in Insterburg.

To my delight, Waldi reappears among these replacements. He has been on an NCO course and now wears the appropriate silver braid. He was assigned somewhere else to begin with, but he has managed to get transferred to become our section leader. He's surprised to find that Fritz Hamann and I are still here, but is delighted to be with us again. He tells us that our *Oberleutnant*—the Prince—had supposedly submitted the paperwork for us to be awarded the next highest medal, but after his death this had not been sent on by the *Spiess*. Turnip told him this when they were together in the convalescent unit. We knew nothing of this, but we weren't particularly surprised. We know how these things go, and realise it always depends upon the individual judgement of a superior. What makes the difference—and Fritz thinks like I do—is that our most fervent wish is that we can survive this damned war. We've made it so far, and with God's help we can make it to the end. Unfortunately, this piece of luck was not granted our good comrade Waldi.

28 July. Waldi has changed a lot. Now that he wears braid, he has more responsibility and has to set a good example for the new men. But he doesn't! He's nervous and apprehensive, and although he tries to hide it from the others, he can't hide it from me. I can see the problem: he's been away from this murderous war for too long, and he has to get used to it all over again—used to the fact that death is all around us but we nevertheless can't bury our heads in the sand.

Once, when we were attacking through a forest where the enemy had dug in, Waldi was nowhere to be seen. We had to pull back because of heavy counter-fire, and I found him taking cover in the same place he was before the attack. Thinking about this, I believe that Waldi had sensed in his subconscious that something awful was about to happen.

Some days later, when we had organised a few bottles of brandy from a local distillery and emptied them after the fighting, he made some very strange remarks, which, at the time, I interpreted as just a few sentimental comments made under the influence. He talked a good deal about his friend Fritz Koschinski, who had been killed during the battle for the Nikopol bridgehead. He also talked about the death of his grandmother, and claimed to have heard the tolling of her funeral bell, although she had been dead for a long time. This conversation came back to me the next morning when I had to witness Waldi being caught by a burst of enemy machine-gun fire and falling dead to the ground. A young relative of our earlier commander—a young Prince too— also fell for *Führer, Volk und Vaterland*, as it is so nicely worded in the obituary notice.

5 August. This evening we were relieved by another unit and drove for the remainder of the night. In the morning we occupied a house at the Szczucin bridgehead, and we've spent the entire day resting up.

There is everything that a soldier's heart desires in the many supply depots in Galicia. We are living like the proverbial maggots in the bacon; ammunition, which has been in short supply, is now available and we can stock up, and even a unit equipped with the so-called 'stove pipes' for close-range anti-tank use can now be resupplied.

6 August. Today my state of mind has sunk to zero level. I genuinely believed that I'd become strong enough to be able to eliminate all thoughts of anything threatening or unpleasant, but that, plainly, is not the case. As if something is driving me, I have to think about all the friends who have died beside me, and to recognise that, among a very few, I am still alive. I am convinced that God has heard my prayers, but then I also know that others also prayed and, in spite of that, perished. What is the secret, and the purpose, that might explain why God decides upon different fates?

7 August. Even mere survival at the front is difficult, and it can be traumatic. It cannot be denied that a survivor's nerves can slowly become brittle. I have also become restless and apprehensive, and I have the feeling that it will soon be Fritz's and my turn. The war at the front line doesn't allow anyone to escape, and, in the uncertainty of the situation, the many new faces around me and the constant changes in leadership make me even more insecure and fearful. Beyond that, I am of the opinion that our leaders are no longer able to do anything about the enemy's enormous capabilities. It follows, therefore, that all that is happening is a series of fruitless attempts to plug the holes in our defences where the enemy has broken through, not with more weapons but with human beings—something which for the average soldier is tantamount to a death sentence.

Although today, as usual, I'm trying to keep my mind on the enemy situation and on my upcoming engagement, I can't deny that within me an inexplicable fear is rising like a heatwave, creating nervous unrest throughout my entire being. I can't rid myself from this feeling that something terrible is about to happen to me. It has taken root in my brain so strongly that I believe it's a kind of premonition. When I think back, I have always experienced this restlessness before being injured, and it was not until I had healed that I regained my composure. This time, however, the feeling I choose to call a premonition is stronger than ever before. I am therefore thankful when orders come to mount up, because it takes my mind off things.

Our unit is to be transferred to another sector with all available vehicles. Just before we get to a village we have to secure an embankment sloping down to the Vistula. There is no sign of the enemy, but we know that he's already tried to cross it at various places

Stretching from the edge of the village down to the Vistula is a harvested cornfield, and at the edge this drops down for a short distance to the river. The farmer has not apparently had time to gather in all the sheaves: most of them are still lying on the field, and they serve as camouflage for our positions, which are on the upper ridge of a hollow. In front of the field of stubble is a narrow band of a meadowland bordered by bushes, some trees and a small wood. The river itself lies beyond this copse and cannot be seen from where we are.

Following orders, we position ourselves in front of the village and begin to dig our foxhole. The ground is hard and dry from the sun. It's a hot August day and the sun is baking our hides. In spite of heavy perspiration the digging is no problem for *Obergefreiter* Dorka, my assistant gunner and myself—I have mentioned once before that Willi Dorka and I have already dug hundreds of foxholes in the ground. But now we nearly throw up our last cup of coffee when an *Unteroffizier* comes over and tells us that an officer has given orders that we are to move our heavy machine gun further to the front, in the sloping cornfield. We can't believe we've heard him properly: why should we exchange a position with a great field of fire and good protection for one which is easy for the enemy to spot? Whoever gives these kinds of orders can't, God knows, have much in the way of front-line experience. The *Unteroffizier* is also unhappy—he is supposed to position himself in the field off to the right with his light machine gun. With gritted teeth we begin to dig our new hole. Sweat runs out of our buttonholes, but deep in the earth it is moist and cool. After we have made our hole, we camouflage it with sheaves of corn and disappear into the depths.

As it gets dark, restlessness overtakes me. As a rule we relieve each other from watch every two hours, but today I will probably not be able to sleep, so I take the first shift right away and will only wake Dorka when it is necessary. A gentle night breeze wafts over from the Vistula, and at first I find it quite pleasant.

There are no clouds in the sky and the stars are glittering under a deep blue canopy. The smell of newly harvested corn rises from the field and is heavy in the air. The smell awakens memories—I am reminded of home and the enjoyable albeit brief time of time spent harvesting duty, with my girlfriend Traudel. She was a real farmer's daughter, and once told me that the corn was for her the symbol of growth, development and fulfilment. I know what she meant, but at the moment I'm oppressed by the smell of the ripe corn mixed with the rather mouldy reeds from the Vistula river bank, which the wind wafts over to us. Slowly a milky fog from the river bank creeps through the forest across the meadow and up to us. After a time it grows thicker and the suffocating vapours float back and forth like ghostly beings in the wind.

I peer into the fog and jump at each insignificant little noise—fieldmice, no doubt, moving around in a sheaf of corn, just busy running about. Still, a restless feeling remains in me. As a matter of fact the restlessness increases when I realise that we're alone in front of the cornfield without anyone to the side of us. Even the other machine gun, with the sergeant, is somewhat behind us.

The fog creeps slowly higher up towards us, and now it's so thick that we can only see the outlines of the village. The moisture deposits itself on the machine gun and makes me feel chilly. I turn up my collar and squat deeper into the foxhole. We have covered the bottom of the hole with straw. Dorka is sitting curled up in one corner with his back leaning up against the wall. He is breathing deeply and I can hear him quietly snoring. I let him sleep, even though he should have relieved me from my watch long ago. I'll wake him up when I feel tired.

As I am about to cover the machine gun with a canvas because of the damp, I clearly hear squeaking noises and also voices in the fog. The Russians! I shudder. I hold my breath and listen. They are slowly approaching. The squeaking sounds like wheels turning on dry axles. I wake Willi Dorka carefully. He jumps up as usual and wants to say something. I just reach across to lay a hand over his mouth, then we listen together.

We assume that the Soviets have got their anti-tank guns or rocket launchers across the Vistula and are now moving them further forward. They are not being very quiet about it, and we reckon they have no idea that we're lying right here in front of them. If they get much closer we might be able to surprise them by opening fire and perhaps chase them away from their guns. We did this successfully once in Romania with two ATGs. Dorka removes the canvas cover from the machine gun and I get in position behind the weapon. We wait and stare into the fog, but it looks as if they're not coming any closer. Then suddenly we hear other noises. The Russians are hacking and shovelling in the ground.

'Dammit! They are digging in their guns directly under our noses,' says Dorka, annoyed, and then he adds: 'What a mess! What should we do now?'

'Nothing for the moment,' I answer nervously. 'The fog's too thick. We don't even know for sure exactly where they are, and we just can't just fire into the fog at random. But they can locate us quickly and can easily finish us off.'

'Yeah, but we have to do something!' Dorka is excited and steps from one foot to the other. 'When they have dug themselves in, then God help us in the morning. At this range they are going to spot us straight away.'

'I know,' I say, and feel how my thoughts about tomorrow morning drive my heart up into my throat. 'It's obvious that we can't stay here,' I say to Dorka. 'The best thing would be for you to go back up to the young *Oberleutnant* and ask him where we should move to. Maybe he'll send down a strong force to surprise the Russians while they're digging.'

Dorka dashes out of the foxhole and runs up to the houses. Shortly afterwards he returns, and I can hear him cursing quietly.

'What did he say?' I ask, expecting something bad.

'The bastard said we've got to stay put,' Dorka spits out angrily.

'That can't be true! Did you tell him how close those guns are to us?' I ask incredulously

'Of course! He said he already knows that the Russians are digging in their guns in front of us. We're to stay here until the tanks come.'

282

'And exactly when are they supposed to be here?'

'He didn't say. But the *Unteroffizier* to our right rear is hopping mad as well. He reckons that the silly arse knows full well that no tanks are expected—they were assigned to another sector yesterday.'

Well, then, we might as well write our last will and testament! Just how can an officer be so irresponsible? As soon as the fog lifts, they will be able to reach us with their shelling. Judging from the noise they're kicking up, the Russians must be close enough to chuck stones in our hole. We won't stand a chance if we stay in it. It's a death warrant— that's the way I feel right now! Who could be so idiotic as to let someone come here and give a stupid order that will decide whether we live or die. If this officer, whom I don't even know, didn't make this decision out of incompetence, then, clearly, he has decided to sacrifice us in the interests of his own safety.

I mumble this last sentence to myself, but Dorka hears it and says with a grimace, 'I reckon the idiot has his pants so full of crap that he thinks we can hold the Russians up long enough to allow him to escape. We should upset this bloke's plans and go back to our first position, up there at the top of the field.'

'Are you mad, Dorka?' I stop him in his tracks. 'This miserable fellow would sure as hell have us in front of a court martial in no time. We can't do anything else but wait this one out and trust to luck!'

I say this, although I know that our lives are now worth less than the straw we are standing on. I have been on the front long enough to be able to size up a situation correctly and to know that belief in luck is a very weak subterfuge. Here only a prayer can help us—to ask God that he will be with us in this bitter hour of our wretched lives. Unlike me, Dorka is a Catholic: while I pray silently, he crosses himself and prays with trembling lips. He reminds me of Swina that time in Rytschov. Swina was very religious, but, even so, God had not preservied him.

The fog becomes even thicker towards the morning. We are straining our eyes to see through the milky soup and listening anxiously to the

Russian commands and muffled calls which reach our ears. We've had a brief respite, but other than praying there is nothing we can do. All the experience amassed during the war is not worth a tinker's cuss when you sit in a rat trap like this, from which there is no escape.

Slowly, over the next hour, the fog begins to lift. First the houses behind us come into view, then the first rays of sunshine hit the stubble field. I look for the light machine gun position diagonally behind me and recognise the sheaves of corn heaped around it. Somebody raises a hand and waves, and I wave back. I reckon the LMG will be brought in position first, when it is needed. Until then they can keep it hidden. Our HMG, on the other hand, must, because of its mounting, stand ready in position, all set to fire. We have lowered it and camouflaged it well with straw, but at this range and on this slope we can expect the enemy to see it immediately we open fire.

And so it is! As the wind removes the last vestiges of fog in front of us we are staring directly into the barrels of four guns. The range is about 100 metres. They must have discovered our positions or else just fired first where the sheaves of corn are stacked up. As the muzzles flash, we feel the blast in our faces—that's how near they are. There is a sharp explosion, the sheaves are blown into the air and our machine gun is now in the open.

'Anti-tank guns!' yells Dorka, thunderstruck, and crosses himself.

At the same moment a second shell hits the mound and shatters the HMG to pieces. Dorka yells and clutches his throat. He looks dumbstruck at his bloody hand and presses it against his wound. Panic-stricken, he jumps out of the hole and runs up the field towards the village. Right behind him another round explodes and rips off both his legs. His backside is thrown into the air and falls, covered in blood, on to the ground. Only seconds have passed, and as I again look towards the front another flash comes from a gun barrel. The shell hits in the mound in front of my position at full force and covers half my hole with dirt. I pull my legs out of the dirt and press myself tightly down on to it. Then the next round explodes immediately in front of me and sends a glowing splinter towards me. I feel a heavy impact on my upper right arm and some light splinters hitting my chest. Blood immediately starts running warm down my arm and dripping out of my sleeve. For a moment I am numb; then I feel a burning sensation, and pain.

You will bleed to death here in this hole! I think, and then I am gripped with a terrible fear. Just get away from here! The fright drives me out of my hole. I press my left hand over my wound and dash away. Instinctively, I do not go the obvious way—up to the houses—but, propelled by terror, I run to the right, towards the copse. I know that the direct-fire gunners must first physically shift their aim in order to pick up a new one—in this case me. The shells start to land around me only after I have been running for a bit. They are firing at me as they would at a rabbit—so I behave like one, by constantly zigzagging. I carry on like this, to force the gunners to adjust their sights all the time.

But I am running out of steam. My lungs are heaving like a pair of bellows and I sense a light dizzy feeling. I can't stop the bleeding with my hand. The blood is running continuously out of my sleeve and is now soaking my trousers. Anti-tank shells are exploding to the right and to the left, the dirt showering me in the face. Wheezing, I keep on running in zigzag fashion, running for dear life, afraid of being blown to bits by the next shell. But the trees in the wood are coming closer all the time— and then there are only a couple of paces left! Finally I can hide from the enemy gunners. Their shells are exploding like mad in the trees, causing trunks and branches to snap like matchsticks. Well out of breath, I run further into the woodland then fall to the ground.

I am safe, but I'm not yet saved! I stand up again, but my knees are weak. The blood I have lost has weakened my body. But I must carry on! With my last ounce of strength I run further through the wood and, under cover of the hill, back into the village. There are only two hundred metres left to the edge of the village. My knees shaking, I reach the first houses.

There are several vehicles between the houses, and two officers are watching the sloping ground down to the Vistula. The enemy's ATGs are now firing into the village, but they are receiving considerable counter-fire from our heavy mortars. When the two officers see me, they wonder why I am coming from that particular direction. I explain to them where I was wounded, and that *Obergefreiter* Dorka was killed. Neither the *Major* nor the *Rittmeister** knows there is a forward HMG position in the stubble field, thinking that the trenches at the edge of the village represent the most advanced line. They are surprised that I've managed to escape, bearing in mind my wounds, from the ATG fire. Then I collapse in a heap, and a driver just manages to catch me. The *Major* orders the driver of his VW jeep to take me to the medics.

Besides two medics, the *Oberartz*† of the battalion is there. He already knows me, because he was the chap who sewed up my upper lip at the end of April. He greets me like an old pal and immediately cuts open my sleeve.

'This time it got you pretty good!' he says as he lays open the large wound in my upper arm and sees the two smaller splinters in my chest. 'The one in the arm seems to be a real big bastard, but as far as I can work out it didn't hurt the bone,' he says.

He attends to the wounds and at the same time removes a small splinter from my chest which had embedded itself under the skin. Then he bandages my arm tightly to my body and says in a fatherly way, 'Now, off you go to the main collection station! They will find you a support brace and then you are off home.' Jokingly he adds, 'Including the scratches, this is your sixth wound, right? I'm sorry, but for your Gold Wound Badge there are still no diamonds like there are with the Knight's Cross!'

It is a while before the medic leaves, because two more wounded come in. I use the time to ask the medic to write a few words to Fritz

---

* Captain.
† Head doctor.

Hamann, who is lying with his LMG somewhere in front of the village and will miss me before long. Now, with me falling out, Fritz is the last member of our troop of October 1943. I never saw him again throughout the war.

8 August. At the main collection point, as the *Oberartz* said, they fit me with a so-called *Stukaverband*, immobilising my arm. The splinter has not been removed: it will be dealt with after it has been x-rayed at a military hospital back home because it looks as if it has entered the bone. Only in the hospital train do I begin to realise that I've been lucky getting out of this mess. Though for how long? Anyway, I will first enjoy my stay in hospital. The wound does hurt, but what is that compared to the hell which lies behind me?

The hospital train takes most of the wounded to Grottkau, a small village in Upper Silesia. There we are off-loaded and taken to a spotlessly clean military hospital.

CHAPTER FIFTEEN

Vultures over Nemmersdorf

AUGUST 30. My hospital stay in Grottkau, which began on 9 August, was a period of convalescence for me. After the 5cm long splinter had been removed from my right upper arm, my wound healed up pretty quickly. Instead of the unpleasant 'Stuka' cast, I can support my arm in a simple sling. In company with a wounded *Feldwebel* from an Army AA unit, I explore the bars of the town and manage to get hold of something alcoholic instead of the usual whey beer. The rest of the time I'm either playing cards or reading a book.

While in hospital I also get a visit from my mother, to whom I pass on the notes I've written since I my last home leave and have continued writing while on the front lines in Romania. Her gifts of tobacco and cigarettes come at a very convenient time for me as a heavy smoker, since our rations of these items are getting less and less.

4 September. Today I am joining the convalescent company in Insterburg for the second time: owing to the tense war situation my convalescent leave has been cancelled. I can't feel anything at all from my wound: it's only a deep round scar, about double the size of the dial on my watch. I don't know anyone in the room in the convalescent barracks to which the orderly room had assigned me, but an *Oberschnäpser** tells me that

---

* Soldier's slang for *Obergefreiter*.

there are supposed to be some soldiers here from the 1st *Schwadron* of our regiment. I find some, but I don't know them. So many new men have passed through our unit recently; many were with us for only a few days before they were killed or wounded.

Some days later, to my enormous surprise, I meet someone in the grounds I had given up for dead. It's little Schröder, who had got shot in the head by a Russian sniper in my foxhole on 1 January 1944 and whom both the medic and I had thought had no chance of survival. In spite of this, the medic had let him be taken off to the main medical station. Although his face is fuller and he has a scar the size of a dinner plate around his left ear, I recognise him immediately.

It's a very happy reunion. Schröder tells me that after he was wounded he had woken up in the rear-area hospital. His recovery had taken a long time, but his life had been saved. This is a miracle when you consider that a piece of his head almost the size of a fist, from his temple to his left ear, was shot away. Schröder is now at another convalescent barracks, awaiting discharge.

I spend many an hour with him before he is released. While we reminisce about the days at the Nikopol bridgehead, thoughts and images of Katya continuously surface. We all had always considered her our guardian angel. We wonder whether she survived the arrival of the Russian troops. For Schröder the war is now over, but he has had to pay a big price for it. He will have many health problems for the rest of his life—partial deafness, irregular eyesight and periods of dizziness.

8 October. As well as Schröder, I also by chance meet our *Ober* in the barracks. After his seventh injury he was transferred to a training company, in which he is still serving. I can tell that he's also had it up to here, continuously being assigned to front-line duty. Although I had never aspired to becoming a leader, the *Ober* managed to get me assigned to his company as a recruit instructor.

9 October. The rabble to be trained in our company consists of a mix of older East Europeans of German ethnic descent, most of whom were heads of families, and naval personnel, who because of the shortage of ships for them to go to are to be retrained to become tank infantry soldiers. Because of the undisciplined attitude of the sailors, many of whom had served in the *Kriegsmarine* for years, instructors who were highly decorated combat veterans were preferred because these were the only people the sailors would respect. Even so, it was not always easy for us instructors to find the right tone of voice to use in order to get the message across to this group.

10 October. The Russian front has moved a bit closer: the Soviets are said to be on the north bank of the River Memel. There is talk that our training company will be assigned to duty in Poland, at least, in that part of it which is still free of Russians.

16 October. The enemy is attacking with strong tank units and combat aircraft from Lithuania, and manages to create big salients in our front lines in many areas. Our barracks are placed on alert and we receive fresh ammunition. It is still hard to believe that we will move from the simulated wargames in the barracks to serious conflict. But reality has arrived: the enemy is about to invade and occupy our homeland. What a disgrace for the fighting troops!

21 October. The Soviets are supposed to have penetrated to within ten kilometres south-west of Gumbinnen and on the road west have reached the little city of Nemmersdorf on the River Angerapp. Everything in the barracks is thrown into confusion. Vehicles with officers in them dash back and forth, their commands echoing through

the barracks grounds. Old trucks with wood-burning gas generators drive up to be loaded with new recruits not yet trained. These trucks have up till now only been used for supply and other basic training duties. We are now loaded on to these vehicles, and we have to squeeze down on to the floor amongst all the ammunition boxes and sacks of wood.

After a short distance the roads are getting so choked with refugees and their carts, horses and wagons that our column has to make wide detours through forests in order to reach the specified combat sector near Nemmersdorf. We dismount during the afternoon and advance on Nemmersdorf on both sides of the road. Surprisingly enough, there is no combat noise to be heard, but then further discussion is suddenly interrupted by enemy tank fire. The enemy is standing about two kilometres to our side and shooting on the street. Everyone immediately seeks cover in the ditch.

Under cover of the darkness we move nearer to the village and dig in on a small hillock. The Russians are reported to have taken over the trenches that in recent weeks were excavated by the *Volksturm** and the local civilian population in order to defend the village. Our training company is going to storm these trenches with shouts of 'Hurrah!', we are told.

The night passes quietly, but the recruits are nervous and can't get off to sleep. For them and the former sailors it will be their first engagement.

22 October. A hazy fog covers the fields this morning and the only view of the village is a few dim outlines of houses. Our company is located on the right flank and awaiting orders to attack. However, even before our orders arrive, the recruits from the other company are storming forward yelling 'Hurrah!' They receive heavy machine-gun and rifle

* Roughly equivalent to the British Territorial Army.

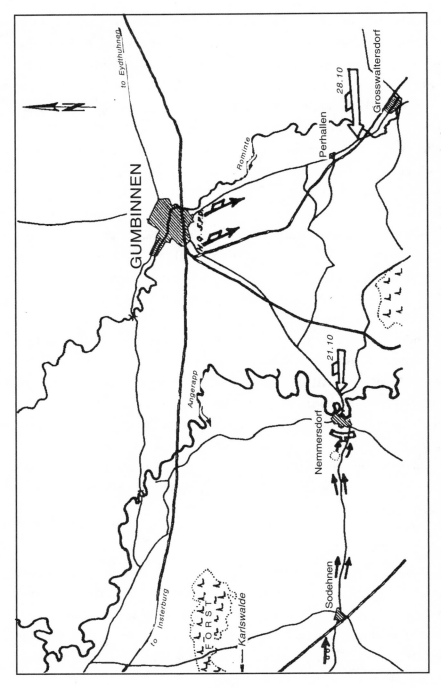

Out of the barracks in Insterburg and into action towards Nemmersdorf.

fire in return. I can hear lots of voices calling out for medics. As we also start to attack, the counter-fire is no longer as strong, but, even so, we suffer three slightly wounded and one seriously wounded from my group. The losses from the other companies could be considerable— together with some officers, it seems that a large number of NCOs and soldiers have been killed or wounded. The enemy suffers heavy casualties in the trenches; the rest try to get away, but they are captured one by one.

We don't meet any more Soviets as we sweep through the village. Instead, we discover terrible incidents involving mangled bodies, reminding me of the atrocities committed by Soviet soldiers on their own villagers which I saw during our retreat in the spring of 1944. Here it is German women from whose bodies they have ripped clothing, to shame and then mutilate them in the most inhuman manner. In a barn we come across an old man whose throat has been drilled through with a pitchfork so that his entire body is hanging on the barn door. In one house all the feather cushions have been cut open and smeared with blood, and among the feathers lie the dissected bodies of two women and two murdered children. The sight is so terrible that some of our recruits run out in panic and vomit.

It is impossible for me to describe all the terrible sights we have witnessed in Nemmersdorf. I can't find the right words, and it is repugnant to have to talk about the horrific acts perpetrated on innocent women, children and old people. For a moment I have to think back on what the recruit said when he saw ravens and crows and so convincingly spoke about the 'buzzards being over Nemmersdorf'. Was it a coincidence that, at exactly that moment, such a large flock of birds was in the village? Or was there more to it? A premonition, perhaps? Unfortunately I can't discuss this further with the young man in question because he was the one who was badly wounded this morning during our assault.

23 October. After the battle for Nemmersdorf we learn that the local National Socialist Workers Party office hadn't warned the population soon enough about evacuating the village. The people were therefore surprised in their sleep by the Soviets and couldn't escape. The party bigwigs, however, were all able to get away in time.

25 October. By concentrating strong German units, the Soviet troops are again pressed back and the front lines once more stabilised. Our reserve battalion remains for a few more days to secure the Nemmersdorf area and reoccupy the strongpoints and trenches. This morning we are relieved and return to the barracks in Insterburg. Over the course of the next few days there is a general disintegration of the Insterburg training area. The training companies are finally going to be deployed.

27 October. Today we're leaving, but no one knows where we are off to. A number of rumours are flying about, one mentioning front-line duty, another further training and deployment in Poland. In the meantime some of the ex-naval personnel have been detached and replaced by former *Luftwaffe* personnel.

29 October. The uncertainty is laid to rest. We are off-loaded in Lodz, Poland, and march, singing, through the gates of a Polish barracks— our home for the next few weeks.

CHAPTER SIXTEEN

From Poland to a Fool's Paradise

NOVEMBER 10. We have been in this former Polish barracks for almost two weeks. The place is built of red brick with a high wall all round. Heavy frost has arrived in the last few days and we have been issued with warm overcoats. Each morning we sing along while we march with the training companies through the streets of Lodz towards the training ground outside the city. This area, which belongs to the barracks, is very large and is equipped with dug-outs for protection against tanks. The training for the sailors and recruits is hard, but relatively pleasant.

No one can complain about the food—only the tobacco rations fall short, and for heavy smokers like me they are inadequate. It is therefore hardly surprising that some of the soldiers try to get in touch with the civilian population in order to get hold of Polish *papieros* cigarettes—the ones with the long filters—from the black market for resale to other soldiers. This trade was not without its risks, and in one unit a warning was given out that this type of contact had already got some men into trouble.

Black market trading is illegal, so it takes place mostly in obscure or uncontrolled areas. However, German soldiers are often lured into these places by Polish Underground personnel for the express purpose of being murdered. Virtually every day we hear about soldiers who had been found dead or have just disappeared without a trace. In our barracks building there have been two incidents in which recruits disappeared and were never found. According to statements from their colleagues, they hadn't deserted.

7 January 1945. There is a air of breaking up within the barracks once more, and we are driven to the railway goods station and loaded on to a train. We're not told where we're going and the rumours are flying. All sorts of theories are put forward, although we as instructors know from the battalion commander that we will not be dispatched to the front as training has not yet been completed. We travel generally at night, and because of the continuous bombing raids on the cities we only stop when we're in open countryside. Our journey takes us through Berlin and Hamburg and further north to Denmark. When we reach Aarhus we're off-loaded and driven from there to a small village.

10 January–6 March. Our training company is billeted in a newly built school near the port of Aarhus. We are very well accommodated and have enough space in which to carry out our training and weapons instruction. Outside it is freezing cold and a light dusting of snow covers the fields. The garrison is well placed for training the recruits as it's only a few minutes to the range for gunnery practice.

After our first look round the village, it's rather like being in Paradise because we're able to buy a lot of things which we've had to do without for a long time. We have taken a particular fancy to the cakes and cream puffs available from all the bakers' shops. I don't think I will ever again eat as many cream puffs as I have pushed down my gullet these last few days.

Our stay here in Denmark has started off really nicely, but then a series of unexpected loathsome and provocative acts become the routine, and for me and some of the others finally an unbearable torment. The reason for all this is the new company commander, who doesn't know enough about combat training and leadership. We got a sample of this the day we arrived. Because, in his opinion, our company had not dressed ranks properly when the *Transportführer* reported to him, he made us stand in the freezing cold in front of the school for an hour; only then did he accept the *Transportführer's* report and dismiss us. This was a pretty selfish demonstration of his authority. He made himself look ridiculous.

He was a comical-looking *Leutnant* who belonged to the old 'spit and polish' brigade and who recently, mainly out of pity, had been promoted from *Stabsfeldwebel* to officer rank. In his case, the compassion was probably well-directed, because he had at some time unfortunately lost his left arm and been injured in one eye, which had gained him a Silver Wounded Badge and the Iron Cross 2nd Class. The loss of his left arm in no way prevented him from using his right arm in the manner of a jumped-up drill sergeant, neither did it stop him constantly patting us in order to correct our body posture as we were submitting our combat reports in front of the recruits. To show us up in this way was bad form, coming from a superior in the presence of recruits, to whom it must also have appeared pretty silly. As a result of his constant nagging and touching of the instructors and recruits—correcting a shoulder which might sag a half a centimetre or correcting a salute because the raised arm did not reach above the eyebrow—he was soon known only as '*Holzauge*' ('Woodeye') to us and to the recruits.

Over the next few weeks Woodeye gave us the creeps with his constant pettiness and fault-finding, diminishing more and more the desire of everyone to serve in his company. Once, when we were pitted against a unit of Danish partisans who had blown up a railway line, we learned from a *Wachtmeister* from another company that our company commander had only been commissioned a few months ago and that this was the first company command he had had. Apparently he had never understood that service as a company commander required a new outlook and a different attitude. Woodeye may have looked like an officer, but as a result of his childish demeanour he was just a brainless drill sergeant.

8 March. We have been here in Denmark for almost two months, and orders come for our recruits to be assigned to the front. Even though we've been expecting these orders, they nevertheless do come as a bit of a surprise. I'm immediately faced with a dilemma: should I remain here and let myself be exposed to the whims of a stupid officer, or volunteer to go to the front with the recruits? Following a conversation with our *Ober*, who very wisely keeps out of any controversies but who nevertheless wants to talk me into staying, it becomes clear that he can't do anything to change the way the company is run. I therefore decide to do my duty at the front rather than continue to be exposed to the unpleasant atmosphere here.

It isn't an easy decision to make, but it does characterise the bitter disappointment which I feel I'm suffering in this degrading situation. As I tell Woodeye my decision, it's clear that my leaving the company in this manner is to his personal disadvantage. In his plump, sanctimonious manner, he refers to my Gold Wounded Badge and my other decorations, and furtively asks if I have considered things properly, as I have already done more for the Fatherland than many others have. For this, I really ought to punish Woodeye and stay put, but I know that it is precisely because I am a mere *Obergefreiter* with high honours that I bother him, and that this irritates his enormous ego.

10 March. Our training company—now designated a *Ersatz-kompanie**—has boarded on a train and has reached Hamburg. We are picked up from the station and taken to a barracks. Another company

* Replacement company.

arrives after us—like us, it has been trained in Denmark—and with it is Gerhard Bunge, with whom I trained in Insterburg in 1942. Bunge had decided to go on for additional training and had in the meantime become a *Fahnenjunker-Feldwebel*.* He had completed his tour of duty at the front line and has been decorated with the Iron Cross 2nd Class and the Bronze Close Combat Badge.

He tells me that our division has been fighting in East Prussia, but exists now only as a combat group. We are to be supplied only with new uniforms, as we are replacements for the élite 'Grossdeutschland' unit, greatly decimated in combat near Stettin, on the eastern side of the Oder.

Bunge is right. Back in the days when I was a recruit, I would probably have been very proud to wear the narrow black sleeve insignia with the silver inscription 'Führerbegleitbrigade Grossdeutschland'.† Now the designation 'Grossdeutschland' seems more like a joke, not least because this supposedly élite unit is now nothing but an bunch of half-trained HitlerYouth members, re-trained *Kriegsmarine* and *Luftwaffe* personnel and elderly ethnic Germans from Eastern Europe who can only speak broken German—a dreadful bunch the like of which I have never seen, even in 1942 after the flight from Stalingrad.

14 March. We have got our new uniforms and have been issued with weapons and equipment for our assignment at the front, but, having received orders to depart, we now get orders to stay where we are. Apparently there is not enough transport available, and so we're told to await further instructions in the barracks. Is this a last brief respite before the final curtain? We use the time to get to know the *Reeperbahn* (the infamous red light district in Hamburg)—but what a disappointment! Many of the houses are bombed out. One place which

---

* Officer Candidate Sergeant.
† Führer Escort Brigade, Greater Germany.

provides us soldiers with some entertainment is the Hippodrom, but after half an hour there is an air raid alarm. Everyone runs to a basement, or to the underground bunkers. This is my first experience of the massive Allied air raids on Hamburg.

The war is now everywhere! It destroys cities and people from the air, and the horror is reflected in people's faces, which are furrowed with fright, sorrow and sadness. They all appear years older. The war shreds nerves and daily demands wounded and dead. It tears friendships and families brutally apart and brings them unspeakable unhappiness and suffering.

Woina kaput! Just as Katya had expressed this wish, full of desperation and pain, at the Nikopol bridgehead, so also must the people here with us have said it a thousand times—the longing that this wretched war might end quickly. But it doesn't stop; it rages on. It destroys everything around it, except war itself. All the fanatics, who are now under pressure, will either lose face or be brought to book. Many people still believe them; they understand how to juggle and twist the events. They believe in the top-secret 'wonder weapon' everyone is talking about. I am sceptical—very sceptical—because in the past so much has been promised and not delivered. But one thing I'm certain about—I have no desire to stick my neck out. I feel that, for us, things are moving inexorably towards a conclusion. Soviet troops stand on the Oder and the Allies are about to cross the Rhine.

19 March. Our marching orders came two days ago. Then we were loaded in a train and taken to Stettin. We came under enemy artillery fire near the railway which resulted in one dead and two wounded. While we were off-loading everything was in uproar, with people running around like headless chickens, and we old hands were hard put to it to hold things together. After months resting I will have to get used to being at the front again, and get used to the fact that Ivan has his claws

in me once more. So how long will it last this time? And how will it all end?

20 March. After a tiring march we reach the unit to which we will be subordinated. In a large village square we are welcomed by an officer, some *Feldwebel* and several *Unteroffiziere*, who immediately begin to sort us out and organise us, the replacements. A somewhat older *Major*, with the Iron Cross badge of the First World War, seems surprised to see me with the fresh troops. He comes over to me and says, 'How come old boy?

I look at him and think that he might be right—if he means my age. I pull myself together as usual and say, 'If *Herr Major* is talking about my combat experience, then I admit I have a few things behind me.'

He nods and asks directly where I was involved and what I had been doing up to now. In the end I tell him that I would feel happiest behind an HMG.

The *Major* shakes his head. 'I'm sorry, but all the machine gun positions are assigned, and the *Gruppenführer* positions were filled just two days ago.'

That of course could mean that things become very hot for me. Disappointed, I reply, 'Then I will probably be assigned to the front with rifle in hand, *Herr Major?*'

He laughs at my comment and slaps me on the shoulder. 'Of course not!' he says decisively. 'That would be *too* much. Besides, I don't like to see good men go to the dogs.'

That sounds good, my brain says to me, and he becomes a much more interesting sort of bloke. The *Major* pauses and I see that he is considering something. Then he asks, 'Can you ride a motorbike?'

'*Jawohl, Herr Major!*' I answer quickly and with pride. 'I hold all Army driver's licences up to armoured personnel carriers.'

'Great!' the *Major* answers and nods, satisfied with my answer.

'As of tomorrow you will lead the motorcycle courier section at Regimental Headquarters—is that clear? After few days I will put you in charge of the section, okay?'

His suggestion comes as a bit of a surprise, but I answer without hesitation. '*Jawohl, Herr Major!*'

What else could I, an ordinary *Obergefreiter*, have said? Decline? If I'd done that I might have annoyed him—and heaven knows where he would have sent me. Motorcycle courier might not be so bad. I might not be exactly over the moon about it—up till now I've only had only a vague idea what it might entail. I shall have to wait and find out how the next few days develop.

21 March. They are in a hell of a hurry. Today I've got my motorbike and my courier equipment. At the moment, the motorcycle courier section consists of five men, and we are quartered at the regimental headquarters. The HQ, with an *Oberst** as commander, is located in the basement of a school. The companies are about two kilometres in front of the city and are in action with the enemy all the time. There is a continual coming and going at Headquarters, and for the first time I am experiencing the hectic atmosphere of a regimental command post. Up at the front, the enemy is continually trying to breach our defences, but he is always thrown back. His heavy artillery is firing without let-up into the village, and quite often the shells land close by.

In spite of the fact that the front-line units are constantly in touch by radio, we as couriers are employed where important orders are involved. On the first day all my couriers are on the road, so I too have to get into the saddle. It's not long before I'm cursing my new assignment. What from the *Major*'s point of view seem to be an advantageous position turns out to be the exact opposite: I'm exposed to more danger on my motorcycle than I ever was at the front, in a

* Colonel.

foxhole, fighting the enemy. My men and I have to make our way through soft ground and deep shell craters, all the while dodging exploding ammunition. Once, on this the first day, the ground in front of me suddenly collapsed because of a heavy shell impact, and I and my motorbike dived headlong into the hole. As I groped my way out of the crater, a second heavy shell exploding nearby threw me back into the crater again. I was lucky—a tractor came by and hauled me out with a cable.

With the engine roaring and me bent low over the handlebars, I race towards the front to deliver my orders within the allotted time to the company involved. This is a bit of a problem because the company in the meantime has been forced to move elsewhere as a result of enemy activity and I have to ask for directions in order to find them. Then there is a hellish drive through mortar fire and a rain of bullets, at the end of which my overcoat is shredded, but miraculously I come away from it all without any serious injury.

26 March. The dangers and exertions of the courier journeys through craters and deep mud is a very risky game of life and death, but I'm involved in it for only five days. During this time two of my couriers withdraw because of injury, and their replacements have to be instructed. Prior to this the devil was, as they say, afoot. After a major offensive by our side—which brought no results—the Russians in turn attacked us. Our courier section was heavily involved, and I again cursed the *Major*, who had so grandly announced he would not let me 'go to the dogs'.

I have no protection at all on this bloody motorbike, and I am forever dismounting and haring across open fields to get to the units I need to meet up with. As I go to my machine and remove the leather straps on the side pack where I keep my food, I hear the howling of a grenade and immediately afterwards an explosion quite near the school. Splinters bury themselves in the walls. I can hear one of them fizzing through the

303

air and I instinctively duck—too late! It has my name on it. It makes only a light impact on the rubberised courier coat, but then I feel a hard smack over my left elbow. I can feel the pain and see the blood seeping out of my sleeve, but I suddenly feel freed, as if a heavy weight has been lifted from me. And I am aware of the fact that once again, as before, there was a premonition.

CHAPTER SEVENTEEN

Better Dead than Siberia

COMPLETELY at ease, I walk back down into the basement and the assistant surgeon gives me a first-aid dressing. A large splinter has bored through the flesh above the elbow joint and lodged against the bone. The doctor believes that it has not affected the bone itself. As the *Major* is not at the moment at the command post, I walk over to the Regimental Commander and, in accordance with regulations, report my injury. As he gives me his hand, I get the feeling that the *Oberst* is rather glad for my sake that I have been granted a *Heimatschuss*. However, some of those present are jealous and obviously envy the fact that, after less than a week here, I can leave the combat zone because of an injury that is not life-threatening.—I know because several of the men are calling out after me. Even though they may not show it openly at the command post, I can see that they all have their noses full of the war and certainly only fight because they have, as German soldiers, taken the oath of allegiance to the flag and are sworn not to desert.

I can't free myself from this obligation either, although I no longer believe any of the propaganda. I don't think that there's anybody who, at this stage of the war, seriously believes that it will work out in our favour. The fighting which is still being conducted by the troops is just a last stand—a last gasp before defeat. But no one dares to express this view openly. Although I am among friends, I'm not necessarily among the like-minded. For example, on the way here we saw military policemen along the road who would brutally shoot dissenters, or even hang them publicly, as a deterrent.

One of my couriers is bringing me on the motorbike to the medical station, where shortly afterwards I am loaded into an ambulance which is supposed to take us to Stettin. We aren't safe, however, until we have passed the Oder Bridge, which is outside enemy artillery range. The bridge has been damaged, and so we have to wait until nightfall before we can finally cross it in safety. I feel better now—for the first time in a long while.

27 March. The ambulance brings us to a large military hospital in Stettin, filled to the brim with wounded. The two medics only off-load the seriously wounded and those who cannot walk unaided, and don't concern themselves with me or two other slightly wounded. With all these hectic goings-on it is impossible for us to find a doctor who can even inspect our injuries, so we doze through the night in a packed corridor and are delighted when, in the morning, we are served hot coffee with bread and marmalade. As I am only able to use my right arm, a fellow with a head injury helps me slice the bread.

28 March. Still no one attends to us during the morning, although a Red Cross sister looks after us and gives us some painkillers. She tells us that the city is in the middle of trying to evacuate the wounded to other military hospitals in the west and that we should therefore try to get away on one of these hospital trains.

'Away to Hamburg!' calls an *Obergefreiter* from our group wearing a headband. It turns out that he is Detlef Jansen, from Bremerhaven. I and several others are in agreement as we have only one wish—to get as far away as possible from the Russian front. Even if we have to be

306

taken prisoner, then we'd much rather it was by the British or the Americans.

29 March. We, along with four other wounded, only get as far as Schwerin before we are stopped by the 'chain dogs',* taken off the train and 'controlled'. They are swine! They have no consideration for our injuries and brutally rip the bandages off our wounds, even though we display our injury postings very obviously on our uniforms. When we protest, they fall back on the excuse that it is 'regulations', and that by doing so they catch deserters and malingerers on a daily basis. We can only grit our teeth and let ourselves be bandaged up again. What annoys us most is that these buggers take themselves so seriously that they take no account of even distinguished front-line soldiers who, after all, have stuck their necks out on their behalf.

10 April. I have been in a military hospital in Jena for the past few days. Everything is quiet and peaceful here. The hospital is located in a former school on the edge of the town. My bandage has been changed and my festering wound cleaned up. The splinter is supposed to be removed because it gives me trouble.

The food here is excellent, although the smoking requisites are in rather short supply—we each receive one pack of tobacco. This is hardly enough, so we try to dilute it with blackberry leaves. It tastes awful! An older soldier who has been here for some time and knows his way about brings us some special herbs which he finds in the forest around here. These are dried and then mixed in with the tobacco, so we can stretch our ration. The question is whether our lungs can stand the mixture in the long run.

* Slang term for the Military Police.

12 April. Literally overnight, an atmosphere of disintegration has come over the hospital. It is going to be evacuated. Today I am finally able to contact to the anti-aircraft unit near Apolda where my girlfriend Traudel has been serving. Her unit is also in the middle of packing to move off somewhere, so I can only talk with her for a few minutes. We never make contact with each other again.

13 April. I have decided to join a group of wounded going to Plauen in Vogtland, but here again it is the same problem—an over-full hospital. No one worries about us; everybody is concerned about only one thing—getting to safety.

I get to know a *Gefreiter* who comes from Marienbad in the Sudetenland. He tells me that his parents own a small watchmaker's shop there. This conversation reminds me of the soldier who had his leg amputated over Christmas 1942 and who had been my neighbour in the hospital train after the death run at Rytschov. He told me that *he* came from Marienbad, and described the beauty of the place in such glowing terms that, there and then, I made up my mind to get to know it. So, as fate spins its web, I now find myself quite close to this lovely health resort. I didn't take long to decide to join the young fair-haired *Gefreiter* and a few others who were also trying to get there.

14 April. Last night we stayed in Eger and received ample marching provisions. We were lucky enough to get a lift from the railway station for a good part of the distance, in a truck that was going to an army supply depot. We walked the rest of the way. The weather has been cool for days, but to make up for that, sunny.

The walk, which took us through wonderful pine forests, did me good, and I could breathe the woodland air deep into my lungs. I would have felt good all over had it not been for the pain of my wound, which because of all this increased activity, had begun to fester and produce pus. I am therefore thankful when we reach Marienbad, where I can go to a hospital to get treatment.

21 April. The time here passes much too quickly, and we would all like to slow the clock down if it were possible. We follow the advance of the enemy front on both sides with the greatest interest. Everyone hopes that the Americans will get here first; indeed, many want to try to get to the American lines on foot. But they are not near enough yet. Still, everything is quiet in Marienbad and roundabout.

The front-line units engaged with the enemy have begun to pick up all the soldiers who have finished their convalescence. I am not yet fully recovered, so I'm staying here for more treatment. My wound is still festering; even the bone itself is apparently deteriorating. Good! I don't have a problem with that, because the pain is quite bearable.

29 April. Yesterday the rumour got about that the Americans will come from the west and possibly be here in the Sudetenland before the Russians. We breathe somewhat more easily and hope that this will come true. Marienbad is wholly a hospital town, with no German soldiers stationed here. It will therefore be surrendered to the victors without a fight. However, there are German troops in the outskirts of the town and in the forests.

There is talk about some over-enthusiastic group commander putting up some sort of resistance to the American troops. No doubt there will be, in this endgame, some brain-damaged troop leaders who will follow Hitler's orders to the letter and fight to the last round of ammunition. They can do what they like, but I hope they do it alone, without endangering everybody else! To fight the Americans now would not only be crazy, but also a betrayal of all the wounded in this town. It would mean that the US Army would be held up, and perhaps not get to Marienbad before the Soviets do. If that's the case, we fear for ourselves and the civilian population. God preserve us! If we have to go to prison, then let's hope it's with the Americans, who, contrary to the Soviets, treat their prisoners in accordance with the terms of the Geneva Convention.

30 April. We can all feel that the end is at hand. Even the food supply has been interrupted, and some have begun to clear the depots. I had my treatment in the hospital today, so I didn't learn until quite late that a uniform depot had been emptied. The soldiers are all running around in new uniforms and boots. I managed to get a pair of brown shoes which were too small for someone else.

1 May. *Gefreiter* Biernath from our guest-house and *Obergefreiter* Vogel from our room have suddenly started to learn English from a book. They are practising the words they will use when they meet up with and welcome the Americans. The rest of us don't like what they are doing: we consider the two of them to be turncoats, who after our defeat will immediately offer to work with the enemy in order to perhaps secure some advantage from it. I don't know if you should make judgements. Perhaps they bear no resentment towards our enemies, to whom we will now be delivered without any recourse to law. They were with an anti-aircraft unit and so never learned about the terrors of the front— lucky them, to have survived the war in this manner—and so they will also be able to forget the war very quickly, unlike me and the many others who have escaped the hellish inferno of the Eastern Front and now stand in front of a heap of shattered remnants. Within me there is a feeling of indescribable disappointment, and I feel hatred for anything which has to do with this war.

4 May. Over the last few days stragglers have been arriving in town in a steady stream, but they are immediately picked up by combat units and driven away. The surrounding forests are now supposed to be full of these stragglers, all fleeing west so as not to fall into the hands of the Russians. Three days ago we heard about the suicide of Adolf Hitler and Eva Braun. We were shocked that the proud leader had decided to shirk his responsibilities in this cowardly way. But within a couple of hours he is forgotten: we have our own problems. It is reported that the Russians are not far away and will soon be here. We therefore sleep very uneasily, hearing the roar of artillery fire from both sides getting steadily nearer.

5 May. The day starts cloudless. The sun has warmed up the fresh green trees and the bushes and creates clean shadows on the well-kept footpaths. The grass in the parks and in the gardens is dark green and the hedges along the paths are in full bloom and exuding a wonderful aroma. It is a beautiful spring day and a wonderful one—not least because news has now reached us that today Marienbad is to be turned over to the Americans without a fight. We therefore await a bloodless entry by American forces within a few hours.

We are curious about the Americans. When we hear that they're approaching the town, I go with a group of soldiers along the street and stand, with them, outside a big hospital. Soldiers injured on the Western Front tell me that the Americans are very well equipped but much more pampered than we are. Without their abundant rations and the huge amount of heavy-weapons support they enjoy, they would never have been able to measure up to German soldiers, nor would they have survived in combat like them. But why make comparisons? They are the victors, and we will soon meet them face to face.

We can soon hear the rattle and droning of tank tracks drawing slowly nearer. Then we see them! I wonder why it is that so many soldiers are sitting on the tanks, as if they are about to open fire. As they come closer, a shiver runs down my back. They look like the Russians; only the uniforms are different. They are kneeling on the tanks and holding their sub-machine guns at the ready. Their faces are hard, and they have a tense and a watchful glint in their eyes—something I know so well. As they pass our group, they aim their weapons at us. I can see their eyes sparkling, and in their dirty faces I recognise their preparedness to kill; but I also recognise fright. Can't they see that we all have bandages on? No one thinks about resisting. Or is it that they have respect for the German soldier and are therefore very nervous? I hope none of these cautious white and black figures with stern faces will go berserk and pull his trigger. We therefore keep quiet and make no movement until they have gone past. Then, all of a sudden, a couple of women and girls are standing there with flowers. The ice is broken!

6 May. Our freedom is over: as of today, orders are that all German soldiers are confined to barracks. You can still hear some exchanges of fire from the forests around Marienbad; apparently some combat groups there are still resisting. Our hospital is now guarded, and no one is allowed out without a pass. The guards fire live ammunition and don't ask questions. In front of our boarding-house a jeep with two black, gum-chewing GIs is parked. Tomorrow the hospital will be checked for SS men and convalescing soldiers.

8 May. Today we are being transferred from our boarding-house to a large military hospital with the posh name 'Bellevue'. Yesterday the Americans transferred many convalescents and soldiers from the Waffen-SS on to trucks and took them off somewhere. The result is that the hospitals are no longer so full.

9 May. There no longer is any salt in our food. The thin soup tastes terribly flat. People say that the Czechs have confiscated the salt. We assume that it is to punish the loser. When I look out of the window, it makes me wonder where all those Czech soldiers have come from. In the meantime, the end of the war has come about with the official signing of the surrender by *Grossadmiral* Dönitz.

13 May. Everything is suddenly happening much too quickly, and we've no time to think. Given time, I and many others would undoubtedly have tried to escape. Yes, there were murmurings about being turned over to the Russians, but everyone hoped for a fair deal from the Americans—that they would not be so unfeeling as to turn their prisoners over to the Red Army. But this morning, when we're called into formation in the hospital and wait for transport, we know that our hopes have been dashed. On the way to a barracks we meet up with a number of women and girls who have heard about our move and are looking for members of their family, and friends. They wave frantically to us, but none of us waves back. We're all sitting on the trucks in silence, with pale and stony faces, unable to comprehend how our hopes of a fair imprisonment can have changed overnight to a terrible, deadly future. Travelling to Russia means nothing less than imprisonment in Siberia!

A terrible word! It hammers away inside my head. Can the Americans begin to imagine what the word 'Siberia' means? Do they understand the fear, horror and hopelessness that this word conjures up? We who have fought against the Soviets—we can imagine what awaits us in Siberia.

In the barracks area we receive our first taste of what lies ahead. We are led into rooms furnished with beds comprising bare wooden planks, with just a blanket on each. We are still guarded by American GIs, but all this changes when a goods train pulls in at the end of the

313

barracks and some Russian soldiers emerge. I shiver! The very faces and uniforms that I have always feared! I had thought that I could forget all about them, but now I know that I can't. If I'm not seeing them in person before me I'll be seeing them in my nightmares.

We have to line up, and a translator comes over to us. He demands that everyone who was in the SS step forward. Only a few men do so. Next to be called forward are those who have only fought on the Eastern Front. He warns us to own up, since our units can easily be checked. I just keep quiet. My brain is working feverishly as I try to figure out a way of getting out of this. I am quite determined not to allow myself be taken to Siberia: I'd rather get shot running away, as happened to two other soldiers who tried to flee when they entered the camp.

14 May. I know from previous experience that I get a fever every time my wounds get infected, so I reckon I have to organise a new infection. The grenade splinter created a sort of little tunnel from the point of entry to the bone, through which pus would drain. A thin layer of skin had now grown over this hole, and it is this new skin that I now have to open up. I manage to lay my hands on a rusty nail. I realise that things could turn serious, but in my desperation I would rather die from blood poisoning than be sent to the hell of Siberia. I choke back the pain and puncture the recently healed skin with the nail until the blood oozes out, and in order to speed up the infection I poke several centimetres of gauze bandage into it as well.

15 May. My plan has worked. During the night I had terrible pains in my arm, but this afternoon my head is hot and I go down with a fever. As I make my way to the medical station I am dizzy and start to black out. The medic puts me on a stretcher straight away and gives me an

examination. All I can remember after that is telling the ambulance driver to get me to the hospital in the Bayrischer Hof, which he does. From that point everything is a blank.

17 May. This morning, as I wake up, I am bathed in sweat. I have been having nightmares about the war and all its horrors. Gradually it dawns on me where I am—I'm lying in a clean bed in the hospital in the Bayrischer Hof with three other wounded, in a light and airy room. A friendly nurse is bringing coffee. She gives me a cup. It tastes like bean coffee but is thin and flat, as if it has just been reheated. As I try to sit up I note how weak I am and that my left arm is swathed in a thick bandage from elbow to upper arm.

A doctor comes along. He asks me why I am out of bed. I wonder if he's the one who treated me? As if reading my thoughts, he says, 'That was a hell of a length of bandage stuck in your wound. I had to make a long incision above the elbow. I just caught you in time: another two hours and you wouldn't have made it.'

I go to say something but he hushes me up and says with a twinkle in his eye, 'It's okay. I looked in your passbook and I know why you did it!'

3 June. The time has flown. The hospital has been gradually emptying and there are now only a few left needing treatment. The food has improved, but we don't get tobacco any longer. Some of the patients have got into contact with the outside world and managed to get hold of American tobacco every so often—rescued from ashtrays by German employees working for the Americans!

Personally, I've traded in my decorations, one at the time, to the Americans for Lucky Strike, Camel or Chesterfield cigarettes. Both white and black GIs are crazy about German medals, and they'll probably boast about them when they get back home. They even come to us in the hospital here and try to outbid each other in cartons of cigarettes for our awards. What use are all these trimmings to me? They have never meant very much, although other people's do to them. I've already said why. And now, since we've lost the war, they are only worth their weight in the metal they are made from. Best of all, I am given a couple of cartons of American cigarettes for them, helping me, as a heavy smoker, get through a difficult time.

6 June. Unpleasant things generally take you by surprise. So it is today. Just after breakfast I'm told that I am being discharged from the hospital and will be picked up by a truck around noon to be taken to a prisoner-of-war camp. Although my wound has healed, my arm is still pretty useless and I have to wear a sling. The open truck in which we are driven takes only about half an hour to reach the camp.

The camp is really nothing more than a barbed wire enclosure, a more or less grassless field with some American guards patrolling around the outside. Every now and then they flick their half-smoked cigarette butts over the fence and chuckle when some miserable looking German soldier rushes over, picks them up and then starts smoking them, passing them round from one man to the other. Many of them wait by the fence to get hold of a cigarette end, and sometimes the guard will get some entertainment by taking out a cigarette, lighting it, and then after a few puffs deliberately throwing it on the ground and grinding it out. It makes you sick!

11 June. Every day a handful of prisoners whose home is in the American-occupied zone, or who can give the address of their family there, are released. In this latter case, this is specifically added for those whose home, as indicated in their soldier's passbook, is in a Soviet-

occupied area. As I can provide this proof, I get my release documents today, and I am now walking with a group of discharged soldiers past the black guard, through the gate, into freedom. After a few metres I stop and look back at the dirty, miserable-looking figures camped on what looks a bit like a ploughed field. For the first time it dawns on me that everything has actually gone quite smoothly. I could have vegetated here for ages inside this barbed wire enclosure, so I thank God that I can put this imprisonment behind me. It was not just the filth and dirt, or the stupid waste of time, but, much worse, the humiliation and the degradation I have had to endure from every lousy guard.

Now I'm released from all of this—I'm free! And with every step I remove myself further from the camp, I free myself from the burden which for the last few weeks has weighed me down. Gradually I begin to rebuild my hopes, and I start to look at my surroundings in a new light.

I look at my old Army-issue trousers, the bottoms of which are now all frayed. They don't really match the new brown lace-up shoes I am wearing. I'm glad I got hold of the new shoes that time in the depot—who knows when I might have found a new pair? Just as I am about to clean them up with a rag from my pocket, a dark shadow appears. I look up and am startled: in front of me stands a Czech soldier, demanding in broken German that I give him my new shoes. I simply ignore him and try to get away, but he takes his Russian Kalashnikov and pokes the barrel right in my chest. I can see his hate-filled eyes and know that he will not hesitate to pull the trigger. I am his enemy and he is the victor. I belong to him, and he can shoot me if the fancy takes him. So I hastily pull off my shoes and give them to him. In the meantime the Czech had also taken off his worn-out shoes, which he throws in front of me. With a satisfied grin he pulls mine on and marches away.

How I would love to run after this rotten bugger to get my shoes back. But he was armed, and he wanted some revenge. There was nothing for it but to grit my teeth and put on his shoes, if I didn't want to run around in my socks. This meeting with the Czech militia proved to me very clearly how helpless the loser is and how deep the hate and the thirst for vengeance reside in those who were our enemies.

Woina kaput! The fervent wish of many people has come to pass, and the war is finally over. But will it also be over in their hearts? How long will it be until the hate and the craving for revenge is buried? Yes, I know, there are people who, despite the atrocities, have put aside hatred and seek closer bonds with their enemies. It is they who give me new hope.

But when will people realise that it is possible for any of us to be manipulated by domineering and power-crazed individuals who know how to motivate the masses in order to misuse them for their own ends? While they keep well out of the way, in safety, they have no hesitation in brutally sacrificing their people in the name of patriotism. Will mankind ever stand together against them? Or are those who died in the fighting dead forever, and will the reasons they gave their lives be forgotten?

I will never be able to forget those I knew. They are the constant reminders that I was very privileged to survive them.

It is no less than my obligation to tell their story.